# Sunrise in Spain

Finding the Good Life Hiking the Camino de Santiago

Theresa A. Fersch

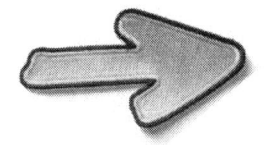

# Dedication

To my husband Brian, who inspired and enabled me to hike the Camino. To my cousin Christina, who taught me the importance of living in the present. To my good friend Jess, who helped make this book possible. And to my mother, who honestly believes I can do anything.

# Contents

# PREFACE

We were curled up on the couch together, watching a PBS documentary on the Appalachian Trail, when my husband Brian said to me, "You know, I'd like to hike the trail when I retire." It was a casual enough statement, but it got my attention.

"If you want to hike the trail, could you do it now? You never know if you'll live to retirement." That may seem like a morbid response, however this is how we'd come to live our lives.

Allow me to back up a bit.

In 2007, after only two months being married, Brian and I moved from everything and everyone we knew in the Washington, DC area to a small town in New England. We both had the desire to see another part of the country and we knew we should move while we were still young and able. We had no friends, no family, and I didn't even have a job in New England when we uprooted ourselves.

We experienced total culture shock. We moved just off of a busy metro line outside of DC to what we initially considered the "wilds" of New Hampshire. Everything was different: from the way strangers interacted in public to the extreme weather conditions. It was a difficult year and a half for two newlyweds, but we were determined to make our new life together work. We were madly in love, and that was all that mattered.

We decided the only way to adjust to our new lifestyle was to fully immerse ourselves. We began making friends, exploring the area, and taking on new hobbies. On New Year's Eve I made the resolution to try something new every month, an idea I got from a good friend of mine back home. Soon, I was trying something new every week. Up until then I wasn't exactly an adventurer; "trying new things" consisted of dining at a restaurant that just opened in town.

But over time, the more I broadened my horizon, the hungrier I became for new adventures. I learned that with every new experience I could better relate to the world I live in. "Trying new things" suddenly meant pushing myself completely outside of my comfort zone. I tried to learn everything from knitting, to sculpting, to racing my Mini Cooper, to building a bar in my basement, to building a friction fire in Vermont, to field dressing large game in New Hampshire, to fly fishing in Maine, to dog sledding in Canada. The more "unlike me" it sounded, the more appealing it was. So hiking the Appalachian Trail perfectly aligned with my new way of thinking.

There was one other driving force behind my response to Brian. During those first few years living in New England together, several loved ones passed away. Between the two of us, we lost seven friends and family members in five years. I was beginning to think that burying loved ones was the dreadful norm for adulthood.

A defining moment in my life was when my 23-year-old cousin passed suddenly. She was young, vibrant, and had her whole life in front of her. She was also the only family member who called me regularly just to see how I was doing, which I should have appreciated even more since I was so far from "home."

It was my birthday several years back, and I was having an absolutely horrible day at work. She called around 2:00pm, probably just to wish me a happy birthday. But I was completely absorbed with a conflict I was dealing with, so when her name popped up on my caller id, I said under my breath, "sorry cousin, I have a life" and I ignored the call. I was so consumed with something that didn't even really matter, I had forgotten what was important. I cruelly snubbed her, and I never bothered to get back to her. I took for granted having someone in my life who cared enough to ask how I was doing in the middle of the day. She passed away that very night. While I was sitting in bed, frustrated and angry into the wee hours, my cousin died alone in her bedroom. I will never be able to change those final moments of our lives together; I will never be able to take back that terrible decision to choose work over family. I continue to be haunted with the question, *could I have changed the outcome of the terrible evening if I'd just bothered to call her back?*

The experience changed my life in ways I'm still learning about. For one thing, I developed a new motto, and I repeat it often: *I don't live to work. I work to live.* I will never put work before my personal life again. I also found myself clinging to my husband and dog, fearing I'd lose them. I was suddenly very aware of my own mortality, and more importantly, the mortality of my loved ones. I rushed out to California to celebrate my brother's graduation from college. I flew down to Virginia to celebrate my sister earning her Ph.D. I suddenly felt I needed to be everywhere for everyone. Every day felt like a blessing not to be wasted, to the point of anxiety.

I learned that continuing my ever-expanding adventures was one way to release some of this nervous tension. I was suddenly aware of just how limited our time is, and the saying *life is short, do it all* rang through my head repeatedly.

It was the culmination of these recent life experiences that led to my response to Brian's comment regarding the Appalachian Trail. There was no better time!

We decided together that night that we would do everything in our power to enable him to hike the trail. He began planning immediately. Less than two years later, Brian spent just over six months hiking the entire length of the Appalachian Trail, from Georgia to Maine: 2,185.3 miles. Meanwhile, I maintained our life at home, sent him care packages, and occasionally visited him in the trail towns along the way. It wasn't easy being a "trail widow" while he was gone, but it was worth it to know my husband was living his life to the fullest.

When he returned from his journey, nearly seven months later, he was a new man. He was still the same loving, silly, compassionate man I fell in love with, but his own love for life had deepened. He reprioritized what was important to him; his strengths became even stronger, and he was dedicated to being the best husband and man he could be. It was clear that he had gone through some transformation, but I didn't fully understand what he had experienced.

What I did come to understand is this: hikers have the extraordinary opportunity to experience life as it is meant to be lived. They are freed of their possessions, fears, and anxieties. As their burdens lighten, they are better able to be engage with others and the world as God intended. There is love and mutual respect. They are on equal ground with everything and everyone around them. Income, vocation, homeland, race, gender, religion, physique, ability. All these things that mean so much to people everywhere else in the world mean nothing on a long-distance trail.

Brian told me when he returned, "You have to do something amazing. You have to have your own adventure." This is how I found myself at 34 years old in the middle of rural Spain hiking the 790km Camino de Santiago, a pilgrimage that dates back over 1,000 years. Initially, we considered hiking the last 100km together. This section of the pilgrimage is considered the official Camino one must hike to gain "credit" for their spiritual journey. We discussed how we would have to take approximately two weeks off of work to hike this last section.

Embarking on this spiritual pilgrimage together would be a great way to renew ourselves and our marriage. But I began to feel that usual itch. *Life is short. Do it all.* It occurred to me that I may have few opportunities like this in my life. I asked Brian, "If I'm going to hike the Camino, should I do the whole thing?" Without hesitation, he responded, "Yes. And you should do it alone. It'll change you." We still wanted to enjoy the Camino together though, so we decided that while I would hike the entire Camino Frances (the most popular of the routes), he would join me for the last 100km. And so began my planning.

I read that the Camino is transformative and spiritual in nature, however, I wasn't completely convinced I personally would experience the adventure in the manner so many books described. As it turns out, I had absolutely no idea what was in store for me.

I maintained a blog from the time I began planning my trip until its completion in June of 2015. Initially, I kept the blog as a means for keeping in touch with my loved ones and colleagues as they cheered me on from home. I thought of my blog as a letter to them, wherein I shared my deepest thoughts, feelings and experiences as they played out. And now, I am sharing with you a very sincere part of myself.

In the interest of full disclosure, I have gone back through my blog and added the adventures that I did not write about while on the trail. Sometimes, after a full day of walking, I did not have the desire or energy to thumb away on my phone for hours at a time, describing every detail. In those instances I took notes of what happened so I could add the details later. While 98 percent of my book was written in near real time, some of it was added later. Also, while I have kept the names of all the main people I met along the way, I have changed some of the secondary individuals mentioned.

I have read several stories of people who have hiked the Camino and then wrote about their experiences upon their return, and I noticed that the majority of the writings are very positive; the hikers wrote about their new outlook on life and how miraculous the Camino is. While I, too, found the Camino life-changing and spectacular, I also found it very difficult and I struggled all along the way. I think writers forget about the tough parts when they reflect back on their journey and only remember the beautiful moments.

While I considered altering my blog for this book to paint a more beautiful and perfect picture of myself and my transformation, omitting the struggles from my story and the sea of human emotions I experienced along the way would leave me with half-truths and a hollow account of my experience.

If you are looking for a romantic depiction of the Camino, or a story that tickles, tantalizes, and flows like a melody, this book is probably not for you. I am not a poet. I am a realist and an adventurer and I am choosing to share everything with you as I experienced it in the moment. The praying, the kindness, the sharing, the drinking, the hypocrisy, the cockiness, the gratitude, and the love: it is all here, in all of its rawness. It is my hope that in reading about my experience on the Camino de Santiago, it will inspire you to do something amazing for yourself.

# CHAPTER 1

## BEFORE THE WAY

*Just What We Needed. Another Long Distance Hiking Blog.*

So there I was, intending to hike the Camino de Santiago over the course of May and June, 2015. The Camino is a 500-mile pilgrimage that begins in Saint-Jean-Pied-de-Port, France, travels across northern Spain, and ends at the shrine of the apostle St. James the Great, which is in the Cathedral of Santiago de Compostela in Galicia, Spain. If all worked out, I would continue my adventure from there all the way to the coast of Spain to a small town called Finisterre.

What was I thinking? If you had asked me a year ago if I would ever take a trip like this, I would have laughed at the idea. In fact, when I first heard about the Camino de Santiago back in April 2014, seriously considering hiking it was the furthest thing from my mind. My husband was only one-third of his way up the Appalachian Trail and I was still adjusting to my life back home, alone. But when Brian returned from his trip with a renewed sense of self and livelihood, I began to more seriously consider taking a similar journey for myself.

Initially, the thought of hiking 500 miles alone in Europe scared the living daylights out of me. How could I possibly manage? But once I realized the unlikeliness of finding someone who was willing and able to take that much time to hike, and the more I read about the Camino and prepared myself physically and mentally for the challenge, the more I came to realize walking this pilgrimage alone was the only real way to accomplish my goal. I wanted to prove to myself that I could do it. I wanted to just show up in Europe with nothing more than the gear on my back and my ambition and find out what I was capable of. I was also eager to see what this adventure would serve up for me. I had no idea what to expect, and that in itself was exhilarating.

A word about my blogging: As I prepared to embark on my journey, I accepted the inevitable; I'd been made aware that it's impossible to have a long distance hike without a blog of some kind. I had hoped to minimize the amount of time I stayed"connected" while hiking the Camino, but I was aware that, at the very least, I needed a method to keep my loved ones aware of my status.

So to the extent that Spain's Wi-Fi access would allow, and as long as it was not pulling me from my trail experience, I promised to stay in touch. I may have posted a quick "here's where I am" update or if possible, I'd create a gallery of scenic pictures along the way. But I couldn't promise my blog wouldn't be reduced to a few drunken photos of myself as I toured the wine country. In all honesty, I tended to enjoy wine more than blogging.

*It was official; flights were booked!*

I got approval at work for my sabbatical, and I purchased my plane tickets to and from Madrid. It was real now. I had also made reservations for my first two nights overseas. Once I arrived in Pamplona (train tickets from Madrid to Pamplona still had to be purchased), I would have to be picked up by bus and taken to

Pensión Corazón Puro, which is a hostel located somewhere between Pamplona, Spain and my starting location in Saint-Jean-Pied-de-Port, France. The service includes dinner, a place to sleep for the night, breakfast the next morning, and a ride to St. Jean where I would obtain my Camino credentials (a small passport book) and immediately start hiking.

As a security minded individual, this adventure was already testing my limits. Finding a business online and trusting a stranger to pick me up at a train station, take me to their place, feed me, give me a place to stay the night, and then give me a lift to my destination the next day contradicted nearly everything I'd learned up until now. But I suspected this was just the first of many perspectives I would be forced to reconsider on this journey.

I had also managed to secure a reservation with Orisson, which is a small albergue about eight kilometers into the Pyrenees Mountains. This is a highly desirable stop because the most difficult section of the Camino happens to be at the very beginning. Not only is a hiker less conditioned for hiking at the beginning of her trip, but the trail itself is more difficult there, with few stops along the way. The hike up the Pyrenees mountains is extremely steep. Orisson is really the only place someone can stay for the night without having to walk the entire 25km to the next town. So I was relieved to learn that they still had availability; this will be my second night's stay in Spain but my first on the Camino itself.

I hadn't determined yet how I'll find a place to sleep after the first two nights. There seems to be two mindsets on the trial with regard to sleeping arrangements; the first line of thinking is that it's best to make reservations. Some people make reservations well in advance with the hopes that they can maintain the pace they scheduled for themselves, and some call ahead the day before they arrive in each town.

The other mindset is that this is a spiritual journey, and part of the experience is having faith in God that there will be "room at the inn." I wasn't sure what mindset I'd have, but I suspected it would be a little of both. I had plenty of faith in God, but not as much in myself. I suspected I'd make reservations a day ahead until I got a feel for the trail and my own pace. Perhaps, once I'd gained confidence in my own journey, I'd feel free to be more spontaneous.

*Testing My Gear:*

The weekend's weather was finally decent enough that I could test my gear for the first time. I spent all day Saturday creating a gear checklist and finding the best way to pack my bag. At this point, my pack weighed about 16 pounds. I was hoping to reduce the weight before I left but at this moment, I was not willing to discard anything I packed. For example, Brian insisted that six ounces of deodorant would be useless to me on the Camino, but I was just not prepared to part with hygiene.

As for my pack, after spending some time adjusting the straps, it fit pretty well. This was a relief because there are very few extra small women's packs available on the market that would be appropriate for my 4'7" frame, and my Osprey Tempest 40 was the second one I'd tested. If this one did not work out, there was only one other pack I could try.

That Sunday we drove out to Odiorne Point in Rye, New Hampshire to do a short three mile walk along the coast. I'm sure I looked ridiculous trudging through two feet of snow by the beach with a 40-liter pack on (I did get a few strange looks), but I didn't care. Making sure my pack fit before I left would increase my chances of finishing the Camino.

Following my hike, I noticed three things I'd need to address:

I'd have to add some foam to the lower back of my pack because after only a few miles, the rubbing irritated my skin (postscript: this never ended up being a problem on the Camino).

My ankles would have benefitted from some muscle strengthening. They were definitely strained from walking in the snow and over the rocky beaches. While the Pyrenees mountains wouldn't have snow, they would have a similar rocky terrain (postscript: the path over the Pyrenees was not rocky).

Finally, I had foot pain that I knew I'd be forced to contend with along my entire journey. I had recently learned that the muscles in the back of my legs had never fully developed. They are too short and therefore are always over extended, which causes foot pain whenever I stand, walk, or run. I tell people it's like having permanent plantar fasciitis because most people can relate to that. I had been to three specialists and two physical therapists hoping for a solution, but no one could help. Within only 20 minutes of walking with my pack on during my practice hike, my feet were agitated much more than usual. I was hoping this would be a blessing in disguise, though. Many people get addicted to hiking long miles every day, and they push themselves to the point that they either injure themselves or they miss out on the best parts of the adventure. My underdeveloped legs were actually going to force me to take things very slowly. This would give me more time to appreciate the Camino and take care of myself.

Of course after the very short hike, we had to celebrate. So we finished the day in Kittery, Maine with raw oysters and martinis!

## Bon Voyage Party

I was less than two weeks from my start date and the closer I got, the more driven I was to practice hiking. On Sunday, my friend Liz and

I walked the Rail Trail from start (Nashua, NH) to finish (Ayer, MA). All in all, we walked almost 14 miles. I was more confident now that I'd be able to walk long distances. That said, I wouldn't know if I could maintain that kind of stamina for multiple consecutive days. I suppose I'd find out when I was faced with the Pyrenees Mountains.

What I didn't know about Sunday was that our walk served as a distraction so Brian could prepare for the surprise Bon Voyage party he planned for me. I returned home (all exhausted and sweaty) to a house full of my closest friends and a fabulous Spanish-inspired paella Brian grilled for everyone. I couldn't have asked for a better going away. It filled my heart to know that I would have so many supporters cheering me on from home. This would surely keep me going when times got tough. Once again, I thanked Brian for always providing encouragement.

Practice hike with my gear

Celebrating with martinis and raw oysters

# CHAPTER 2

## LONGEST COMMUTE EVER

Finally, it is May 15, 2015, and I'm on my way. I have spent so much time planning and thinking about this trip that I am emotionally drained, but ready to do this.

*Boston Logan Airport*

No more than 20 minutes after arriving at the airport, I ran into another solo Camino hiker from New Hampshire! Her name is Dolores, and she would be starting her walk the day after I start mine. Like me, she reluctantly chopped her hair off so she wouldn't have to worry about it. I had no idea why, but this made me feel like we have the world in common. Just two chicks roughin' it through Europe with bad hairdos. I was so excited to meet a fellow pilgrim, I could barely contain myself!

"So Dolores, what are you looking forward to most on the Camino?" I asked my new friend with excitement in my voice.

"The solitude."

Okay then. Point taken! I chuckled to myself. What are the odds of meeting the one pilgrim who isn't interested in meeting others? Nevertheless, I throttled back my enthusiasm and only spoke to her when she spoke to me.

We actually did have a very nice conversation. What made our meeting notable was that even though Dolores is taking a completely different mode of transportation after arriving in Madrid, she happened to have written instructions that would guide me from the airport to the train station, the one part of my trip I am most unsure of. I felt so fortunate to have run into her when I did. I've heard from other hikers that pilgrims should never worry about their journey because "the Camino provides." I don't know if that is true, but so far things are looking good!

## Two hours Later

I have just found out via the internet that another pilgrim named Melisa is sitting in the same terminal as me! She posted on the American Pilgrims on the Camino (APOC) Facebook page that she was at Boston Logan and she couldn't wait to meet her new "trail family." I responded immediately with a description of myself and told her to look for me. As I searched around the room, I caught my sights on a woman about my age who was also clearly looking for someone. I waved wildly at her and she waved back with equal excitement. We greeted in the middle of the gate terminal as if we already knew each other. I imagined everyone staring at us assumed we were long lost friends! Dolores was sitting close to me so I introduced them and the three of us began chattering away about our trip. I am thrilled.

I learned that Melisa is from Austin, Texas and has a layover in Boston. She said once she arrived in Madrid, she planned to take the subway to the train station even though it requires multiple transfers. I considered joining her but was hesitant because I didn't study the subway system at all and had planned to avoid it altogether.

The advantages of traveling with her are: 1) I wouldn't be alone in a new country and 2) she spoke some Spanish. After taking some time to contemplate during my seven-hour flight and after consulting with the Spanish woman I was seated with, I decided I, too would like to experience the subway system.

## *Finding Our Way Around Madrid Airport*

Dolores, Melisa, and I waited for each other to debark the plane and walked through customs together. We were supposed to enter the little rooms separately, but the three of us walked in practically arm-in-arm. The authorities didn't seem to mind though; I think it was because they are accustomed to naive pilgrims coming through the airport. Melisa and I said goodbye to Dolores as she boarded a bus to Pamplona, and we headed for the train station.

Thank God we stayed together. Everything worked out, but nothing came to us easily. From buying food, to using an ATM, to purchasing metro tickets, to finding our way around, to paying to use the bathroom, it all took time and effort. Having a buddy made it comical instead of stressful.

The subway is one of the cleanest I've seen and is very easy to navigate. However, once we reached the train station, we spent the next three hours completely confused. If it weren't for Melisa's Spanish lessons, I would have had an extremely difficult time getting around. Employees were not friendly even when she spoke Spanish, and they seemed to have little incentive to help two Americans. We talked to nearly ten people just to find the trains - in the train station! How was that the challenge?

## *On the Train to Pamplona*

Okay, this isn't fun anymore. I have been awake for over 24 hours, traveling for over 18, and am still hundreds of miles from my destination. I am tired, I am hungry, and I stink. The good news is, while I almost lost my travel buddy, we learned that the only really nice guy at the train station happened to be the supervisor for my train. I'll spare you the details, but Melisa and I spent those three hours at the station trying to get her on my train, which was supposedly full. I purchased my tickets in advance but Melisa tried to buy hers when we arrived at the station, but no one was willing to help us, so when the time came I wished her luck and boarded without her.

I was hopeful when I saw two empty seats directly across from me. The train obviously wasn't full, despite what the people at the ticket counter told us. But I quickly lost hope as the train started moving and Melisa never arrived. Sure enough though, about 20 minutes after leaving, I received a text from Melisa saying the man let her on the train at the last minute. So she snuck into first class with me and the two of us are traveling in style.

Side note: the countryside is beautiful. Lush green fields in the foreground, snowcapped mountains in the background, and little villages tucked into valleys scattered across the landscape. That said, I am too tired to care. Ten-minute naps are my new favorite thing.

## Two More Hours Later

Who buys children first class tickets? It's like a freakin' playground in here! Rugrats running up and down the aisle, playing patty Spanish cake, squealing like they had a full night's sleep. I can't even take it right now.

## Pamplona to Bizkarreta

The fourth leg of my trip was much better. I was to meet a man named Istvan who would shuttle me to his pensión in a small village called Bizkarreta. The Pamplona train station was bustling with people, but Istvan gave great instructions for finding him outside in front of the building. He actually found me first, since I told him I'd be the shortest adult he'd probably ever meet. That always works.

We took winding hilly roads to Bizkarreta, population 160. Along the way, I saw sheep and cows grazing on steep hills, and even some pilgrims as we drove past part of the Camino.

The couple who own the pensión are from Hungary and have hiked the Camino multiple times. They were extremely kind and hospitable. I had my own room, a shared bathroom, and access to a common family room which was overrun by some very boisterous hikers. I could tell they've been hiking the Camino for a while now as they were very comfortable with themselves. I was still adjusting to my surroundings and feeling quite tired so I wasn't very talkative. I did spend some time with them at dinner, but for the most part I stayed in my room, read, and tried desperately not to fall asleep too early. I was guessing it would take several days to get over the jetlag. It was very cool and rainy, so I don't regret carrying my jacket for a moment. It looked to be a dreary start.

I couldn't see much out my window because it was very foggy, but across the street from the pensión was a steep hill peppered with cows. They were all wearing bells around their necks that rang out and echoed off the village buildings. It almost sounded like music.

Melisa, my Camino amiga

Train to Pamplona

# CHAPTER 3

## DAY 1: 7KM FROM SAINT-JEAN-PIED-DE-PORT TO ORISSON
—
### EXCITED, NAIVE, AND SOAKING WET

After getting a small bit of sleep last night, I was feeling much better this morning. I woke up at six and joined the other pilgrims for a simple breakfast provided by my gracious hosts. The noisy Americans who had their massive suitcases shuttled from place to place for them were still in bed, so I had time to visit with the ladies who came in late, last night including a solo hiker named Jenny. We were to ride together over the border to Saint-Jean-Pied-de-Port, France, where we would start our journey.

I had a moment of panic when I couldn't find my money as I was leaving. One downside of carrying everything on your back is that if you want one thing, you must unpack your entire bag. So there I was, with everyone waiting for me as I tore my bag apart in the foyer looking for my credit cards and 200 euros. They were very sympathetic though.

In the night another couple came in but had lost all their credit cards at the airport. They were a disaster. Sadly, I don't think they'll make it on the Camino. They were so frazzled last night and still in bed when I left this morning. I did find my money, though, and we all left with our spirits high. We were so energized by what we were about to embark on. It was cold, windy, rainy, and foggy, but that didn't bother me in the least. I knew the Pyrenees would be a challenge and I would rather hike it cold than in the heat.

The ride into France was beautiful. The massive rolling hills covered with lush greenery reminded me of Costa Rica. When we arrived in St. Jean, I thanked Istvan for his hospitality. I knew the Camino would have me passing back through his town in three days' time so I made reservations to stay there again - in three days. I have no idea what day that will be because I've already lost track of time.

He reminded me for the third time that, if for some reason I changed my mind, to please call and cancel my reservation. As he shook my hand and he wished me luck, I realized he didn't think I was going to make it. On the ride to St. Jean, he was saying he could tell who would finish the Camino and who would give up. I would normally take this as a sign – someone with a great deal of experience betting I wouldn't make it three days in.

But I reminded myself that I'm usually underestimated. There I was, this short woman all by herself (there were lots of comments in the house about how small I was, so it was clearly on their mind). For some reason, people presume to know a lot about me based on my height alone. So I couldn't really fault him. He just doesn't know me. I do, though, and I'm not worried. If I quit, it will be by choice - or if I fall off a cliff. I didn't bother to correct him though. I could do that when I see him in a few days.

We all gathered up our packs and walked toward the pilgrim's welcome center. Jenny and I entered the office together and rifled through the box of scallop shells. Every pilgrim walks with the symbolic scallop tied to their pack. The shell represents the many Camino paths that all lead to Santiago. I also had to purchase my credentials (or Camino passport), which is a small accordion style booklet pilgrims carry and have stamped at every stop. You must have a full passport when you arrive in Santiago to receive credit for the hike. You also must have a pilgrim's passport to stay in the albergues along the Way, which are sleeping accommodations specifically for pilgrims.

I had been told the volunteers at the office spoke all languages, but the only woman there that early in the morning spoke French. Unlike most others I've encountered so far, she was very friendly, and we fumbled through the conversation together. I purchased my shell and immediately dropped it. It has a big chip in it now and I suppose I could have traded it for another, but would a shell really be mine if it didn't look like it had been dropped? No. So I tied it to my pack proudly and gathered up my credentials.

As I pulled on my pack, another pilgrim informed me that the office was strongly advising pilgrims not to take the Napoleon route. When a pilgrim passes over the Pyrenees Mountains, she has one of two routes she can take. She can walk straight up and over the mountain (the Napoleon route), or she can walk around the mountain (which is still very much up and over the mountain, though not quite as directly as the Napoleon route). The Napoleon route is known for its harsh conditions, especially at the top, so my instinct was to heed the local's advice. Unfortunately, the albergue I booked for tonight, Orisson, was on the Napoleon route. So I had to go up and over.

I was just contemplating my predicament when Melisa walked in. We were so happy to meet again and greeted with a big hug. We introduced each other to our newfound friends. Melisa had met Misha, the Australian, and Angie, the American the night before in a really nice albergue right in St. Jean. From their description they had a wonderful experience.

They all had a chance to get to know each other and discuss why they chose to hike the Camino. It was a simple group exercise facilitated by the volunteers running the albergue, but it helped foster close relationships very quickly. It reminded me of the tight relationships my husband formed while hiking the Appalachian Trail. I am happy to see that the Camino also has the magical power to bring its hikers together; I hope I will be able to form bonds like that somewhere along the Way. There's something special about trail families that I don't quite understand, but would really like to. I forgot all about my worries of hiking over the Pyrenees.

As we were exiting the pilgrim's office, Misha told us about this amazing foot cream that reduces the chance of blisters. I have heard about it, but hadn't seen it yet because it is only sold in Europe. Jenny ran into someone she recognized, so we said goodbye to each other and I eagerly walked with Melisa's group to the pharmacy up the road.

St. Jean is a beautiful little town tucked away. I took in the cobblestone roads lined with old shops and homes, the small river running through the two streets that made up the town, the fresh fruit sold outside of the stores, and the smell of freshly baked bread. Wow, so this was France!

The three of us stopped multiple times to figure out what gear we should be wearing and carrying. It began to rain slightly, so we needed rain gear, but we would be sweating soon from the steep hike up the Pyrenees, so our jackets were unnecessary.

As we were fumbling through our gear, Melisa ran into an American woman she was originally planning to hike with. But Melisa already hooked up with Angie, Misha and me, and the other woman met up with two guys named Stephen and Nikolai. Stephen is from Memphis and Nikolai is from Germany. They all just met on the first day, too. So I guess the two women decided to stick with their hiking families that naturally formed. We all greeted each other, wished each other luck, and went on our way.

After the pharmacy, we stopped in a little shop to pick up some snacks. I had so much adrenaline coursing through me. I was excited, nervous, and scared all at the same time. As I was picking out my snacks, I bent over to get something from the bottom shelf and cracked my chin on my hiking poles. It wasn't quite a tearjerker, but I knew it would leave a mark. I tried to play it off like nothing happened, but I had an instant goose egg hanging from my chin.

"What happened to your face?" Melisa said. I told her the stupid thing I'd just done and we all laughed. We joked that I found the first way to die on the Camino - stabbing oneself with a hiking pole. I carefully purchased some fruit and headed out onto the cobblestone street to wait for my hiking buddies to finish their shopping. We then headed to a beautiful church at the end of the road. It felt good to say a prayer and center myself in preparation for what I was about to do. I prayed for the strength, health, and the courage to hike the entire Camino.

We hiked out of town, chattering on most of the way. The Pyrenees start off with an immediate ascent. As we got to the top of the very first hill, I saw a massive hardbound book that someone abandoned on a stone wall. Apparently, they did not read all the hiking articles that discourage carrying anything that isn't entirely necessary. I laughed to myself, thinking about how quickly this hiker was willing to abandon his or her book. We were only at the start of the Pyrenees, but I had to admire their interest in bringing such an enormous book to begin with.

Sometimes the four of us walked together and sometimes we hiked by ourselves, but we were always within sight. The hills were merciless as we switch-backed the whole way up to our first stop at Orisson. Sometimes it felt like we were walking straight up, and there were few breaks from the steepness. We were walking along a road most of the way, though, so at least the terrain was smooth.

I stopped many times, mostly to catch my breath and give my calves a break, but also to take pictures of the clouds rolling in over the hills, and the farm animals who didn't seem to notice us. It was quite a sight, though I suspect it would be absolutely spectacular on a sunny day. The fog was obstructing the views heavily. Still, I thanked God for the cool weather.

And then came the rain. We were drenched. My toes were squishing in my socks and, despite the strenuous walk, I was shivering from the soaked pants that clung to my legs for dear life. Angie and Misha trudged onward but Melisa and I took frequent breaks.

"Oh, look, Theresa, a worm."

"Lovely. Let's stop and make sure it makes it across the road safely."

Any reason to stop the pain in my feet was fine with me. I frequently stopped and leaned over my poles in an attempt to remove some of the weight from my strained feet. There was a moment when we got splashed by what had to be cow dung. We were trying to avoid walking in it as it liquefied and flowed down the mountain, but when the massive tractors blew past us on the road, there was little we could do. We were a mess.

At one point Melisa and I were talking about giving up. We stopped and whined to each other that we would die out here in the rain and fog. We only had about five miles to hike for the entire day, but we were so cold and wet (and covered in manure) and the discomfort of walking straight up the mountain was turning into pain that spread up and down my legs. We had to keep going, though. We gathered our strength and carried on, realizing we didn't have a choice.

It is kind of scary when you realize your only alternative to dying right there on that steep mountain is to keep putting one foot in front of the other. There's no going back. It's all or nothing.

We walked only about fifteen more feet from where we wanted to forfeit and suddenly the albergue Orisson came into view through the dense fog. It was right there! We were excited to see that beautiful old building and laughed at the fact that we nearly gave up just a few feet back!

We burst into the main area to find dozens of drenched, stinky pilgrims chowing down on soup and drinking wine. I checked in and was relieved to find they had not given my bed away, which the place is known for doing on occasion. If I didn't have a place to sleep, I would have to hike another 13 miles to the next town, and I didn't think that was even physically possible.

Melisa and I waded through all the wet backpacks that littered the floor and found a place to rest our own packs. Everything was soaked and the floors were slippery. I walked back to the counter and ordered what seemed like the best cup of hot tea I've ever had. I sat down with it in my soaked clothes at the long table where I spent the next hour chatting with other pilgrims and trying to gain feeling back my frozen toes.

Once it was ready, a very annoyed volunteer showed us our three-bunk room and pointed out the amenities. I always thought I'd be super shy about changing with others in the room, but I learned today that when you're soaked to the bone and shivering, you're not remotely concerned about modesty. I bolted for the showers and deposited the special coin they gave me to begin my five-minute shower. It was the most glorious five minutes of my life! I could feel the warmth flowing back into my extremities. I instantly felt better and completely forgot about how miserable I was just minutes before.

Next, I hand washed my clothes in the sink. Melisa let me borrow a bar of soap she brought with her. This is something I forgot to pack. We then stood in line for the dryer, which didn't actually dry anything. Pilgrims had to run multiple drying cycles to dry their soaked clothes.

Over the next four hours, Melisa and I took turns waiting in line for the dryer and then watching our clothes in the machine. We chatted away with Misha and other pilgrims who were also waiting patiently. Later that evening, after the machine had only half-dried my clothes, I strung the parachute cord I brought from home across my bunk and hung them. I placed my shoes on the heater, hoping to dry them out a bit, too.

Dinner time was great. All the pilgrims gathered to eat, drink, and meet new people. I talked mostly to the four women who were sitting closest to me. We shared with each other our reasons for walking the Camino. I was in awe over how much honesty and openness strangers can have with one another.

While we were eating, the volunteers encouraged each pilgrim to stand and tell the room who they are and where they are from. The very first guy to introduce himself was from Holland and he'd clearly had too much to drink. He yammered on and on until his embarrassed wife dragged him back down to his seat. Several of us joked that it was going to be a very long night if everyone took as long as he did.

Following a great meal (I stuffed myself) I walked out to the patio that hung over the cliff side. I could imagine how fantastic it would be to sit and eat outside on a nice day. The clouds parted long enough for us to see the view that we had been missing, and it was truly beautiful. We saw miles of rolling mountains with sheep and cattle everywhere. Several other pilgrims congregated outside and we stood around and talked until 9:00pm, which is late for pilgrims. But it was still broad daylight so the thought of going to bed was difficult.

When Melisa and I headed back to our room for the night, we found the four other pilgrims we shared the room with were sleeping already. It also felt like a sauna! My glasses steamed up as soon as I entered the room and I knew it was going to be a very long night. There was no way I could sleep in that kind of heat. I live in New Hampshire! That is what it's like to share a room with strangers though; you lose control of your surroundings. Someone took it upon him or herself to crank the temperature all the way up. I also noticed that someone removed my sneakers from the heater, which means tomorrow I'll be hiking in wet shoes. Again.

Pyrenees Mountains

Orisson

# CHAPTER 4

## DAY 2: 18KM FROM ORISSON TO RONCESVALLES

—

## WHERE ARE MY PANTS?

I made it! I passed over the Pyrenees and the toughest part of the Camino is mostly behind me. After packing up all my gear this morning, I got my passport stamped at the Orisson bar and had a quick pilgrim's breakfast before leaving. They gave us toast and orange juice. When we were passed the basket of bread, I assumed it was just the first course but after I scarfed it down and sat patiently waiting for more, someone told us that the Spanish don't eat much for breakfast and this was all we would be getting. I was hoping we would get something like a hardboiled egg. After all, I was about to hike the rest of the Pyrenees and needed protein.

But things always seem to work out here. Just as Melisa and I were complaining on the trail that we didn't get enough breakfast and we were getting hungry, we came across a Camino food truck: a man in a van parked in the middle of the mountain offering drinks, fruit, candy bars, fresh cheese, and hardboiled eggs! We eagerly purchased several items from him and continued on our merry way, feeling renewed.

I purchased a banana, a block of cheese, and a hardboiled egg. I sliced the cheese with my Swiss army knife and shared it with my new pilgrim friends who were nearby, Betty and Markus from Texas.

We all had lots of time to get to know each other the previous night, so by now I recognize most of the people on the trail. It's really great to walk alone, but I also love when I meet up with other folks or when they sneak up on me and suddenly I have a new but temporary walking buddy. You're never really alone on the Camino.

I do tend to walk by myself for the most part, though. My legs are short and they just don't carry me as fast as everyone else, so when I do walk with someone, it's usually for a very brief period of time before they move on.

I paid close attention to how others were hiking. Markus walked well ahead of his wife Betty and would frequently stop and wait for her to catch up. It made me wonder how Brian and I will walk when he meets me for the last 100kms. Until then, I'll have to be okay with the fact that I will probably be hiking this Camino alone for the most part. Melisa and I are walking together, but I suspect as she gets stronger, she will want to carry on without me.

The rest of the way up the Pyrenees was as relentless as the day before, but the distance was much farther. I was so relieved I didn't do the entire thing in one day. I found the hike to be extremely difficult. The Camino is not very technically difficult, meaning you don't have to maneuver your way around boulders or cross streams, but there are plenty of mountains and hills all along the Way. I'd like to say the descent was easier, but my knees would beg to differ. It was just as challenging as the ascent.

Whenever I would start to lose interest or hope, something great would happen. For example, I was trudging along in the thick fog, bummed about not being able to see any of the landmarks on the Pyrenees, when I heard something galloping towards me. At first it scared me. Whatever was creating the noise was huge! Two beautiful horses burst through the fog and ran up to me out of nowhere. They were looking for attention and they were as playful as puppies. They leaned into Melisa and me as we tried to give them all the love and petting they desired. There were many other farm animals on the Way. I couldn't always see them through the fog, but I could always hear their bells. Sheep and cows are plentiful here.

I was a bit disappointed that during all my time in the mountains, the fog was so thick that I missed all of the major features. The guidebook mentioned many things a pilgrim ought to see, but I never saw any of them. Occasionally the sun would poke through and I'd catch a glimpse of the spectacular views I was usually missing.

The good thing was that it wasn't raining, which was a huge improvement from the day before. It was freezing at the top, though. At one point several pilgrims stopped dead in their tracks and we all ditched our packs to dig out our coats. The wind hit us hard, and suddenly we were too cold to go on. We all laughed as we struggled with our frozen fingers to help dress each other. For instance, Pam from California had been hiking in a skirt! She was freezing!

"For God's sake Pam, put your pants on!" we all joked.

The sun did make an appearance towards the end of my walk, though, and the weather was absolutely perfect then. But that was later in the day.

I met my first trail angel today. Trail angels are people who, of their own free will, provide food, water, shelter or anything else a hiker really needs. This angel was a Frenchmen who was squatting in an old tiny shack right on the trail. He had a roaring fire and was making hot tea. Melisa and I stopped in to warm up, dry off, and buy a drink. The glasses he served us with were dirty, but you'd be surprised what you're willing to overlook when you're hiking all day. A few other hikers came and went as we sat there and warmed ourselves by the fire. One attractive young man took a liking to Melisa. The two of them chatted for a bit before he wished us luck and moved on. I pretended to be super interested in the fire while they talked.

We thanked the man for his hospitality and left the shelter feeling energized and ready to go. I continued to trudge straight up the mountain at lightning speed. But one thing I'm learning is that you must take your time on the Camino. Every time I try to speed up, something sets me back - like slipping on a muddy rock and nearly wiping out. Well, as I exited that shelter and bolted up the mountain, I started feeling very nauseated.

I lagged behind as all the familiar pilgrims passed me. When I had a moment of privacy, I threw up everything I had eaten for the day. It was not a proud moment for me, but that's what I get for pushing too hard. I spent the rest of my day being super careful not to overdo it. I found Melisa waiting for me a few turns up the mountain. Another pilgrim who passed me while I was bent over in the weeds walked ahead and warned her that I wasn't feeling well. Apparently news travels fast on the Camino.

We reached a nice rocky area that overlooked the mountainside. Melisa and I stopped to eat the ham and cheese sandwiches the albergue in Orisson sent us away with. We sat on a mound of rocks and watched the sun poke through the clouds over the rolling hills along with a handful of other pilgrims who had the same idea. I rested my feet and dried out my shoes and socks. Brian told me the best the best way to minimize the chance for blisters is to take off my shoes and socks, flip my socks inside out, and let everything dry. He said I should try to do this every couple of miles. The weather had been so bad, though, that we kept moving continuously, so this was my first opportunity to follow his advice. Melisa followed along and did the same.

I'm not sure when it happened, but at some point today, we crossed into Spain. If there was an official *Espana* sign, we missed it in the fog. But nonetheless, we still had to have a mini celebration. When we came across a big stone water fountain, we stopped to refill our water bottles and to take pictures. "This looks like Spain. I think we're in Spain." We really had no idea.

Although the rest of the walk was foggy and soggy, I did have the opportunity to see some of what nature had to offer. For example, we came across many massive shiny black slugs. They were bigger than I could ever imagine a slug to be. At first glance, I was repulsed by the slimy creatures and they nearly made me gag. But Betty would say, "Look how beautiful they are," as she would stop and lean down to admire them. I slowed my roll and looked again. Yeah, I guess they were kind of pretty.

I was also extremely happy to see the beech tree forest. Not only was it a beautiful sight with the fog stretching across the forest and engulfing every tree, but I knew from my guidebook that these trees were not far at all from our stop in Roncesvalles.

We knew we had arrived at Roncesvalles because, out of nowhere, we saw a massive ancient monastery appear. This is where we would spend the night. There was no need to make reservations here, though. The place has over 500 bunks! I learned later that they are partitioned into four beds, though, so it's actually quite cozy.

Upon arrival, I stood in line outside in the cold to scrub the mud off my shoes, which were completely soiled. A woman in front of me kept washing other people's shoes, making me wait even longer for my turn. I found myself getting very frustrated but realized this was just a lesson in patience. I relaxed a bit and quietly awaited my turn.

The check-in process was quite an ordeal. The *hospitaleros* (albergue volunteers) were very friendly and helpful to the masses of people streaming into the building looking for rest. We were asked to drop our shoes at the door before waiting in a very long line to get our passports stamped and directions to our beds. Melisa and I were instructed to find our beds on the second floor.

I am cracking up right now because as I'm typing this in my top bunk with my earplugs in, Melisa just hit me from below and let me know she's going to ask if we can be moved. We won the lottery. We have the loudest snorer ever in our quad. I took a video of it because I don't think anyone would believe how loud it is. Yikes! Earplugs are an essential on the Camino.

Anyways, back to earlier tonight. We ran into Stephen and Nikolai in town, and they were ready for drinks at the only bar. I wanted to take a shower and wash my clothes first, but Melisa was eager to see what this little town had to offer. I decided I should be a little more flexible and just go with the flow. I could worry about chores later.

While we were out for drinks, we all decided to have dinner together. We made reservations at the restaurant in the town's only hotel. One woman really wanted to eat at the restaurant where Martin Sheen supposedly ate during the making of *The Way*, which is a movie about the Camino. But since we already made reservations at the hotel, we all decided to stick to the plan. It was a good thing we did, too. What a great evening!

It was a typical pilgrim's meal: wine, water, soup, bread, duck, and some kind of tart for dessert. We sat at a long table with pilgrims we knew and some new faces as well. Everyone spoke different languages so we worked hard to understand one another. I love that people come from all over the globe to hike the Camino. Our table consisted of people from Canada, the U.S., South Africa, Spain, Italy, and Germany.

There was an impromptu concert by a woman at the next table over who began singing. She had the most beautiful voice that brought a room full of noisy pilgrims to complete silence for several minutes. She was breathtaking. I learned later that she is actually a famous singer from Ireland. I didn't know of her, though.

Later, several of us walked around the small medieval town. The architecture was beautiful and the church was downright scary. Melisa and I walked down three flights of stairs underground into the crypt of the church. It was pitch dark and smelled musty. I only lasted about 30 seconds before I sprinted back out, leaving poor Melisa by herself in the crypt! I really can't put this experience into words. I can't even compare it to anything else I've experienced either.

We then spent the rest of the evening walking around town looking for our pants. That's right. We lost our pants. Our only pants. So we were freezing in our shorts.

Because we had so much trouble hand washing and drying our clothes yesterday, while we were having drinks earlier in the evening we tried to find somewhere to have our clothes laundered. We paid the hotel to wash our clothes for us. But Melisa and I couldn't find Stephen, and he was the one who knew where to pick up our clothes. And it's not like there's Wi-Fi in an ancient town like this. So what did people do before phones? Apparently they walked around town stopping in every building until they found their friends.

We hit up all the restaurants, the churches, and the bars in town. Granted there were only about five establishments altogether. We halted our search for a while when we arrived at the bar and met a nice Dutchman. Melisa is a natural conversationalist. I sat quietly and listened as the two chatted away. Once we finished our wine, we said goodbye to our new friend and continued our search for our missing pants. Fortunately, we did retrieve them from Stephen before the night was through.

A few interesting facts about Spain: soup and lamb are very common dishes here. Customer service is not a priority. Most devices are on timers to save energy (lights, faucets, etc.)

As I was lying here in my bed, I wondered if Melisa was sleeping yet. I looked down at the bunk below me to find her bed was empty.

Where could she possibly have gone? I decided to run to the bathroom while I was still awake. When I entered the bathroom, I saw there was one other woman in a stall.

"Melisa, is that you?" I whispered.

"Yeah, it's me. I figured if I can't sleep I might as well try to poop!" We both laughed at the awkward situation we were in. This would be the second night of no sleep.

Well, that's it for now. I'm surrounded by snoring pilgrims and I need to accept that this is my life for the next eight hours! Good night.

Beech tree forest

Hiking towards Roncesvalles, Spain

# CHAPTER 5

## DAY 3: 21KM FROM RONCESVALLES TO ZUBIRI

—

## FAMILIES ARE FORMED, BODIES ARE BROKEN

Today I walked with several people throughout the journey. We joined up with Cristina from Italy, and I suspect we will be together at least for the next few days. It's great when you find people who fit your hiking style. Melisa and I have been talking about expanding our trail family, and after spending the evening last night with Cristina, we thought it would be great to walk with her. We told her we would meet her by the Santiago sign at the edge of town at 8:00am and we would walk together. The giant sign that reads "Santiago de Compostela 790km."

Well, by 8:00am, Melisa and I stood by the sign feeling like we were the only pilgrims left in town. Everyone had left so much earlier and we realized we should have asked to meet Cristina at 7:00am rather than 8:00am. We got antsy and decided to leave at exactly 8:00am. Poor Cristina showed up at 8:03am and we had already left!

She caught up with us later at a *supermercado* we stopped at, and we apologized to her for leaving her behind. I felt so bad. I probably would have been pretty angry if someone had left me behind like that. She was very easy going, though. She just laughed and said she understood. The three of us continued on together.

But first we stopped in the *supermercado* so Melisa and I could purchase a couple of things. Since I forgot to pack soap, I attempted to purchase detergent but because everything was in Spanish, I ended up buying the wrong thing and didn't realize it until we left the store and I opened the box. I had to carry it 20km before I could ditch it. I really wish I knew Spanish. I miss a lot not knowing the language. That said, it makes things very comical.

Partway through the day, I ran into Istvan, the guy who owns Pensión Corazon Puro where I stayed the first night. We were walking along the road in a little town and he recognized me as he drove by. He stopped to say hello and assured us we were going the right way. It was so nice to see him again. The three of us girls then stopped for a water break before continuing on. I sat in the shade and played with a big beautiful dog that was running around.

Several minutes later when we started walking again, we saw Istvan standing at a crosswalk. It seemed a bit random and suspicious at first. But he pointed us in the right direction, got back in his car and drove off. We realized he had been waiting for us there and wanted to make sure we wouldn't miss the tricky turn. Our Camino angel!

Another man also pointed us in the right direction when we went the wrong way. People are wonderful here. I'm starting to realize that suspicion really doesn't have a place here on the Camino. The locals are genuinely kind and generous.

The local animals seem to be as kind as the people. I shared my Camino cheese with a couple of alley cats. I love that you can find animals everywhere around here and all they want is to be loved. Melisa calls me Snow White now because animals always approach me.

This Camino stuff is getting serious now. We are all working harder and playing harder. Two things happened today. I am becoming stronger and weaker all at the same time. On one hand, my body is learning that walking is just something I do. I'm propelled forward in an almost mindless manner. I get into the zone (especially on inclines). I find my happy place, focus on my breathing and just move. The last two hours of today's hike felt like I was on autopilot.

On the other hand, I'm hurting everywhere. Unlike the last two days, my day began with aches and pains and they just grew worse as the day went on. It was almost comical when we arrived at our albergue tonight. Everyone limped around like zombies. I saw a young, fit man stop at the top of a stairwell and look down the stairs as if he wanted to cry. He was in too much pain to even think about walking down them. I knew exactly how he felt. We all did. Everything hurts. Everywhere.

I've been having a hard time following Brian's advice to stop every few miles. I'm finding that your body hurts so much that you don't like taking breaks because it's so difficult to start again. Your body screams the moment you stop walking, so it's tempting to just keep moving. But, if you don't stop, you run the risk of getting blisters, so it's a balancing act.

So far I'm okay. My knees and calves ache terribly and of course my feet are in more pain than I've ever felt. I don't have blisters yet but I do have hot spots so I will be watching them carefully tomorrow. I will probably bandage them before I get started in the morning.

We are all aware that tomorrow will be a crucial day. We have 21km to Pamplona (where they have the running of the bulls each year), and while it'll be a flat stretch compared to the last three days, this is when we will be truly pushing our bodies. We don't want to break, so we are all being extremely careful. Cristina, Melisa and I may stay in Pamplona an extra night to allow ourselves to heal.

In the meantime, we are having a blast. Today I met so many more people from all over the world. The conversations are engaging and the interactions are hilarious. Everyone is good natured and we all look out for each other.

Today we trusted we would find a place to sleep in the next town. No reservations, no plans. We just strolled into town and looked for an albergue. Actually, we didn't have much of a choice. Remember how I'd made plans to spend another night at Corazon Puro? Well, we were making such great time that we passed it early in the day and decided to keep going.

Istvan and his wife Barbara weren't home at the time, so I called them and let them know that we were feeling good and were actually going to carry on. Cristina, Melisa and I ended up in a small room with a few people including Ginger and Drennan, a mom and son team from Florida. We were a bit surprised to see the boy because we were told only women were allowed in our room.

Melisa whispered, "Is that a guy in the bed above you?"

But I couldn't make out what she said so I awkwardly stood up and peaked over the bunk. Sure enough, there was Drennan. He seemed like a sweet kid. We carried on as usual. You quickly get used to unisex accommodations.

The bathroom situation in the hostels isn't as bad as I imagined either. They are co-ed and it's common to step out of the shower and have a man standing there waiting for his turn. But the showers themselves are fairly private and usually have small changing areas inside, so I've been pretty comfortable with the accommodations.

On our way out to dinner, we ran into Nikolai and Stephen, who were staying in the room next to ours at the same albergue. We all spent another dinner together talking about our day and enjoying the scenery as we sat outside with several other happy people we'd met along the way. Our group split several pitchers of Sangria and we were feeling pretty good by the end of the night. So far, I'm finding that the walking is tough but I love hanging out with everyone in the evenings.

What else can I say about today? This morning I saw how forward Spanish men can be. The owner of the restaurant where we had breakfast walked up to Melisa, blew a kiss at her, put his hands on her face, drew her in and called her "*muy guapa.*" She was completely stunned, of course, but then we couldn't stop laughing. Who does that? Not that I blame the guy. Melisa is gorgeous!

We're the last ones in Roncesvalles

Leaving Roncesvalles

# CHAPTER 6

## DAY 4: 23KM FROM ZUBIRI TO PAMPLONA

—

## DÓNDE ESTÁ LA ESCUELA?

It's amazing how my mood shifts from hour to hour. For the first 10km today, I was powering through it. Minus a few wicked steep hills, the road to Pamplona was mostly flat, so I dashed through most of it. We stopped for lunch in one of the many little towns we passed through, visited with some new pilgrims we met along the Way, and got our passports stamped. But somewhere within the last 8kms, the pain really started to slow me down. I wasn't the only one either. Cristina was struggling with her knee.

I desperately need time to let my feet rest. My chronic foot pain has been nearly unbearable at times but Melisa doesn't seem to have any issues. I tried to race ahead of her sometimes so I could give myself time to sit and take my shoes and socks off while she caught up with me. Once, when I was on my own, I reached a gorgeous wheat field that overlooked a large hill. The wheat seemed to change colors as the wind whipped through, making it dance. It was the perfect place to stop and rest. I asked a nearby pilgrim to please take a picture of me standing in the field before he continued on. It was a moment I didn't want to forget.

As I sat on the edge of the field waiting for Melisa and Cristina to catch up with me, I was suddenly struck with the notion: *I am alone in rural Spain*. I sat in silence without a soul in sight trying to decide how to feel about it. I struggled with my usual self, who is always looking for exit strategies and constantly running through worst-case scenarios in my head. But out here, that just doesn't feel right. It feels excessive. Even wrong. I get the sense that this place is different than anywhere else in the world and that normal conventions just don't belong here. I suppressed the urge to race ahead to find other pilgrims and sat quietly with my thoughts. These fields would keep me company for now. I could adjust to this new way of life. And you know what happened? Nothing. I was fine. I was better than fine. I felt great. I felt my layer of armor melt away under the sun.

I tried once again to walk ahead of Melisa later in the day. As I was plowing ahead, trying to get some distance between the two of us so I could find time to rest, I caught up with some other pilgrims. They were still about 100 meters ahead of me and they were moving fast. If I caught up to them, I might have the opportunity to talk with them and maybe even add a few more people to our hiker family. I marched as hard as I could. My feet were screaming and my shins felt like they might split in half.

When I finally caught up with the speedy hikers, I realized they weren't carrying packs! I spent about 20 minutes keeping up with people who had their bags forwarded to another town. They were carrying itty bitty water pouches on their backs and nothing more. I gave up. I could never keep up with my 16+ pound pack. I took the opportunity once again to stop and wait for Melisa.

While Melisa, Cristina, and I were walking together later, I came across a beautiful scarf lying on the ground. I've seen several instances where people abandoned their things, like the person who abandoned the massive hardbound book on the Pyrenees. But this seemed different. There was no reason to abandon a lightweight beautiful object like this scarf. Although it was a bit wet, I decided to pick it up and wear it into town. The owner would undoubtedly see it and ask for it back. Sure enough, within the next hour, I came across a group of women walking together. One of the young women lit up when she saw me.

"You found it! Thank you so much!"

I gave it back to her and we chatted briefly. It felt good to be able to do something good for someone. There's something about the Camino that just makes you want to be a better person.

Melisa and I were getting quite silly later in the afternoon. We were talking about how we both learned Spanish in high school. Melisa has been exposed to the language more than me over the years, as she lives closer to Mexico. I was telling her that the only thing I remember from Spanish class is "*Dónde está la escuela?*" which means 'where is the school'? We laughed about how useless that is here on the Camino.

After hours of walking, we reached a town and thought we made it to Pamplona. We pulled our cameras out to take a picture of the sign, only to learn that we were still many kilometers from Pamplona. We sat on the bridge over the water and sulked for a few minutes before picking ourselves up and moving on. We decided it would be better for us to stop somewhere nice for another meal (and the pharmacy to get some supplies for our injuries) than to push forward in our condition. We found a nice cafe and chilled out for at least an hour. As we continued our walk, we ran into Misha and a few other familiar pilgrims again. We took lots of fun pictures as we rested on the park benches.

I think we were the last pilgrims to crawl into Pamplona around 4:30pm. Pamplona is a great town. It's like a fort, surrounded by a massive stone wall with only a few entry points. The first thing you'd notice upon entering is there are very few cars. There are also no sidewalks, just wide roads shared by pedestrians and cars. You would also notice that the town is a river of gorgeous people. The Spanish have a subtle natural beauty about them. It's not that they work hard for it and you wouldn't easily spot it from across the street, but when you took the time to notice, you'd definitely see it.

I was very overwhelmed by the city at first. Unlike the other small towns we walk through, not everything here is pilgrim friendly. People don't speak English and because we are still in Basque country, sometimes they don't speak Spanish either. If I were hiking alone, I probably would have stayed at the municipal albergue where the majority of pilgrims stay, but since my two hiking buddies speak Spanish, we were quickly redirected to the heart of Pamplona. Let me just say I was feeling a tad helpless there. I couldn't understand a word of the conversations, which was very frustrating at first, but I found that after a few drinks it didn't really matter. I just went with the flow and we all had a great time.

Today's hike was really hard on us so we agreed that it would be a good night to stay at a private pensión where we could have our own rooms rather than staying in one of the albergues that houses 150 people. We called ahead and found a nice place right downtown. Melisa and I shared a room, and Cristina got the room next door to herself. When we arrived, we met up with a *peregrina* named Margarita who was staying at our pensión. She invited us to dinner so after our usual routine of showering, hand washing our clothes in the sink and hanging them out the dry on our beautiful private balcony, we hit the town.

What a great place! There's plenty going on but the streets aren't so crowded that you can't move around. Pamplona is where they have the running of the bulls every July, and it's obviously a huge part of their culture. The stores are loaded with paraphernalia and it occurred to me that bullfighting is probably Pamplona's largest source of revenue. They even have children's shirts with fake blood and holes in them. I thought they were pretty tasteless, and I'm strongly against bullfighting, but it's very much in your face here.

The menu at the bar we went to was in Basque so we took a guess and ordered several tapas (or *pinchos* as the Basque would say.) The food really surprised me because despite it being outside my comfort zone, I really enjoyed it. One of the bruschetta-looking tapas had anchovies on it and I was hesitant to try it but it was great! It was all great. And of course the wine was wonderful, too.

While we did well ordering the food, what we messed up was the portions. The small and grande portions weren't at all what we expected so the guy came out with twice the food we thought we had ordered... but we ate it all anyway! We have fierce appetites.

Finally, after a long day, I got to sleep in a real bed for the first time in a week. I don't think I've ever slept that well in my life!

Finding peace for the first time

So many animals on the Camino

Pamplona city hall

# CHAPTER 7

## DAY 5: 10KM FROM PAMPLONA TO ZARIQUIEGUI

—

## TO THE Z-TOWN I CAN'T PRONOUNCE

My next stop, according to my guidebook, is Puente La Reina (24km). However, our trio decided we should not try to push ourselves that far. Cristina's knee was very swollen and causing her a lot of pain. Also, the weather is supposed to be cold, windy, and rainy and the trip would take us up and over a fairly steep mountain. So instead, we only hiked 10km to a small town called Zariquiegui. This worked out well because we could do it in a half-day's time, which would give us the morning to explore Pamplona before leaving.

In the morning, we had breakfast at a nice café with Margarita, and then quickly explored the town's highlights. We saw the *cathedral de Maria*, which is absolutely gorgeous. Melisa, Cristina, and I bought some lovely jewelry there. Then we went to the famous café once frequented by Hemingway. He's the one who put Pamplona on the map by writing about their odd bullfighting tradition in one of his books. The town was never the same again, so they continue to celebrate his memory.

The café was filled with lots of interesting local people, including a very attractive local guy who clearly had an interest in hikers. He chatted with us for a bit as we waited in line to order. Then we walked around the third-largest bullring in the world. I'm glad I won't be anywhere near here on July 7th, when the bulls run through town and are routed directly to this stadium.

Prior to leaving town, Melisa, Cristina, and I stopped into a pilgrim's store which was filled with hiking essentials. I talked Cristina into buying some nice hiking poles for herself. At first she protested that they were expensive, but soon she realized they really were necessary considering the trouble she'd been having with her knees. I picked up a small wallet for myself. It's not great but it will allow me to hold my money in my pocket so it will be easier to access when I reach small towns and want to quickly purchase some food or drink. Until now, I have just kept my money in a ziplock bag to protect it from all the rain we've walked through.

The hike out of Pamplona wasn't bad. We walked along a highway exiting town for quite some time, but I didn't mind the traffic. The rest of the walk was beautiful. We passed through a couple of small towns and some modern Pamplona suburbs. The three of us hiked spaced far apart. I tried to hang in the middle to make sure I didn't lose sight of Melisa in front of me and that Cristina was still okay behind me. I pulled out my umbrella and used it for the first time. That, in addition to my oversized rain jacket, was quite a sight. Melisa and Cristina thought I looked ridiculous. Melisa took pictures while Cristina laughed at me.

"I've never seen anything like it, "she said in her thick Italian accent.

We were feeling hungry partway through the walk, so we stopped on some park benches in a Pamplona suburb and shared our snacks. I still had some leftover cheese, Melisa had apples, and Cristina had bread. We ate our lunch and chatted with a couple of pilgrims before they continued on. I was tired and hurting but really enjoyed the social interaction.

As we were walking, we passed a memorial. Actually, we have passed several so far. Many people have passed away while hiking the Camino. In fact, we just learned that someone died on the Pyrenees Mountains the other day. The man was passing over the mountain only one day after we did. I believe he had a heart attack just near the shelter where Melisa and I stopped in for some tea. Apparently several nearby hikers carried his body into the shelter.

From what I understand, the man was hiking with his wife and a couple other friends. The group took a break for a day or two after he passed, but then continued on the Camino. They felt the man would have wanted them to make it to Santiago. Melisa and I talked about the strength it must take for a woman to say goodbye to her husband on the Camino and then continue walking. We sat on the bench next to the memorial and rested. I reflected on how fortunate I am to have this amazing opportunity and prayed, as I do a hundred times a day, that I'll be able to continue my journey.

While the three of us girls were laughing and talking along the way, several pilgrims passed us. The first question we always ask is, "Where are you from?" One guy as he was passing said he was from New Hampshire! I was so excited!

"Where in New Hampshire?"

"Merrimack." Wow! This guy lives fifteen minutes from my home! I was so excited to meet him and thought for a second how cool it would be to make a new friend at home while in Spain. But the guy was not interested! I told him where I was from and he just kept on walking. I actually felt rejected! How could he not want to talk to me? The other girls laughed at me. Melisa had a similar experience with a woman she met from her hometown. I guess not everyone on the Camino is as interested in making friends as we are!

I'm noticing accommodations are always a surprise on the Camino. Our bedroom today consisted of three children's beds stuffed into someone's messy craft room. I couldn't complain, though, because my alternative option was to cram into a 10x12 room with four bunks! The food in the attached restaurant was the best of the pilgrim meals I've had so far.

Prior to dinner, I hung out in the albergue kitchen area talking with other pilgrims. I sat with a nice German couple for a while and they shared their private stash of wine and German chocolate with me. Eventually, I made my way around the small room meeting everyone else. I met Christof and Renate from Germany, and their friend Roswitha. They seemed very shy and didn't talk for most of the night but I think it's because the rest of us at the table spoke English. The other two Germans retired early for the night.

We also ran into two English girls who we had seen back at the Hemingway café. I wanted to say hi to my fellow pilgrims then, but I was too tired to make the extra effort. When I went back through my pictures of Melisa and Cristina in the café, I could see the girls in the background. It was cool to have another opportunity to hang out with them. They were loads of fun. I loved their accents and their different use of familiar words. They kept referring to themselves as tramps. Melisa and I just giggled. That must mean something very different to them.

A couple comments about long-distance backpacking: one of the things I had heard can be difficult when sleeping in the same room with many people is that some choose to get up at 4:00am while you want to sleep longer. I've been fortunate enough not to have had that problem yet. The issue I have, which is more difficult, is that our 6:00am wake up is too early for most everyone else. Apparently I'm that jerk. My pack is full of garbage bags, plastic bags, and zip lock bags, so any movement I make in the morning is really loud. I have to bring my bag outside of my room so I don't disturb anyone.

The other issue is that to obtain anything from your pack you must remove everything. So I find myself spending a great deal of my time packing and unpacking. And every time I do so, I run the risk of losing something. I've gotten into the habit of always looking behind me before leaving a location to make sure I didn't leave anything behind. I suppose I'll get better at packing and unpacking eventually.

I'm getting a wicked headache now for some reason so I'm off to bed.

Third largest bullring in the world

My rain "costume"

Many people have passed near or on the Camino

# CHAPTER 8

## DAY 6: 24KM FROM ZARIQUIEGUI TO CIRAUQUI
—
## ALTO DEL PERDÓN

When we woke in the morning, it was clear that Cristina needed a day of rest, so she stayed in bed and Melisa and I carried on without her. I was sorry to leave her behind and I really hope I'll see her again one day. As with most days, I started out refreshed and ready to go. I had my pilgrim meal, a croissant with Nutella and *café con leche*. I know it's not much but it's all the albergue had to offer.

Today was a milestone day. Melisa and I climbed up to a windy mountain ridge lined with dozens of windmills. It's also the site of the famous iron pilgrim figures, *Alto del Perdón*. The view heading up the mountain was gorgeous and I was glad that we didn't try to walk it yesterday when it was drizzling and foggy. We started early in the morning, so the sun was just rising behind us and there were dark storm clouds in the foreground. When we reached the top, the town below was highlighted in the sun's early rays. Several of us made it to the top around the same time so we got lots of great pictures of each other with the statues and the quaint village below.

Coming down the other side of the mountain, we were rewarded with multiple rainbows stretched across the landscape. The ground was very rocky though, and I had to be very careful with my footing. Throughout the day, I passed a variety of fields filled with wheat, peas, dill, honeysuckle, cherries, figs, corn, almonds, artichokes, grapes, and olives.

We walked with a woman named Mary for a while. Mary started her hike in Le Puy-en-Vela, France, so by the time she reached St. Jean, where I started, she had already hiked 500 miles. She had this hiking thing down. I had a lot of admiration for her. Mary, Melisa, and I had fun trying to identify all the plant life along the Way - tasting, smelling, touching. I felt like a little kid the first half of the hike, full of joy and not a care in the world.

This afternoon at one of our stops, I saw the café was selling bracelets made of pretty blue ribbon. The bracelet was something of a map with each of the major Camino towns listed from one side to the other. Right now, only a few of the towns mentioned are familiar to me but I suspect as I continue on my pilgrimage, I'll start to recognize more of the names.

Unlike my blissful morning, the second half of my walk was very difficult. I'm really struggling with my feet, which I knew would be a problem. I knew my chronic foot pain would slow me down but until I test them, I really don't know what my limits are. I think I found my limit. I've been increasing my hike by about 1km each day. Today's 24km hike was extremely hard on me. There were some very steep slopes, but they were nothing like the Pyrenees. I think having only a few hours to rest in the evening and long days of hiking day after day is really destroying my feet.

Also, Melisa is on a tight timeline. She only has two weeks to hike as much of the Camino as possible so she's moving pretty fast and she doesn't seem to need to stop like I do. By the time we stopped to rest in the town before our destination, I was nearly in tears. I was climbing a steep hill with the sun beating down, my head pounding, and my feet screaming. I was feeling very sorry for myself.

Fortunately, the town had a wonderful water fountain with fresh ice cold water. I downed two bottles of water and sat in the shade for a few minutes. This gave me enough strength to walk the remaining 3km to Cirauqui. Melisa is a powerhouse. She just kept moving.

What an adorable town Cirauqui is! Everything is extremely old and made of stone. I've seen very few residents here. Like most of these towns, it's super quiet with the exception of church bells. Melisa and I went to the bar in the basement of the albergue with Annette, a nice American woman we walked with today. Annette works for the U.S. government but is stationed in Italy. The three of us had pre-dinner and drinks and played around with our guidebooks. We also took silly pictures of ourselves in our goofy town clothes. We joked about how sexy we all look in our socks and crocs.

Random thought: You know your life has become simple when you see a pretty postcard, think, *I should mail that to someone*, and then quickly dismiss the idea because the thought of purchasing a stamp and signing the card before mailing it seems too complicated for you to figure out. Your daily pace really seems to slow down out here. The Camino feels like life boiled down to the essentials. It's simple and sweet.

The highlight of my day in town was when the supermarket up the street reopened after siesta and I could buy food for dinner. Since I didn't have anywhere to cook and the store had such a limited selection, I ended up with the strangest food pairing. I got sliced ham, yogurt, canned artichoke hearts, peanuts, clementines, and an apple. I could have had the dinner the albergue was serving but I needed a non-structured evening to recover from today's hike, and dinner is usually full of joyous people. Tonight, I just didn't feel like socializing. I noticed as I walked down the road to the store that the entire town smelled like the garlic soup the albergue was making. I believe their bar/restaurant is the only food establishment in town.

Another cute thing I saw was a little boy who came running into the shop to buy baseball cards. You could tell it was a weekly or monthly routine for him. He stretched his little arms up and over the counter to give the man his quarters and the man handed him a pack of cards. Then the boy dashed off.

The man I assume was the store owner. He was also the town butcher. I was struck by the standard of cleanliness (or lack thereof) in this establishment. The butcher's once-white apron was covered in blood stains and so were the chopping blocks behind the counter. The floor was littered with what I can only assume was crumpled up receipts. I would never purchase non-prepackaged meats in this place, but for some reason I felt the filth gave it character.

After purchasing my food, I walked another 20 feet over to the medieval church for some meditation time. I felt a little foolish walking in wearing my puffy coat, cargo shorts, socks, and croc sandals, but the locals didn't bat an eye. I suspect they are accustomed to pilgrims barging into their sanctuary. I prayed for many things, but as I do in every church I step into each day (and there are many), I prayed for my body to hold strong over these next few difficult weeks.

The Camino is said to have three sections. The first, through the Pyrenees and beyond, breaks and rebuilds your body. The second section, through the Meseta (which is hundreds of kilometers of fields, devoid of civilization), is said to break and rebuild your mind. And once your body and mind are reborn, the Camino then works on your soul. I am really hoping I can make it through the first stage. I believe it will be the hardest for me.

Melisa and I have decided we are going to continue on separate tomorrow. Every day we reevaluate our situation. "I'm content with how our hike is going. Are you?"

"Yes, things are good."

Up until now we have really enjoyed hiking together. That said, she's on a tight schedule since she only has two weeks in Spain, and I currently feel like a broken horse that needs to be put down.

Tonight, without even having to say it, I think we both knew we would have to go our own way tomorrow. I told Melisa I will only hike with her to the next major town 14kms and stop there for the day. From there, she will continue on without me.

I'm a bit nervous to be alone. It was just reported that an American woman who went missing on the Camino a month before I started is thought to have been abducted by an active sex trafficking ring. This is pretty much the worst thing I could possibly think of, and I hate that I live in a world where men allow these things to happen to women. Adventurers should be free to explore this world we live in without the fear of others taking advantage of them. This goes the same for men and women alike. It is infuriating that I'm at higher risk just because I'm a woman. So I'm continuing my hike but admittedly, I do so with fear. I prayed tonight that I would find other Camino buddies to walk with me.

Alto del Perdón

Cirauqui on the horizon

# CHAPTER 9

## DAY 7: 14KM FROM CIRAUQUI TO ESTELLA

—

## ALL ALONE IN SPAIN

This has been the toughest day yet. The hike was short and sweet. But upon arriving in Estella, I decided to stay while Melisa would move on. We wished each other luck and I headed into town. I struggled with my decision because it was so early in the day to stop walking, and I hated saying goodbye to Melisa. We've had so much fun together these last several days. But I also knew I would most likely run into people I know since this is one of the major stops mentioned in my guidebook. If I want to find a new hiker family, this is where I need to be. The downside was the town is huge (compared to most towns I go through with a population of perhaps 150) and probably harder to get around without my Spanish-speaking travel buddy.

Let me start by saying there is probably nothing intrinsically wrong with this town and I'm sure many people find it lovely. That said, I hated it. I couldn't find anything I needed and everyone I asked refused to help me or even talk to me. I'll give you more detail on that later.

I did manage to find an albergue pretty quickly thanks to the well-marked path, but after being checked in for about five minutes I knew I had made a mistake. The accommodations were not bad by any means; the place was clean and had everything a pilgrim would need, but I had a very strong sense that I should stay at the municipal albergue instead. Municipals are usually much larger than the quaint private albergues and I knew I'd have a better chance of seeing people I know there.

I used the translator on my phone to ask for my money back. The volunteer working there was very understanding and returned my six euros without hesitation. I lied to him, though. I told him I had checked into the wrong albergue because my friends were in the municipal albergue on the other side of town. I didn't have any friends at the other albergue, but it was the only good excuse I could come up with for my sudden need to leave a perfectly decent albergue.

I then attempted to find an ATM by asking for directions but failed. They don't like pilgrims in this town and no one speaks English. At least not to me. I tried asking in Spanish and people acted as though they didn't even notice I was speaking to them. I felt invisible. The experience made me realize how humiliating it must feel when homeless people ask for change and the passersby completely ignores them. It's so alienating and dehumanizing. I will never ignore anyone again.

I went to the information office thinking they would help me there. After all, it's the information office, right? That's what they do. Much to my dismay, the woman working in the office was extremely rude. She made several annoyed comments about the number of pilgrims who come in with questions for her. After she made me wait 15 minutes while she puttered around the office; she wasn't helpful at all. She gave me a map and pointed to a machine that I learned when I got there was not an ATM but was for money wiring. I searched the surrounding area looking for an ATM but I was unable to find one on my own. After a few final attempts to ask for help from the locals, I gave up.

I ran into a few familiar faces throughout the day, which kept me going, but overall I spent my day choking back tears and hating myself for taking on such a difficult challenge. I'm injured so I struggle on the trail, and my Spanish is weak so I struggle in towns. I don't sleep at night and I never order food right. What else is there to look forward to? Oh, and showers suck, too!

For the better part of the morning, I sat on a park bench just where the trail intersected the town next to a nice little river. As I tried to relax in the sun, I ran into several people. I saw Markus and Betty again! I hadn't seen them since the Pyrenees. They were taking the day off. They looked rested and clean and it was comforting to see them again.

I also ran into Annette. She wanted to find the wine fountain at the end of town. That's right, a wine fountain. It's like a water fountain but it pours wine, provided by the generosity and kindness of a monastery. I thought, *Just what I need!*

So I grabbed the cup I had brought specifically for this landmark and we started hiking towards the end of town. I'm going to have to walk this same route tomorrow, and normally I would be dead against walking something twice, but I figured the fountain was worth seeing twice. Epic fail. We asked an albergue volunteer for directions and he told us the fountain was only about 1km outside of town.

We walked 4km more only to find the fountain was actually much farther from town than either of us were willing to walk. We turned around and headed back into town empty handed. My feet are giving out on me earlier and earlier each day, and I'm having serious concerns about whether or not I'll be able to complete this trip on foot. Adding extra mileage just seems like a really bad idea right now.

We arrived back in town sober as a heart attack and found the only restaurant open during siesta - a pizza place. As Annette found a place to sit, I went to the bathroom to wash my hands. There was no soap though. There's never soap. As I stared at myself in the mirror, I began to cry. What have I gotten myself into? How am I going to do this? What was I thinking? I'll never make it. I prayed out loud for strength, courage and support. Then I cleaned up my face and walked out. *I can do this.*

I was relieved we were at a pizza place. Finally, something I can do! Even I can order a slice of pizza right? Wrong again. I thought I ordered just a slice but somehow I managed to order an entire pie for myself. When the man brought out the massive pizza, I was really annoyed and tired of all the surprises this town was throwing at me. That is until I started eating it and realized I could eat the entire thing without taking a breath between bites. Apparently I was starving. I started feeling better immediately. I was still miserable, but at least I didn't feel like the world was ending anymore.

Annette and I said our goodbyes as she was catching a bus to the next major town. Apparently I'm the only one dumb enough to try to walk this whole thing. I walked back to the municipal albergue where I checked in and decided what I should do next. I texted Brian several times and apparently my messages were pretty pathetic because he called me!

"Baby, what's wrong? What happened?"

I told him nothing specific happened but nothing was going right and I was having a terrible day.

When he realized I was safe and just having a tough time getting around town, he suggested that I should come home. "Why would you even suggest that?! You're not being supportive!" I knew he actually was being very supportive but when presented with the thought of actually quitting … I don't know. It just felt awful.

"Baby, I think you're going to be just fine. And I have no doubts that you're going to make it all the way."

We talked for a few minutes before I told him I loved him and we hung up.

My room was starting to fill with people and it was getting later in the evening. I had to figure out where I could wash and dry my clothes. Yup. That lifted my spirit. Hand washing my clothes in freezing cold water outside on a cold windy day. This is how is choose to spend my time away from work. I'm such an idiot. I was just thinking this when I heard someone call my name. I turned around to find Nikolai standing in the yard. He and Stephen were staying in my albergue. I told him I was so happy to see someone I recognized and we chatted for a bit. Stephen was having his afternoon nap so we agreed to all meet for dinner together later.

The evening turned out much better than the day. I had a real salad (vegetables aren't as popular as meat), Spanish Lamb, some amazing tort thing, and beer from the tap. We also ran a few errands on the way back. Stephen needed another pair of shoes. Who doesn't like shoe shopping? While we were walking around, I asked the guys if they would be interested in walking together tomorrow. I told them that I walk slowly so I didn't expect them to walk with me the whole time but maybe we could meet up in the towns. Neither one of them thought it would be a problem so we all agreed we'd meet in the morning and start walking together.

When we returned to the albergue, the three of us found our clothes were still wet on the drying rack, which was located in the courtyard in the back of the albergue. Ginger, the nice woman from Florida who I met in Zubiri, let us throw our clothes in her drier for the last 15 minutes since she was done using it. It was weird doing laundry with two practical strangers, but comforting at the same time. I'm not the only one doing this.

Side note: as I'm typing this, a man just stripped naked in front of me like we're two dudes in a locker room. How did I get stuck with the room full of men and why is that not nearly as awesome as it sounds?

Just one of many Camino markers

Still in Basque territory

# CHAPTER 10

## DAY 8: 22KM FROM ESTELLA TO LOS ARCOS

—

## HIKING MY OWN HIKE

Today was a much better day! I got a good night's sleep and I met the guys for breakfast. They were in no hurry at all. I have been pushing myself really hard and trying to keep up with Melisa and I think that may be why I have been struggling with the hiking so much. We walked across the street for croissants and coffee before beginning the hike. Stephen is not a morning person which kind of relieved me. I'm not either.

Apparently the woman working in the cafe was not a morning person either. She was clearly in a bad mood. But I've already learned that here in Spain, servers don't have to be nice to you just because you're the customer. You will be forced to tolerate whatever mood they happen to be in, for better or for worse.

So when the young woman completely ignored me and refused to serve me after several minutes, I stood up on a stool so I could actually see over the counter like a normal human being and I called out to her, "*Perdón!*" in a manner that begged attention. She reluctantly served me. I've learned not to be rattled by these bleak interactions, though. I took my seat with the guys in the back of the tiny cafe and enjoyed my breakfast.

After we finished our coffee and perked up a bit, Stephen joked that maybe we need a second. Nikolai chimed in that we should indeed have another. I was feeling a bit anxious to get going. If I was with Melisa, we would have been well on our way already.

"Really? You want another?" I asked.

"Why not?" came the reply.

Good point. Although I was chomping at the bit to get moving, I wasn't going to push them. It was my first day with my new hiking family and I wasn't about to create waves, but also, maybe they had the right idea. Maybe I should take it slow and enjoy myself more. After our second coffee, we strolled through town in no rush and I have to say, it was really nice. I got some cool video of us walking through the old stone streets.

I finally got to the wine fountain, *Bodegas Irache*! It was just as I imagined. I filled my adult sippy cup and strapped it to my chest so I could enjoy the wine throughout the day. The guys were nice enough to take pictures of the event for me.

The morning started with fresh brisk air I could have walked in all day. It was really ideal for hiking. We passed more fields of wheat lined with big beautiful trees. Stephen and I jumped into one of the fields and pretended to swim through the wheat while Nikolai took pictures of us. It was a fun filled, silly morning.

Later in the afternoon, the sun began to cook me a bit, and I was very happy to have my umbrella. It attaches quite nicely to my pack so I can walk hands-free. I thought most people would find it silly, but several people made comments that they wished they had one as well. Nikolai teased me about it a bit, but I didn't care because his left arm is covered in blisters from too much sun exposure! He seriously could have benefited from an umbrella earlier in his trip. As we hiked by some random pilgrims who were taking rest, they pointed at my umbrella and cheered me on. I was so glad Brian convinced me to bring it.

Several hours into our hike, I began to feel hot and tired. According to our map, there was nothing by way of cafes until we arrived at our final destination. But as we were walking, I saw in the distance those beautiful bright red chairs that are a sure sign of some kind of rest area.

Sure enough, there was a temporary food truck set up in the middle of the field. I was so hoping the guys would want to take a break as badly as I did. Without a word, they veered off the path and headed straight for the food truck. I didn't even have to ask. We were all on the same page. Most of the tables were already taken by other pilgrims who were basking in the sun, resting their feet on the chairs, and taking in their much needed drinks and snacks. We already had all the snacks we needed between the three of us so we just ordered beers and found a place in the grass to spread out.

We met two other cool hikers, a mother/daughter team from the states, Dotty and Kristen. They both had southern accents like Stephen. The three of them spent about 20 minutes just making fun of themselves and giving the rest of us a southern language lesson. Stephen is a parody of himself. He throws on the deep southern drawl and "pretends" to be an obnoxious American tourist in the middle of Spain.

"*Dos cervezas por favor*. And make it fast, boy!"

Of course he's the most polite gentleman so he would never actually speak to anyone like that. It was great to sit in the sun and laugh until my abs hurt. Then Kristen and Nikolai had a contest to see who could stand on their heads the longest. Everyone was in a great mood and being super silly. It was wonderful.

I learned today that I need to walk The Way at my own pace. The trip was much more enjoyable today. It helped walking with the guys because they didn't tear ahead of me at all and they wanted to stop at every single bar and cafe we passed which gave my feet a break. And we still made it into town by 3:30pm.

Every time I got to the point where I didn't think I could take much more, someone in a truck filled with drinks and snacks would be set up in the middle of a field. We took advantage of every one. I even had a much heavier pack today and the hike was still easier. The last 10k had no food stops or water fountains so my guidebook advised I take extra snacks and water.

When we rolled into Los Arcos, I was hurting, but not terribly since I had plenty of breaks and walked at my own pace. We found an albergue run by some German women. "There are three of us. Do you have three beds?" They did! ...in the attic. We followed one of the volunteers all the way up to the top floor of the albergue to find three mattresses on the floor of a tiny room with a five-foot ceiling. In the corner of the room was a huge open "window" that exited onto the roof. Actually, it was just a big hole in the wall. Perfect! Oh my God, how low my standards have dropped. I was just thrilled I only had to share a room with two men I already know. I didn't even mind the spiders who lived on the wooden beam just two feet over my head.

Actually, in all seriousness, I don't think it's that my standards are dropping. I've just reprioritized what's important to me. I'm not so concerned with how nice a place looks. I'm more concerned about how kind the *hospitaleros* are and how friendly the people I'm spending my time with are. These are the things that matter most to me.

After taking showers and settling in, the three of us walked to the center square where lots of pilgrims were basking in the sun and drinking local wine. We had a pint and listened to a local man play his guitar and sing for us.

We were told Los Arcos would have a running of the bulls in the morning but when we asked our waitress about it, she just laughed at us and said we misunderstood. We were pretty disappointed since apparently there was a running of the bulls this morning in Estella and we missed it. Now that I think about it though, I'm wondering if these were just Camino rumors. That's probably why the waitress laughed at us like we were idiots. It was worth asking though!

Dinner was interesting. The food was terrible but we were seated family style with a man from Italy. So there we were, two Americans, a German, and an Italian, miming our way through dinner facilitated by a pitcher of sangria. It was awkward, but fun.

So yes. Overall, today was significantly better than yesterday. I enjoy being in rural Spain rather than cities, I enjoy being in the company of others rather than alone, and I must walk at my own pace rather than someone else's. I'll have to keep that in mind if I'm going to continue to enjoy my Camino.

Interesting facts: siesta can last anywhere from 11:00am until 5:00pm. We've been looking for an open *farmacia* for Stephen all afternoon. He's having problems with his sinuses and needs medicine.

Also, I learned today that people who have hiked the Camino often come back and volunteer at their favorite hostels for two to three weeks at a time. The German women we met at this albergue were volunteers.

My new Camino family

Wine fountain - *Bodegas Irache*

# CHAPTER 11

## DAY 9: 19KM FROM LOS ARCOS TO VIANA

—

## EVERYTHING HURTS

Everything hurts. Everything hurts … everything … hurts. I'm going to go into graphic detail about my body since it's all I can think about right now.

First, the blister. I lost that battle. For days, it's been somewhere between a hot spot and a blister. I was trying to discourage it by using Compeed, which is a second skin sold in the EU. It worked for a while, but this morning I could tell I was definitely getting a blister. I clumsily applied moleskin and tape hoping that would make things better rather than worse. But by our very first stop only 3km in, my toe was turning colors.

Stephen is a paramedic, so he took one look at it and pulled out his kit. Using a suture needle and the accompanying silk thread, he pierced the two blisters that had formed, ran the thread through, tied them together, put antiseptic on it, and explained to me that the thread will help slowly drain the blister and would work its way out as I walked. I felt so fortunate to have befriended a paramedic! And how kind of him to be willing to work while on vacation.

Nikolai, the sadist, recorded the procedure so I now have an educational video to reference for future blisters. I put my sock back on and was supposed to carry on as usual. It felt like I had a stone in my sock the whole time. Stephen also said he highly encouraged me to put Vicks Vapor Rub on my feet. He said my feet need to stay soft, which is completely opposite of what I've always heard. I thought you wanted callouses. I thought you wanted dry feet. I argued with him for about two seconds before agreeing to try his method since he doesn't have a single blister himself.

We then walked to a *farmacia* where we were shocked to discover that the pharmacies here in the EU sell surgery grade suture materials and drugs. I purchased a whole kit. The man working there was so sweet. He didn't speak a word of English, but he knew what I was buying the kit for. He threw in free bandages and wished me a *"Buen Camino."* Buen Camino is what we all say to each other and what we hear from kind locals regularly. We don't even have to tell them we are pilgrims. They can spot us (or perhaps smell us) from a mile away.

As for other bodily issues, I won't go into much more detail, but apparently chafing is a very real thing. Imagine throwing a handful of straw into your clothes before a long walk. That's exactly what it feels like. This is a new experience for me. Fortunately, some of my other hiker friends encouraged me to get medicated cream from my doctor before leaving for my trip. I also brought a stick of Body Glide, so I think I can manage this problem before it gets out of hand.

Anyway, back to my hiking. I felt ok for the next few kilometers, with the exception of my usual persistent foot pain. But after several hours of walking, my blister was really starting to hurt. I found myself favoring my right foot, knowing full well that walking off kilter would surely cause something else on my body to stop working. Sure enough, within a mile, my left knee started barking at me. I really don't want to mess with my knees, because several people I know have had to end their Camino due to bad knees. So I worked hard to push through the blister pain and walk normally. I also realized I hadn't been using my poles, which could also have been the reason for the sudden knees ache. FYI: use poles. Yes, they are ugly; yes, they are annoying. They will save your knees, though.

Eventually the blister pain numbed a bit. Actually, I don't know if it numbed or if it was just overpowered by other pain points, but for whatever reason I was no longer concerned about the blister. I was experiencing my usual foot pain at a whole new level. Our final destination was in view when I suddenly felt a sharp sting up the inside of my right leg each time I placed my foot on the ground. I took three steps like this and was completely done. I could not take another step with that pain. I stopped and did some ankle stretches. I must have looked pretty pathetic because the guys took one look at me and stopped without question.

I was so grateful for how they handled it. I didn't have to say anything, and they didn't make me feel bad. They just stopped and took in the views, giving me some personal time to compose myself. While I was dealing with the stabbing pain in my foot, Stephen saw a field of wildflowers off the trail a bit. He wanted to go check it out so I told the guys to go ahead without me. The thought of walking further than I already had to seemed impossible. But he pleaded with me to trust him and to come with them.

I mustered up some strength and moved onward. Not far off the trail was a breathtaking field of red poppies. They stretched as far as the eye could see. We practically frolicked through the field looking for a place to rest. We found random spots and laid down on the beautiful bed of flowers. It was magical and a break in our day that I welcomed wholeheartedly. I'm so glad Stephen pushed to move off the trail for a few minutes. If I hadn't had my mysterious leg pains, we probably would not have seen the field. Most pilgrims missed the sight altogether and it was definitely a highlight of my day.

Now that I'm stopping in the towns more commonly visited, I see the same pilgrims on the trail. You feel like a rockstar when you climb your way to the top of a hill and find a temporary structure full of snacks, booze, and familiar faces. They cheer your arrival like they haven't seen you in ages and hand you a beer. By the way, my alcohol tolerance increases with my consumption. I couldn't get drunk if I tried.

I love our frequent bar stops. We bask in the sun (or hide in the shade of the trees) and eat anything we can get our hands on. Today we had one stop in particular that I think will be quite memorable. When we arrived, the place was full of pilgrims I recognized: Ginger and Drennan, Dotty and Kristen, Christof, Renate and Roswitha, and several others! They all cheered when they saw Stephen, Nikolai, and me strolling in from a distance.

The gentleman running the food stand was celebrating his birthday. His whole family was there enjoying the day with him. They brought their newborn baby and dog which gave us a lot to talk about. The man was feeling very generous and handed out all kinds of free chocolate goodness. I'm pretty sure I won't lose weight despite my daily exertion because I never say no to anything. I eat everything people have to offer, whether I like it or not. I just eat nonstop. Once we all felt refreshed from the abundant drinks and snacks, we all took silly pictures of each other. It was a moment I won't forget.

By the time we reached town, I was limping and lagging. I felt so pathetic, but I was hurting so bad I didn't care. We checked into the nearest albergue and I was escorted to my room of 20 or so beds. The room was dark and reeked of dirty pilgrims. The woman showed me my bed. It was the top bunk pushed up against another bunk in the middle of the room where a man was already sleeping. Apparently, I was expected to sleep right next to him. I was too tired and hurting too much to care though.

I dropped my stuff in front of my locker and headed for the shower. I learned the trick to showering. Close your eyes. Close your eyes and imagine being in a huge private bathroom with glass doors that overlook the ocean. I enjoyed every second of it, which incidentally lasted longer than two minutes since this shower didn't have a timer like some. I milked that thing for all it was worth. Longest shower ever.

I returned to my dank bedroom all clean and feeling better and realized there was no way I was spending a night there. I went back to the hospitalero sitting at the front desk and told her I would pay anything if they had rooms with fewer pilgrims. Six floors up - six floors (where there is no Wi-Fi) - there was a bed in a room with only about nine others. I paid the four extra euros, said farewell to my napping buddies, and hauled my crap all the way up to the very top floor.

Now, let me remind you how much pain I'm in. This should give you an idea how determined I was not to sleep in that first room. The room on the sixth floor was very nice. There were only a few beds and the room wasn't fully booked. The bikers I shared the room with were also very polite, courteous, and clean. There are many pilgrims who experience the Camino from a bicycle. Since they travel so much faster than hikers do, they tend to have their own cohorts; hikers and bikers don't intermingle too much.

Viana is an old town that is absolutely beautiful. It's a bit dirty, but the architecture is amazing. Tonight, a bunch of us met at a restaurant for dinner. We found it because the owner was riding up and down the Camino on his motorcycle handing out business cards. Little did we know that he and his staff get very frustrated at how obnoxious pilgrims are. He and his waitstaff seemed to be angry at everything we did.

I ordered the cheesecake, which was on the menu, but for some reason it confused them beyond belief. They started yelling at me and when they finally brought it out, I kid you not, the owner threw the spoon at me from the other side of the table. I was striking out with customer service today. They don't work for you, you work for them, so don't piss them off. It shook me at first, but I was having so much fun with everyone that I got over it quickly. "It's all a part of the experience, Theresa!" as Stephen would say.

We saw Ginger and Drennan again. They were just finishing dinner as the three of us were arriving so we only got to chat with them for a few minutes.

You never know which language will prevail in the evening. Tonight it's German. I understood about one percent of what's going on. Stephen and I were trying to figure out how alcoholic the shots were. Apparently you can't say no to Germans. I had about five shots.

Tonight we hung out with Christof, Renate, and Roswitha, the nice folks I met the night before Melisa and I reached *Alto del Perdón*. I'm glad I had more time to get to know them. When I met them the first night, they were super quiet because everyone was speaking English. Tonight was their night.

Everyone was teasing me because apparently I pronounce Renate completely wrong. I have a German friend named Renate and apparently I have been saying her name wrong for years and no one ever bothered to correct me. The Germans thought my pronunciation was so funny that they made me record it on their phone!

Everyone continued to drink into the night, but I began passing on the shots after a while. I don't think tomorrow's walk will be very easy with a hangover! They got all teary eyed as they shared stories about why they were hiking the Camino. Most people have very powerful motivations for hiking 500 miles. Some people hike to grieve the loss of a loved one, some are running from or towards love, some are at a crossroads in their life and are looking for answers. I was struggling with my personal boundaries, though. I didn't think anyone would be interested in my story even though they were all being so open about their own. No one asked me directly about my reason, so I sat quietly and listened.

Actually, while the others chatted in German, it gave Stephen and me a chance to talk for a bit. As much as I've enjoyed walking with him, tomorrow is his last day on the Camino. He will continue on to Barcelona to meet some friends. Tonight he was telling me how much he's going to miss the Camino and he showed me a text he sent his girlfriend. He told her that in just the few days he's been on the Camino, he's had a great deal of positive experiences and the thought of leaving already makes him want to cry. I hugged him and told him I was so happy I got the chance to meet him. We promised to stay in touch.

By the time we were done at the restaurant, we were all very close. We walked back to the albergue together. The Germans were singing, dancing, and laughing the whole way. They kept joking that all Americans ever say is "oh my GOD!" They walked through the streets yelling this at the top of their lungs. So funny. They're fantastic people.

Poppies

Bread on the left, wine on the right

# CHAPTER 12

## DAY 10: 10KM FROM VIANA TO LOGROÑO

—

## PEP TALK

God I wish all hikes could be as short as today's.

What an absolutely beautiful country. I wish I had the words to describe some of the views I see, and I wish I had a better way to share the spectacular pictures and videos I have. Every ten minutes of walking leads you to a completely different view.

Yesterday, I was walking through wheat fields one moment, watching the crop change colors as the wind blew through. The next minute I was walking through a vineyard; and after that, I was lying in a field of wildflowers. I just can't get over how amazing everything is here. There's so much space and everything is so green.

Even the industrial areas have something to offer. Some people complain when the path forces us along highways, but it's not as bad as I thought it would be. First, there aren't nearly as many vehicles here as in the U.S. so the highways don't even compare. Second, they are always lined with colorful wildflowers. I like to slow down and run my hands through them. And if the exhaust ever gets to be too much, you just bury your nose into the flowers and take in their fresh scent. Even the graffiti is friendly and encouraging. "*Buen Camino!*" "Keep walking fella!" I saw such cool Camino artwork on an overpass that I just had to take a picture.

On our way into our next major town, we passed through the vineyards where the wine we drank last night came from. We also passed a famous blind trail angel just before we reached town. She sits outside of her house with her two dogs and provides snacks to pilgrims passing by. I had forgotten the stories about this angel until we met her. I was so grateful to have the opportunity to walk by while she was outside.

The heart of Logroño is huge with an interesting mix of medieval and modern styles. We arrived very early, but stopped here for the day since it's Stephen's last day on the Camino. He'll be taking the train out of here tomorrow morning, so some of us are going to hang back with him and go to a Pilgrim's Mass together tonight. Not only that, but the next major stop is many kilometers away and I'm not in shape to do the whole haul in one day. Talking with Christof and Renate, I believe they could use a rest as well. They stayed in our albergue last night and seemed to need as much rest as I did.

We ran into the sweet Dutch couple who we affectionately call "Holland." We met them the first night on the trail. He was the drunk man who kept standing up during dinner to address the whole restaurant and she kept dragging him back down to his seat. More great people. They were also at the memorable stop yesterday where we celebrated the man's birthday.

The five of us strolled around until we found a café. Some kind locals helped us since we looked completely lost. But first, we had to get food on our way to get food! We stopped at a sweet shop and ate our treats on our way to the café. I bought two baked hearts with coconut topping.

When we found the café finally, we lined the wall with our packs and found a place to sit. The great thing about cafés here is they display their pre-made sandwiches and pastries so all you have to do is point. The bad news is without a description you don't always know what's hiding in them. I asked for the vegetable sandwich, but didn't realize they hid anchovies in the middle. Oddly, I liked the anchovies I had in Pamplona, but these were salty and terrible. Nikolai must have ordered the same thing, because I noticed he was wincing with every bite. We snickered as we realized at the same time that we both ordered something we didn't want. But of course I still ate the entire thing. Calories are great!

The Dutch couple decided to continue on since it was still early in the day, so I may or may not bump into them again. They're much older and tend to walk shorter distances so I'm hoping I'll see them.

We found an albergue and dumped our packs before hitting the town for more food. Because we arrived so early, the place had not been cleaned yet. It was filthy. I could tell that hundreds of pilgrims blew through it early that morning. We hoped it would be cleaned before we returned later in the evening. While the three of us were settling in, I admitted to Stephen that I was having serious doubts that I would make it. I'm always in pain and I struggle the whole way. He was very kind but he didn't sugarcoat it.

"Theresa, this is the really tough part. This is where you have to push yourself. This isn't supposed to be easy. You can do this. You just have to keep moving," he said.

I teared up a bit while I listened. He was right. I have to suck it up and just keep moving.

We walked around town most of the day, sightseeing. First, we walked to the bus station where Stephen would have to go the next morning, so he could purchase his ticket and familiarize himself with the station. Then we headed to the nearest post office so Nikolai could mail his brother a birthday card. We took lots of fun pictures in the botanical garden in the middle of the city and ran into some interesting pilgrims. Then we found a café outside and did some people watching.

I have noticed several things over the last few days. First, older women dye their hair bright funky colors, which I think is super cool. I wondered how I could pass that tip on to elderly American women. I would love to see that at home. Second, city dogs live much better lives than country dogs. We pass many dogs on the Way and sometimes it's very hard to see how they live. Many of them are chained to a wooden box day after day with little to no human interaction or exercise. It's difficult to know there is nothing you can do about it. In some cases, the feral dogs live better than the domestic dogs. The city dogs, though, are spoiled! And third, regardless of where you are, whether you are out in the county or the center of a big city, you will find dandelion particles floating all through the air.

While strolling around town, we caught sight of an amazing painting on the side of a building. It was a massive image of a shirtless old man. His torso was covered in the Camino stamps we get in our credentials booklet every time we arrive in a new town. The three of us stopped for several minutes to admire all the stamps represented in the painting.

After seeing a good bit of the town, we returned to our albergue to find it in much better shape. Stephen took his required afternoon siesta while Nikolai and I did everyone's laundry. Nothing is ever done quite easily though. It took us many attempts to get the machines going and we had to ask for help from multiple pilgrims and one volunteer to figure out why the machines were so finicky. By the time we succeeded, we felt like masters of the universe. High five!

For dinner, we met our extended trail family - Roswitha, Renate, Christof, Ginger, Drennan, and Maria the Mexican from Texas, who accompanied Ginger and Drennan. This time, we ordered a real meal instead of the somewhat bland pilgrim's meal we've been eating these last few days. The food was absolutely to die for. The meal came with two bottles of wine and bottled water.

By the time we finished dinner, we realized we missed Mass so, unfortunately, we weren't able to attend. We did all enter the church and say our prayers before moving on, though.

Stephen, Nikolai, and I then had coffee outside on one of the popular streets in town. This was the last night all three of us would be a trail family, so we wanted to spend as much time together as possible. It was a quarter to ten when we realized we were about to be locked out of our albergue. Most of the hostels lock down at night for safety reasons, and if you're not there in time, you sleep outside. We didn't realize how late it was because the sun was still shining that late *en la noche*!

Miles of vineyards

# CHAPTER 13

## DAY 11: 30KM FROM LOGROÑO TO NÁJERA

—

## FIRST 30 KILOMETER DAY

I did it! 30km - 18 miles - with a full pack. My longest day yet. I am so relieved because originally I was planning to do a few 15km days but, at that pace, I wouldn't make it to Santiago by the time I have to leave Spain. But I learned today that I can do the long miles as long as I give myself ample time and take substantial breaks.

This morning after our pilgrim breakfast (a prepackaged croissant and coffee), we said our goodbyes to Stephen. As we left the albergue, he went right, and Nikolai and I went left. I'm so happy to have met him and hope we will cross paths again one day. As a parting gift, he gave me all of his foot repair gear which I've already started using! I hope you are having a blast in Barcelona, Stephen!

Nikolai and I continued along the Way. I planned to stop in a town only about 20km down the road, and Nikolai said he didn't mind walking with me. I thought for sure he'd ditch me as soon as Stephen left. After all, he's healthy, has absolutely no pain, and can really pack in the miles. Here I am, broken and slow as a sloth. But we talked it over and decided we would stay together as long as it works out for both of us. For me, I like having a buddy to walk with especially through towns. For him, he'll be forced to slow things down and enjoy the scenery. I am happy for the company but I have learned that I need to walk the Way at my own pace. I won't try to keep up with anyone again.

As it turns out, with the breaks appropriately timed, I was able to go the full 30km to the next major stop, which was way further than I expected from myself!

Every time someone is added to or eliminated from a trail family, the dynamic completely changes. This is the most fascinating part of hiking to me. I didn't know how our family would change with Stephen gone because he always led the way and he did most of the talking. For the last three days, Nikolai had been very quiet, so I assumed he was shy. But I quickly learned that he has lots of interesting things to say. He explained that when Americans are together, they speak much faster and he spends all his time trying to understand the conversation rather than participating. But when it is just the two of us, he keeps up quite well. He said he'd like to take the opportunity walking together to learn more English and that he would probably ask a lot of questions.

He pulled out his translation book, checked it briefly and asked me, "Do I go on your nerve?" I laughed. No, of course not. I enjoy the company!

We agreed we should look for others to join us again since our people have slowly been dropping off the Camino due to injuries or deadlines. Sure enough, the Camino provides. We ran into Ginger, Drennan and Maria in the middle of a vineyard. We were sitting at a picnic table in the shade of a food truck when they caught up to us. We were so happy to see them, we cheered them on like they just won a race. They stopped and joined us at the table.

Maria introduced me to wine and Coke, which is similar to but cheaper than rum and Coke. It was pretty good! As the five of us sat at that table by the food truck randomly placed in the middle of the vineyard, I stored the moment in my long-term memory and thanked

God for such an awesome experience. We all walked together for a good part of the day and ended up staying in the same albergue.

All day we walked along roads and passed through industrial areas. The trail was flat though so it was an easy hike. We also spent hours walking through vineyards. I now know why wine is cheaper than water here. There are acres and acres of vineyards across Spain.

Nikolai and I passed the time chatting away. His English improves by leaps and bounds every hour. He told me he learned English in school but this was his first opportunity to actually practice in the real world. We spent the whole day just talking about the English language. There's nothing but time on the trail, so why not? I spent about a half hour just trying to explain the difference between *yet* and *already,* which proved to be more difficult than I thought it would be.

At one point he asked me why I chose to hike the Way. He was the first person to ask me this question. Everyone was talking about their reasons a few nights ago at dinner but we both chose not to share at the time. I told him that I didn't really have a compelling story. I'm walking the Camino because I can. I'm walking the Camino because I should.

It was then that we realized we had something in common. He, too, is walking the Camino because he was driven to do something extraordinary with his time. Unlike others who have these powerful experiences in their lives that directly guided them to the Camino, we are simply here because we could be.

He explained that his journey actually did not begin in St. Jean like most of ours. His journey began at his home in Germany. He biked 900km in France before taking modern transportation to St. Jean. He explained that while he wished he could have biked the entire distance, his knees gave out on him and he had to stop partway through France.

Centuries ago, pilgrims did not have the modern day conveniences of trains, planes, and automobiles, so most would begin their pilgrimage at the front door of their home, wherever that may be. Despite biking only part of the distance between his home and St. Jean, in essence, Nikolai has more in common with the original pilgrims than the rest of us.

I was in a great deal of pain and shuffling like an old lady by the time I got into town. Ginger's family hikes faster than I do, and we didn't want to lose them, so we walked further and with fewer stops than my feet could handle in the last few kilometers. I know that goes against my new rule to walk at my own pace but I didn't think pushing myself just a little would be detrimental. I was in pretty rough shape, though.

Fortunately, we got what I think were probably the last five beds in town. We were turned away from three hostels and hotels before we found one that would take us. Thank God. It was nice, too. It was another attic but it was large, it had real beds, and the five of us stayed together and shared the room with only two other very nice women. And the bathroom was very clean and fancy. It felt more like a hotel in that regard.

Because we arrived so late, the washers and dryers were all being used, but the albergue owner told us if we go to the albergue across the street, they might be able to help us. We all piled our dirty clothes together, and Maria and I carried them across the street. For a small fee we dropped our laundry off. While there, I ran into Misha, the Australian I hiked the Pyrenees with! She is a strong and fast hiker but she overdid it. Her leg was elevated, wrapped and swollen. She would be forced to slow down. It's amazing how the Camino forces you to slow your roll sometimes. It was great to see her.

Some highlights: Hands down the best moment was when we had to stop and get off the trail for a shepherd and his sheep. I had to take a video of it. It was fantastic. Over 100 sheep (and one random droopy donkey) were rounded up and taken down the street by an adorable shepherd and his four dogs, who were very skilled at their jobs. It was quite a sight!

Late in the afternoon as we were hiking through miles of vineyards and talking, a white van from the opposite direction came towards us. As it approached us, the driver slowed down and rolled down his window. He said something in Spanish and extended a shiny metal bowl towards us. With the curiosity of a child, I cautiously walked towards the man and peered into the bowl. Watermelon!! We both dove in and thanked the man. He was smiling from ear to ear. He knew it was just what we needed on this hot afternoon. Another trail angel.

Also, remember Dolores, the woman I met the very first day at Logan airport? I ran into her again! She made it over the Pyrenees and was walking with her four-person hiker family. She was strong and feeling well.

Apparently I have a bit of a reputation on the trail. I was introduced as "the tiny thing with the massive pack." They seemed delighted and almost surprised to see me still going. It made me realize that even though I'm struggling and I feel like I'm incredibly slow, I'm still out here hiking the hike and I'm running into the same people I began with, so I'm not all that slow after all.

Tonight I taught Nikolai the meaning of "hangry." He was ravenous by dinner, which was evident by his sour mood, and the rest of us playfully teased him that he was experiencing hanger pains. It's a new word that really resonated with him and I suspect he'll be using it a lot. He can never seem to get enough to eat.

Ugh, blisters. I got two more small ones today. I thought that was terrible until I saw other people's feet. Ginger and Drennan win the award for biggest and scariest blisters. Mine are actually in decent shape. They are small and clean. During one of our stops, I tried to use the needle and thread the way Stephen showed me, but I had trouble getting a good angle. I was also a bit squeamish about puncturing myself.

Nikolai saw me struggling, pulled my foot onto his lap, and began suturing it for me without a word. I have no idea why he helped me. How do you properly thank someone for taking care of you like that?

"Hey thanks amigo?" I told him I didn't understand why he helped me but that I really appreciated it. He just shrugged and said "It's ok." I thought when Stephen helped me, he was just doing his job as a paramedic. But maybe there is more to it out here on the Camino.

Let's talk about coffee for a moment. I was not a coffee drinker before coming here, but I drink my weight in coffee every day now. When you take frequent stops, there's not much to do but drink beer or *café con leche*. So I spend the first half of my day walking from bar to bar (which are really adorable outdoor cafés most of the time) and drink nonstop, which brings me to my next topic.

Bathrooms. Forget about them. They aren't here. And if you are fortunate enough to happen upon one, there most likely won't be toilet paper or soap and sometimes not even a toilet seat. So don't get too excited. Going to the bathroom on the side of the trail becomes a part of everyday life. I spent the first two days of my trip dehydrating myself to avoid the discomfort of peeing in public and I spent the third day doing a tinkle dance for about three miles before I couldn't hold it anymore. Now, it doesn't even phase me. You just yell "*baño!*" and jump into the nearest bush while your friends keep walking but at a slightly slower pace.

Sometimes it creates funny situations, though. For example, late in our hike this afternoon after hours of walking through vineyards, we were being really silly. I was taking a video of the scenery and

Nikolai was belting out the soundtrack to Star Wars. Suddenly Jenny, a hiker I recognized from my first day, jumped out from behind a tree in front of us with her clothes half off. "I was hoping you two would slow down!" We apologized and assured her we weren't paying attention. I'm sure the video is quite hilarious. After that, every time we caught up to her, I would yell that we were coming to give her plenty of warning. She was a good sport about it. I'll have to delete that video, though.

That's about it. Nothing earth shattering today but I'm thrilled that I made it through my first 30km day and for the first time I don't feel like crying myself to sleep. Progress.

# CHAPTER 14

## DAY 12: 22KM FROM NÁJERA TO
## SANTO DOMINGO DE LA CALZADA

—

### FINDING MY RHYTHM

Awesome day. Hours of walking in silence, lots of breaks with great friends, a spiritual pilgrim's Mass blessing our journey, and a real bed to sleep in tonight.

Highlights: The breaks were a highlight for sure. While we did not always walk together, I ran into my five-person family at nearly all the stops, which were filled with laughter, silliness, and fun. We had a competition to see who had the heaviest pack. Nikolai won with his 22 kilo pack because he's been traveling the longest. We all took turns trying on his pack. I nearly fell on my back! I could appreciate how heavy the pack was already, though. Sometimes while walking, he would pretend to forget the size of his massive pack, swing around to look at something behind him, knocking me with it and throwing me off the path. Although I'd pretend to be annoyed, I actually wished someone would get a video of it because I imagine it looks quite comical. Anyway, my pack on the other hand was of similar weight and size to Ginger's, but it looked twice as large on my smaller back.

I found my rhythm today, walking along those vast open fields. I'd run my hands along the tall plants that lined the Way and occasionally pluck the seeds and toss them into the fields. I would also occasionally find a spider hitching a ride on my arm which would interrupt my zen moment. Everyone teased me about how I'd flip out over the sight of a tiny spider. "Get it off me!" I would yell frantically to whoever was closest to me, as if they were the one who put it there.

As we walked through miles and miles of fields, I started feeling a bit hungry.

"I think I'm hungry. Are you hungry?" I asked Nikolai.

"Theresa, I'm ALWAYS hungry."

Since there were no food trucks or cafes anywhere for miles, we found a dusty patch off the side of the road, threw our packs down, opened my umbrella, and had lunch right there on the edge of the field. I had bread and cheese in my pack and my hiking buddy had chorizo. Together our ingredients made the perfect Spanish lunch. The simplicity of the day felt so special to me. I was hungry, so I stopped what I was doing and I ate. There was no planning or preparation needed. We sat on the dusty earth and ate our bread and cheese to our heart's content.

Following dinner at a nice restaurant in the middle of Santo Domingo, we all went to a pilgrim's Mass. I found the experience to be very spiritual and empowering. Most of it was in Spanish so I couldn't understand all of it but the parts that were in English struck a chord with me. I was moved to tears as I prayed for continued strength and health along my journey.

I've had a bit to drink tonight so I'm off to bed. I'll explain the evening in more detail tomorrow.

Still a long way to go

Santo Domingo

# CHAPTER 15

## DAY 13: 22KM FROM SANTO DOMINGO DE LA CALZADA TO BELORADO

—

### EVEN PILGRIMS CAN ENJOY HOTELS

So last night's albergue was a total bust. For seven euros, I was placed on the top bunk in the middle of a room with a bunch of smelly bikers who didn't bother to shower before crashing for the night. Their gear was everywhere so there was nowhere for me to put my stuff. Nikolai and I took quick showers and left the albergue immediately.

We went to the hotel where we knew Ginger's group was staying and slouched in the big comfy couches in the lobby as we waited to hear back from them. After about a half an hour, though, it was clear that our texts did not make it to Ginger. We decided to explore the town without them. But while we were strolling about, Nikolai spotted them having dinner so we joined them!

They had gotten into town before us and reserved rooms at the Parador, which is a castle converted to a five-star hotel. This is where we had been waiting for them earlier in the evening. Everything they said sounded amazing as they described their sleeping arrangements. Real beds, soap and shampoo in the bathrooms. It was too good to be true. Long story short, after the teary pilgrim's Mass, a few drinks at the hotel bar, and some major convincing from my trail family and my husband, I decided I deserved a night in a real hotel, too. At first I resisted the urge. I didn't want to spend the extra money and I felt it would be cheating. Does a pilgrim stay in hotels? I texted Brian to get his opinion and he responded immediately. Two thumbs up. He assured me that I'm still a pilgrim even if I stay in hotels and the rest and relaxation would be well worth the money. So we walked back to the albergue after dinner, grabbed our stuff and got a double at the Parador.

In the morning, the five of us met for a wonderful breakfast in the hotel restaurant and got a late start to our hike. Despite being in a hotel last night, I had a hard time falling asleep. This was partially because I had too much to drink before going to bed. Big mistake. I also kept jumping awake fearing that if we left too late in the morning, I wouldn't find a bed to sleep in the next night. When I awoke fully in the morning, I realized my fears were a little unrealistic, but they did manage to keep me up most of the night nonetheless. So while the others were enjoying a long breakfast this morning, I ran back up to my room for a quick 20-minute hangover nap. While resting, I heard Nikolai enter the room and then leave quietly. It occurred to me that they probably all decided to hike on without me. I jumped out of bed and quickly put my pack on. If I hurried, I may be able to catch up with them.

But as I was pulling on my pack, Nikolai reentered the room. He explained that he told the others to go on without us and he also checked with the front desk and learned that we could stay until noon. "So you can keep sleeping if you want." I was touched that he was willing to wait for me but I had a quick nap and I was ready to go. When we arrived in the lobby, I was so happy to have learned that the others also waited for me. I felt so loved! Everyone put their packs on and we headed out together.

Here's a quick lesson in Camino clothing. Nikolai ran out of clean hiking shirts so he chose to start his hike in a cotton t-shirt he normally only wears around town. Within 20 minutes of walking, he decided he was better off hiking in a dirty synthetic shirt than the cotton. He was sweating and extremely uncomfortable. This wasn't surprising though. One of the first things I learned about hiking gear is that one should always avoid cotton. It does not wick away sweat effectively and this can be especially dangerous in cold temperatures. Granted, no one was in danger of hyperthermia on a hot day like today, but his experiment demonstrated to me the importance of having proper gear.

Today consisted of vast open fields with the Way stretched in front of us for miles. Seeing how far you have to walk does two things. First, it makes you realize just how small and insignificant you are in this world. And second, it offers comfort. I used to find it daunting when I could see my path miles ahead. But now when I see a long path, I know exactly what I'll be doing for the next couple of hours. Walking along the path. That's it. Nothing more. Simple.

This is what makes life on the Camino so special. When you see your path stretched before you and your only goal is to walk that path for the next several weeks, you are forced to be present. You can't see your destination so your only option is to live in the here and the now. There are few things to worry about, which gives your mind plenty of time to focus on what's most important in your life. And when you walk day in and day out, it's hard to imagine doing anything other than that. I wonder how I will adapt when I have to go back to my "normal" life which is full of decisions, challenges, and chores. Out here, I just walk.

Most of today was spent walking in total silence. Sometimes we were spaced out along the trail and sometimes we walked together, but for the most part, we walked in silence. There would be a random outburst of laughter about something one second, and the next back to silence. And there's nothing awkward about this. When you spend hours upon hours walking with the same people, there's only so much you can say before you become more reflective.

The silliness that interrupts those reflective moments is one of my favorite things, though. Walking today with Drennan, a 15-year-old, ensured lots of random silliness. He's apparently a big fan of Forrest Gump, so there were many references to that. He's also a Willie Nelson fan, from what I gather.

"Drennan! Pace yourself. We've got 20 more kms to go!" He has endless amounts of energy.

I put my headphones on for the first time today. I was afraid listening to music would pull me away from my Camino experience, but it actually enhanced my senses tenfold. I could feel everything. I could see everything. I could smell everything. We were walking down a slight hill and could see miles of fields ahead of us. The breeze was cool and the sun was warm. I was suddenly struck by the beauty of it all.

I broke the silence: "Just look at this! I love this!" My trail family just smiled and nodded. They understood.

I am seeing now that the Camino really does break you down. You don't have the capacity to be arrogant, stubborn, or miserable anymore. You have to just give in to its ways. And with the amount of physical exertion required on a daily basis, it is impossible not to feel good. Your endorphins are thriving. I find myself randomly happy for no apparent reason. I cannot stop smiling and sometimes I even laugh out loud for no reason at all. It's such a refreshing break from my usual melancholy.

Maria, Nikolai, and I stopped at some picnic tables under some trees in one of the tiny towns we were passing through. There were several local men sitting at one of the tables. We eagerly said *hola* to them but they didn't seem too interested in *peregrinos*. They mostly just ignored us, but they weren't mean to us in any way, so we just kept to ourselves. After all, it must be a bit annoying for complete strangers to pass through your town every single day.

The cats, on the other hand, were super sweet. Maria and I learned that we both love cats. As we were sitting in the shade, the cats would cozy up to us looking for love and affection.

At one point, the five of us passed under some trees and entered a huge open field. Whatever the trees are, they release large cotton-like fuzzies. I wrote days ago that you can find dandelion particles in the air in every town but apparently that's not what they are. Whatever they were, it was beautiful. It looked like snow and it was one of those moments when I wished my husband was there to experience it. There was no way to capture it without being there. It was like walking through snow in the middle of summer.

A man walked by us with a mule this afternoon. I learned later that he walked with his mule from St. Jean to Santiago and was now walking back! Apparently people can rent mules to aid their journey across Spain. It's cool to see but I'm not sure how I feel about it. The mules need to be conditioned, just as people do, and I imagine the trek is just as difficult for them as it is for humans. But they can't tell their human that they are tired and in pain. My hope is that the humans who rent them take good care of these animals.

As for a body update: my feet seem to be holding out okay. I think I may be working on another little blister, but it's too early to tell yet. I also have a really sore throat for some reason. The air is very dry and I had to buy moisturizer and lip balm at the pharmacy. I probably should have purchased something for my throat, too, but buying drugs in a language you don't understand is a bit intimidating. I think I may be coming down with something, though.

Speaking of pharmacies, they are everywhere here, probably to support the large number of pilgrims. There are several in the larger towns. What I can't seem to figure out is siesta. I knew stores close for a period of time in the afternoon, but they seem to also be closed whenever the owner feels like it. They'll be closed at 11:00am sometimes.

We finally got to an open store today, and I bought the many things on my list: tweezers, lip balm, toothpaste, ibuprofen, Compeed, and Vick's Vapor Rub. A pharmacy to a hiker is a candy store to a child. So many delightful things to choose from! Ginger and I walked out with our arms full of goodies.

On a more serious note, there are rumors on the trail that there was another attempted abduction just the other day. An American woman hiking alone was forced into a man's car. She fought back and got away, but these instances continue to highlight a very real problem in the Astorga area. Whenever we hike near a road, I tend to hike closer to people. Maria is here on her own too so I usually keep an eye on wherever she is. We have to look out for each other. (Postscript: This turned out to be a rumor generated by the overactive minds of nervous pilgrims. There were no other abductions or attempted abductions on the Camino than the woman who went missing in April 2015.)

We called ahead to reserve five beds at the nearest albergue called Albergue Santiago. We left late this morning and spent way too much time in towns eating, drinking, and socializing. Drennan is solidly against calling ahead but he lost that debate today. With the exception of Nikolai, who is comfortable with his one-person tent, none of us want to be forced to sleep outside.

We had a ton of fun today, but entering town so late would leave us with little time to do our laundry, shower, get settled in, and eat tonight. Calling ahead worked out great. Because our group is so big, we only had to share a room with each other and the Albergue Santiago was really nice.

My family of five sat out in the cool afternoon sun having drinks and enjoying each other's company. What an awesome day. I cannot describe how happy I am being able to be outside all day and with such wonderful people. Then we all had dinner at the restaurant connected to the albergue. I was still so tired from not getting much sleep the night before, so I went to bed early. Everyone was still eating dessert when I excused myself from the table. Since I had done our laundry for the previous two days, Nikolai offered to take care of my clothes for me so I wouldn't have to worry about it tonight. The next morning, I awoke to find my clean clothes folded neatly at the foot of my bed. I believe that was Ginger's doing.

Arriving at the albergue

# CHAPTER 16

## DAY 14: 27KM FROM BELORADO TO AGES

—

## WE ALL WANT THE SAME THING

Great walk today. We did so well that we walked an additional 4km to Ages. We met a young German couple named Kim and Linus who we may be hanging out with for the next day or so. I think Nikolai was excited to talk with people in his first language. He bolted ahead with them for most of the day while I stayed back with Ginger, Drennan, and Maria. Ginger joked that we may have lost Nikolai to another hiking family. I suspected we would see him again though. Our family is too awesome to go without.

The subtle shift in our family dynamics was great because it gave me the opportunity to spend some time getting to know Ginger. She has a fascinating life story and I felt privileged to learn some of the things she shared with me. I had even more admiration for her after getting to know her.

Ginger, Drennan, and I stopped to rest under some nice trees to take rest. Drennan focused on killing all the ants while Ginger and I worked on our feet. We encouraged Maria to stop with us and take her boots off but she refused. She has a pretty bad blister on one of her heels. I'm afraid if she doesn't take care of it, it'll get worse. I got the sense she was afraid to see how bad the damage was, so she chose to ignore it. I can certainly understand her apprehension. I cringe every time I remove my footwear.

We also ran into the mother/daughter team we haven't seen in several days, Dotty and Kristen. It's always exciting to run into people because you are always aware of the possibility that you could have gone the rest of your life without ever seeing them again.

The Germans slowed down enough that we could walk with them later in the afternoon. I began chatting with Kim. She shared her life story with me so easily. I am always amazed at how open people are on the Camino, and how eager she was to share the deepest secrets of her heart. She is a passionate young woman with a great deal of stress for a 19-year-old.

Although we come from totally different places in the world, we all seem to have the same struggles and we all want the same thing. Regardless of how we behave or what we say, we all just want to be loved and accepted. And here on the Camino, love is freely given and accepted between strangers. Every day I am moved by the power of the Camino to bring people together. I was glad I had a chance to meet this young lady and grateful she felt comfortable enough to talk with me.

We all stopped at the town where we originally planned to spend the night, but we decided to move on to Ages. I felt great from a walking perspective, but I've lost my voice and I have a very sore throat. The next pharmacy is nearly 15km away so I'll walk there tomorrow to get some drugs.

I was feeling a bit testy as we all sat in the little café drinking soda. I felt kind of bad later because I was a bit cold to the German boy. He asked if they could stay at whichever albergue we planned to stay. The others eagerly welcomed them but I just sat quietly as if objecting to the notion. I wasn't actually against hanging out with them; I was just focused on my own discomfort at the moment. Either way, he didn't deserve that. I realized I needed to be extra gracious to both kids that evening so they wouldn't leave our family thinking they weren't welcome.

Tomorrow we will be in Burgos. I was planning on continuing as usual, but Ginger said they all plan to take a day off. It occurred to me that perhaps I should do the same. I've been hiking for over two weeks now without a break. Plus, if I'm getting sick, I should probably rest.

Once reaching Ages, we couldn't find an albergue in town that had room for all seven of us so the two young Germans found beds elsewhere while the rest of us settled into the same place. They did join us for dinner later, though. The bathrooms were a total disaster and I almost chose not to shower. There were no seats on the toilets and there was a big mop bucket full of dirty water sitting in the middle of the tiny space which took up the entire bathroom. I cringed at the thought of that water being sloshed all over the bathroom floor with that filthy mop. There wasn't even a place to hang my things so Ginger stood outside of my shower and handed me my clothes as I needed them. That said, at least the beds were decent.

We all had dinner together downstairs in the albergue's restaurant, so it was the five of us with the two young Germans, plus Dotty and Kristen. Tonight was my turn to be hangry. Everyone else was served their food and had completely eaten before my pizza was served. It was well worth the wait, though. Very good. We had so much fun too! I mostly just listened while everyone chatted because my throat was bothering me so much. Ginger and I FaceTimed our parents and let everyone around the table wave to them. It was a great night.

On a totally random note, Ginger let me borrow the most amazing product on the market today. She is carrying a little bottle of fruit scented hand sanitizer. I'm sure this sounds completely unremarkable, but I was so excited about it and I envied her. What a wonderful little thing. Something to clean my hands that smells good too. I'm going to text Brian and ask him to bring a bottle for us when he comes to Spain.

Stork's nest on the bell towers

# CHAPTER 17

## DAY 15: 24KM FROM AGES TO BURGOS

—

## GREATEST CITY EVER

I didn't sleep at all last night. I was so congested that I had to sleep sitting up most of the night and whenever I dozed off, I would jump awake paranoid that I was snoring or about to fall off the top bunk. By morning, my throat hurt so bad I had to brace myself before swallowing and I had no voice at all. My Camino family was so sweet. Ginger ordered me a hot milk with honey which actually helped a bit. It was enough to get me ready for the day's hike. Ginger is the mother of one, but she is an excellent caregiver to everyone.

Maybe it was because I got no sleep last night, but for whatever reason today was a really tough day. There weren't a lot of hills, but we spent much of the time on asphalt, which is very hard on the feet, and we followed a highway for nearly the entire day which was not relaxing, but rather unnerving. There was a more scenic route heading into Burgos but somehow we all managed to miss it. If you hike the Camino Frances, make sure you take the scenic route into Burgos.

The upside to that is we ran across a McDonalds and just had to stop in for Happy Meals. FYI, American chains are nicer in other countries than in the United States. They had massive colorful touch monitors at the entrance of the store. You place your order there and only walk up to the counter when your number is called. It took us a bit to figure out how the process worked, but it was extremely organized.

But back to the start of the day. Dotty had a bad blister on one of her feet so she took a taxi to Burgos while Kristen walked with us today. Dotty was sure to have the driver honk at us when they drove by us leaving the first town of the day. Everyone cheered her on as she blew past us. It would be hours before we would catch up with her.

The beginning of the hike today was very nice. For our first stop, the six of us had second breakfast together. There was a nice little café with an outdoor seating area with trees and a large, open, grassy field. Maria turned on her phone and started playing Jazz music. I was in a more reflective mood for some reason though, so I found a nice quiet spot in the grass and basked in the sun. Eventually Nikolai found a spot in the grass too. We chatted briefly and then fell asleep for quite a while. Kristen woke us at some point to let us know the group was moving on. I was refreshed and ready to go!

Finally, I've discovered the mystery of the white fuzzies that float all over town. They aren't dandelions and they don't come off of trees. They are spider web particles! I found an article about it in a magazine at one of the cafés we stopped at. While I was busy trying to translate the article, Drennan was pushing Nikolai's English skills by teaching him tongue twisters. *How much wood could a woodchuck chuck* ... It was hilarious. Nikolai is a very smart man but something about him reminds me of a child when he struggles with his second language. He has fun with it though and humors Drennan. Drennan looks up to him like a big brother.

Body update: two blisters today, both earned within the last hour of walking. I was angry the whole time because I knew they were blistering and there was nothing I could do about it. I really wanted to stay with the group and they weren't stopping anymore.

I've learned consuming less coffee and alcohol drastically improves my performance. I wish I could say I learned this from experience, but alas, I am not the brightest crayon in the box. It was Brian in fact who informed me that the reason I feel so sluggish sometimes is due to my alcohol consumption. So I haven't had alcohol in three days and I only drink one cup of coffee in the morning. On our breaks now, I order *zumo de piña* (pineapple juice), which makes me feel more refreshed. Of course I'll probably have some drinks tonight, being in Burgos on a Saturday night, but I intend to sleep in tomorrow, so I don't think it'll be a problem.

Hiking Highlights: My nap was definitely a highlight. Lying on the ground without a care in the world is a treasure everyone should have. Rarely do we have the opportunity to live so carefree.

We walked into one town this morning as the church bells were ringing. They weren't the standard ring we normally hear though. They sounded like music and they never let up. I suspect there was a wedding or some other special event. We also ran into some women in town who were all dressed up. Since I lost my voice, though, I wasn't able to stop them and ask for their stories. Drennan got a nice picture of himself surrounded by the beautiful women.

Walking into Burgos was fun despite my feeling like crap. Ginger and Drennan were singing the whole way. I wanted to join them but I could barely speak, let alone sing, so I just made song requests instead.

Burgos: What a cool town! Burgos on Saturday night is jumping. There were at least three weddings and I don't know how many First Holy Communion celebrations going on. All the little boys and girls were dressed up. The girls wore colorful dresses and the boys wore adorable little sailor suits. They were all so precious! Random music groups set up throughout the town, which drew in people looking to dance and celebrate. Everyone was out and ready for a fun night.

When we finally arrived in town, I was exhausted and in a lot of pain but that all went away (for a bit anyway) when we saw the cathedral. It's considered the most beautiful cathedral on the Camino, and it was so worth the walk. The architecture was gorgeous and the building was absolutely enormous. We only got to see the exterior at the time, but tomorrow we will pay to enter and see the inside, which is supposed to be just as impressive as the outside.

We did not have hotel reservations yet, so we had to walk to each hotel and decide where we wanted to stay. Because the others weren't in pain, they weren't really in a hurry and could afford to be particular about which hotel to stay in. I hobbled behind them hoping they would make up their minds quickly. In the meantime, we kept running into pilgrims in the streets who were already showered and rested. They were so excited about being in town and they were so chatty. I couldn't wait to get my shower and feel the same way, so, at the time, I wanted to shoot anyone who got between me and my hotel.

Like the cathedral though, my room was well worth the wait! It was spacious and included two double doors that opened into a beautiful courtyard, as well as a lovely seating area with a luxurious purple couch. As soon as we arrived, without asking, Nikolai called down to the front desk and ordered a cup of hot tea and honey to help soothe my scratchy throat. He's so thoughtful.

Meanwhile, I took a nice, long, hot shower, knowing that no one would be standing right outside the door waiting for me to finish like in most albergues. We all agreed to meet each other in the hotel lobby two hours later to find dinner so that afforded me plenty of time to lounge around on the comfy couch and text Brian.

Dinner in Spain is very different than in the U.S. It was 8pm and yet we struggled to find a restaurant that was offering a full menu. That early in the evening, all we could find open were tapas bars. We chose a beautiful restaurant that was decorated with hundreds of roses and overflowing with people celebrating a boy's First Holy Communion. It was such a positive atmosphere. At one point some police on motorcycles drove by. They got off their bikes and let the family take pictures of the boy on their bikes. He was thrilled.

Just as we were finishing our amazing tapas, our new young German friends came in. Nikolai stayed in touch with them and asked them to join us tonight. Despite being tired and full from tapas, not everyone was ready to turn in for the night. It was 9:30pm on a Saturday, it was still daylight out, and there was so much excitement in the air. So several of us found some live music by an outdoor bar and ordered drinks.

Despite all the fun I was having, I was continuing to feel sicker and I was having trouble swallowing again. We all stayed together as we walked through town looking for an open pharmacy. I still don't understand why stores are open/closed at such random times. When we found a pharmacy that was open, it was in the middle the liveliest section of town. I felt like there was a party in the store. It was very small and filled with happy people who were overflowing from the plaza. Normally I would be energized by this, but tonight I found it very frustrating because I had to find a way to communicate my ailments to a man who did not speak English. I was so grateful for Maria because she helped translate for me and the man gave me some meds. I wasn't confident he gave me what I needed, but I was so desperate to feel better that I swallowed the pills without hesitation.

Some of us stayed out later than others. Ginger and Drennan went back to their rooms first. Maria made a new Camino friend, as she always does, and stayed out with her. Nikolai and I stayed with our two new friends as long as they could stay out. Because they were staying in an albergue, they had a 10:30pm curfew. When I wished them a goodnight, it was more like "it was great meeting you, have a nice life," because odds are I won't see them again. They are in a hurry to finish and will carry on tomorrow while we plan to stay an extra day in beautiful Burgos.

Whenever you say goodbye to people on the Camino, it's very possible you will never see that person again and every single person you meet leaves their imprint on you. They are all special and they all teach you something. I will miss everyone I have met so far even if I only knew them briefly.

Nikolai and I walked around town absorbing as much of the positive energy in town as possible. There was much fun to be had and we didn't want to go to bed yet. We listened to live concerts, tried various drinks, and watched children play with glowing spinners in the streets with their parents. That's another interesting thing I noticed about Spain. The children stay out late, same as the adults.

At one point, we came across what seemed like a band of men in the middle of the street. Several guys were blasting music from their brass instruments so we ventured over to see what was going on. Well, I'm not sure what exactly was happening. All I can report is that a man in a black mesh shirt, leather chaps with holes in the butt, and black wings on his back was scampering around the road on his hands and knees chasing children. The children screamed with delight and hid behind their parent's legs. I have no idea what that was about, but it was quite comical. I took a picture and texted it to Brian. He cracked up.

Although I didn't actually get to bed until after midnight, the town was still full of activity. My room overlooked an outdoor patio where a bunch of elementary school boys had an impromptu concert. They yelled, screamed, and sang until 2:30 in the morning! Many people came out onto their balconies to see what all the noise was but I was surprised that no one actually complained. They let the kids have their fun. I slept with my doors wide open so I could enjoy the fresh air. Eventually I became accustomed to the noise and I slept quite well.

I'd say the funniest thing that happened today was, as usual, due to a language barrier that occurs regularly when people come together from all over the world to experience the Camino. As we were settling into the hotel, Nikolai read that there was a laundry service and the laundry bag was "stored in the closet." As I sat on the couch enjoying the fresh air coming in through the open doors, he tore apart the bathroom (the water closet) looking for the bag. In total frustration he stormed out of the bathroom and said to me, "I don't can do this!"

When I realized what he was struggling with, I casually introduced him to the actual closet which incidentally was nowhere near the bathroom. I think I found it much funnier than he did.

"Sweetie, that's the bathroom. This is a closet."

"What for is this language?!"

Overall I had a great time in Burgos and I'm glad I'll get to spend another whole day here. I could use a day of rest and this is a wonderful town to spend time in. Not to mention my hotel is fabulous. Room service? Yes, please!

The cathedral in Burgos

# CHAPTER 18

## DAY 16: REST DAY IN BURGOS

—

### FEELING BLESSED

I'm feeling very blessed today. Having a day off to recuperate has made me realize several things. First and foremost, I have been blessed with friendship. When I planned to hike the Way, as tough as it was, I was fully prepared to be on my own. I know things constantly change on the Camino, but here I am, 16 days in, and God hasn't allowed me to be alone yet. With the exception of a few hours in Estella, I've been blessed with amazing people from all over the world.

This became even more evident to me today as I ran into so many people I've met along the Way. For example, I saw Rick and Nicole from the Carolinas. I met them our very first day on the trail and they were happy to see Melisa and me together because their daughter will be hiking the Camino in a few months and they were concerned because she is going alone. They told me today when they saw me again how happy they were to see me and that I look so well and so happy. Granted, I've had a day of rest and that does wonders, but hearing that from others made me count my blessings. I told them they didn't have a thing to worry about with their daughter coming to the Camino alone. I actually met my first hiking partner in the airport in the US before I even left the country! The Camino provides! I assured them she would make wonderful friends, as I have.

Second, I am blessed with a strong healthy body. Yes, I've struggled with pain and the occasional blister and I'm now fighting what is probably the worst sinus infection I've ever had, but I hiked for 15 days straight carrying a pack half my size! I couldn't have seen all those sights or met all those people if I wasn't blessed with a strong healthy body.

What can I say about my day in Burgos? Burgos is fantastic. So full of charm and life. I began my morning with a late breakfast in my room. We sat around with the doors wide open to the courtyard eating the big breakfast that was brought right to our door, and watched about an hour of *The Godfather* in Spanish. Then we met the others in the afternoon. We strolled through town and went into the few shops that were still open on Sunday, including an awesome ice cream/candy shop where we all bought treats.

I made multiple attempts at the pharmacies we passed to find different drugs for my overactive sinuses, but wasn't very successful. The drugs I purchased weren't taking effect yet and I was afraid I got the wrong medicine. Last night, I texted Stephen in the middle of the night to find out what drugs he took for the sinus problems he had while we were walking together. He took a different drug. So I wanted to purchase that drug as well.

We all went to the gorgeous cathedral in town and Ginger treated us to the one-hour self-guided tour. There are over 20 chapels within the cathedral for people to marvel over. Some even came with the crypts of important people and dated back to 1200 including clergymen and some of the cathedral's architects. This is a must see for anyone hiking the Camino. Do yourself a favor and spend a day in Burgos!

We had a bit of a scare early in the day. We were all supposed to meet in the lobby late in the morning, but Maria never showed up.

Ginger went to her room and knocked on the door and when that failed, she tried to text and email. We didn't hear anything from Maria for hours. When Ginger checked her room again, she thought she saw a man leaving her room. We thought perhaps she met a friend and did not want to be disturbed, but after hearing nothing almost all day, we were really getting worried. I'm sure the recent abduction heightened our concerns.

Fortunately we ran into Maria later in the day and she was fine. She was out all day exploring the town on her own and forgot that we were supposed to meet in the morning. We all sighed with relief and told her we were worried sick about her. If we agree to meet, we all need to at least check in with each other.

Once we found her, Maria, Nikolai, and I went to a pilgrims Mass in the cathedral. It was nice, but I have to say I don't get as much out of Mass when I have no idea what they are saying. Go figure. Pilgrims who spoke Spanish found it very powerful though; I felt a bit left out.

I fell asleep with the doors to my room open to the patio again. We left the tv on an opera radio station so I was lulled to sleep by those sweet sounds accompanied by the falling water from the fountain out in the courtyard. It was the most peaceful evening. Incidentally, I woke up a couple hours later with the worst sinus congestion of my life. My ears were popping and it felt as though something was tearing apart deep in my ear canal. It was so painful, I wasn't able to sleep most of the night. It did however confirm for me which type of drugs I needed to be on.

Okay, the fluffy white things. I am so over them! They are not spider webs. Everyone teased me because apparently my Spanish is not so great and I didn't read the article right. The spider webs are in Australia and the white stuff here in Spain is some kind of pollen and does indeed come off of trees. I even have pictures to prove it now. But I don't even care anymore. They just taunt me now. This is probably a good time to mention that when you hike for hours every single day, you'd be surprised what occupies your mind. You spend hours focusing on the silliest things. These fuzzy things are probably a good example. I've spent days thinking about them and trying to figure out where they come from. I've also mentioned them about six times now. But my mystery is solved now, so I'm going to have to find something new to obsess about while I walk.

One other thing. I keep meaning to mention the birds here. They scream! I've never heard sounds like that in the US. It reminds me of the Alfred Hitchcock movie, *The Birds*. It sounds a bit creepy and is unnerving.

As we were settling in for the night, I decided to FaceTime my mom to let her know I was doing well. With the time difference, I knew it was much earlier in the day and I wouldn't be interrupting anything.

"Oh Theresa! You sound terrible!" my mom said when I greeted her with my raspy voice.

"It's okay, Mom. I sound much worse than I feel." I could barely speak.

I turned my phone towards Nikolai so they could see each other and I introduced them. My mom has been following my blog, so she knows him well by now.

"Hi, Nikolai! It's nice to meet you. I want to thank you for taking such good care of Theresa."

"MOM! He's not taking care of me!" I protested with my lame voice. I was so embarrassed.

But Nikolai completely ignored me. "You're welcome!" he said to her, smiling from ear to ear.

"He doesn't take care of me!" I knew they were teasing me, but I still felt the need to state my case! They both laughed at me. My voice was weak and unconvincing.

My mom's husband came into view from behind her. "Oh, you must be Nikolai. You've been taking good care of Theresa."

"HE'S NOT TAKING CARE OF ME!" The more I shouted the more my voice failed. The three of them laughed even harder.

"No," my mom corrected her husband when she finally stopped laughing. "Theresa is taking care of him." My mom is always trying to empower me.

"Oh, okay, sure," her husband said with complete disbelief in his voice.

When we got off the phone, Nikolai had a huge grin on his face. "I love your mom."

I threw my pillow at him as hard as possible and he caught it in midair. "You do not take care of me!"

"You are so spoiled," he said as he put my pillow on his bed. "I'm the best friend."

"Give me back my pillow," I pouted.

"No. I like this pillow. I keep it now," he insisted.

I fell asleep without a pillow but filled with laughter and joy. It felt good to know I have people in my life who care about me. Even if they do tease me relentlessly.

Touring the cathedral

Ceiling of one of the Burgos chapels

# CHAPTER 19

## DAY 17: 32KM FROM BURGOS TO HONTANAS
—
## HOLLAND STEALS A BIKE

After a fairly restful night's sleep, I awoke to the strangest sound. As I slowly gained consciousness, I thought Nikolai must still be asleep and snoring. Snoring is a common occurrence on the Camino. It's just something you learn to live with. We are always teasing each other about this so I couldn't wait to tell him that I caught him in the act! But once I was fully awake, I found him standing over my bed holding his phone to my ear. Apparently I had been the one snoring last night and he recorded it as proof! "I DO NOT SNORE!" he mocked me in a feminine, indignant voice. I will never live this down.

As we were leaving the hotel, we met up with Ginger in the lobby. That's when we learned that, unfortunately, we would have to leave Maria behind in Burgos. The blister she had been nursing on her heel became infected and she couldn't walk on it. She stayed behind to see a doctor. We were sad to have to separate, but it was a harsh reminder that every day on the Camino is a blessing. People are dropping like flies. I'm also learning many of those who are still hiking are taking buses and cabs on occasion or having their bags shipped forward to their next destination because they are too injured to carry the excess weight. This really is super hard.

Anyways, I'm going to miss Maria's spark and feistiness: "Les do dissss!" We stopped by her room and had a heartfelt goodbye before carrying on.

Today was a really long day, the longest I've done so far, but overall it wasn't too bad. I've been having all these deeply meaningful thoughts lately but as I write I'm tired and I apologize because none of them will make their way here.

We weren't too far into our hike when I realized it was way too hot for comfort. I pulled out my umbrella and began to attach it to my pack as I've done in the past, but Nikolai gestured to hand it to him. He must have been hot in that sun too because he carried the umbrella over both our heads for the next two miles. We finally reached a shaded rest area with a wonderful water fountain.

Ginger and Drennan were not far ahead of us and were already resting in the shade of the trees. As we approached, Ginger teased me a bit about having a man to carry my umbrella for me. I laughed along with her, but the joke gnawed at the pride in me just a bit. I've been hiking the Camino just as everyone else has and my merits are my own to carry. This is a very hard endeavor that I tackle on my own every single day. Do people think I have it easier than anyone else? I knew Ginger was only kidding, though, and this problem was my own to deal with. So I kept my thoughts to myself, dismissed the joke, and moved on to more important things.

Blisters. That's right. We're still treating them regularly. I worked on the two blisters I acquired walking into Burgos. Ginger and I pulled out our first aid kits and shared supplies and techniques. Meanwhile Drennan took pictures and filled their water bottles in the fountain.

I was concerned about today's hike because there were two options: hike 20km to the town just before the Meseta begins and risk not having a bed because everyone stops there, or push it all the way to 32km because there are no stops in the Meseta in between. The Meseta is a dreaded part of the Camino. It drags on for days and consists of miles and miles of fields, often without a soul in sight. There is also no protection from the sun, which can be dangerous, as the days are getting much hotter. Many people choose to skip the Meseta because they find it dreadfully boring or just really difficult to walk. My group has every intention of walking it, though.

Ginger and Drennan planned to stop at 20km, but I had prepared myself to do the whole 32k, so when we reached the 20km town and there were no beds left, I didn't mind too much. Ginger and Drennan were a bit dismayed, of course. We ran into Holland and his wife again! I must visit them in their country one day. They were so sorry that there weren't beds for us in town and they offered to buy us a cab to the next town. We said no thank you, though. We were perfectly capable of walking.

It was already 5:00 in the afternoon, which is usually when people are settling in for the evening rather than planning to hike another 12k in the heat. Holland ran from albergue to albergue looking for space for us while Ginger and I tried to call ahead to the next town (with no luck and no cell phone reception). Ginger had a bit of a run in with a woman volunteering at an albergue. We asked her nicely to use their public phone and she was emphatic about us not using it for more than one call. Well, we never got to make a single call because the phone was not working. When Ginger tried to explain this to the woman, she yelled at Ginger and told her she could not use the phone again. Ginger was really distraught by it all. The poor woman just wanted to make a phone call.

Drennan waited patiently on a bench out on the street with Holland and his wife while Ginger and I tried to figure out what our next move would be. Nikolai sprinted up the mountain to see the view from the town cross. Many towns have a big cross on the tallest hill. If they're not right on the Camino, Nikolai will race to the top and take pictures while the rest of us relax. That said, we weren't just relaxing today. When he returned, Ginger and I decided the four of us would move on together even though we did not have reservations in the next town.

So there we were walking, mostly out of town when we hear a man yell for us. We turned around and there was Holland on a bike! The poor man just hiked a whole day and now here he was biking towards us!

"I found room for you!" he shouted to us.

"Holland! Where'd you get the bike?"

"I stole it. I have room for you."

Oh, Holland. He ran around telling the town that there were pilgrims with nowhere to go so someone offered to open the small church and allow us to sleep on the floor. He stole a bike he found on the side of the road so he could catch up with us before we hiked too far out. I had planned on moving onward anyways but we were all so overwhelmed by the generosity and kindness of everyone and I wanted to stick together so we all decided to head back to town. "Holland, buddy, you gotta give that bike back," Drennan said. Drennan's a really good kid.

Unfortunately, by the time we walked back into town, the 12 spots open at the church were taken by other hikers who just arrived. Holland felt so bad. He rode around looking for a cab that could at least drive us to the next major town. One guy offered a ride for 20 euros a pop, which was insanely high. He was counting on us to be more desperate than we were.

I could feel myself getting very frustrated. My original plan was to keep walking anyway, and now I've walked at least an extra mile for nothing. I was also becoming extremely anxious that even once we hiked the additional 12kms there was no guarantee we'd all find a bed. The more frustrated I got, the quieter I got, whereas the more nervous Ginger and Drennan got, the louder they got. Ginger pointed this out as they were singing at the top of their lungs and I refused to join them. We were all feeling the tension of the evening. But as it turns out, I was just extremely hungry. Hangry, as it were. I remembered I had a leftover chorizo and cheese sandwich in my bag. I gobbled it down and had enough energy (and patience) to finish my trip.

The last couple of hours of today's flat dusty landscape were still difficult because I was tired and it was late, but we managed to have a good time. Ginger and Drennan walk much faster than I do, so they tore ahead of us. Since there wasn't a single person for miles, Niko and I passed the time sharing our favorite songs with each other. Despite our height difference, we managed to share the same set of headphones so we could listen to the music simultaneously. It was a lot of fun and it made the time pass quickly.

Eventually, we caught up with Ginger in the middle of a massive dirt field. She texted Dotty, who happened to have found a very nice brand new albergue ahead of us called *Juan de Yepes*. Dotty let the volunteers know we were coming in late and they said no problem, they would have a place for us.

When we arrived, it was like heaven. The albergue was beautiful, cheerful, and the four of us shared our own room and bathroom! The place was modern and peaceful. I took a nice hot shower and had dinner with Nikolai outside in the evening air. I was disappointed I arrived so late in the evening (7:30pm, which is super late for a pilgrim!) that I wasn't able to socialize with everyone and enjoy the nice facilities. As usual, there were lots of wonderful familiar faces. I spoke with everyone very briefly to maintain contact, but headed to bed shortly thereafter.

Although Ginger and Drennan sprinted ahead of us towards the end, they were in pretty rough shape when they finished. I could sense Ginger's frustration and fatigue. She let me know that for her son's sake, they probably wouldn't leave as early as we wanted the next morning or hike as far as we planned to. I was disappointed but understood. They have to hike their own hike. I would be sad not to have them as hiking buddies though. They're so much fun.

One thing this trip has taught me is that you really have control over nothing. You don't even know where you'll sleep sometimes. But it's okay. It's all going to be okay. Things always work out. And I'm completely overwhelmed by the kindness and generosity of complete strangers on the trail. Today, Holland was our angel, as were the kind folks who opened the church for pilgrims to sleep in.

I began volunteering for hospice shortly after my cousin passed away. This generosity and sense of community that I'm experiencing on the Camino reminds me what I love about hospice. Everyone is here with essentially the same goals so we automatically have a common bond. On the Camino, a single act of kindness can make such a difference in someone's life. It could be the one thing that allows them to continue their journey for just one more day. And that is priceless.

Ginger, Holland, Drennan and Nikolai

# CHAPTER 20

## DAY 18: 28KM FROM HONTANAS TO
## BOADILLA DEL CAMINO

—

## PRESENT FOR THE FIRST TIME EVER

Nikolai and I woke up early and were hiking by 7:00am. We have our morning routine down to a science. Like most pilgrims, I sleep in the shirt and underwear I plan to hike in the next day. Bringing pajamas just adds unnecessary weight to your pack. So when I wake, I slip into my pants, splash some water on my face, brush my teeth, pack my bag, and I'm ready to go in under ten minutes. Nikolai on the other hand has a whole ritual. He pulls out five full size bottles of lotions, creams, gels and whatever else he carries in his massive pack and spends the next twenty minutes applying them. He wakes up well before me to give himself time to do everything and then wakes me when he's nearly ready to leave. I absolutely love teasing him about it. "Nikolai, you look SO pretty!"

"Leave me!"

Ginger and Drennan were just starting to stir when we left, so we all wished each other a *buen Camino*. They walk so fast it's possible they will catch up with us. I'm really hoping this is not the last I'll see of them.

We ate a quick pilgrim's breakfast provided by the albergue. The freshly squeezed orange juice is always fabulous when you wake up, but I find it difficult to eat as much as I need to that early in the morning. My stomach is not quite awake yet, but you really do need to eat as much as you possibly can. The calories are essential to get you through until lunch time, or at least second breakfast. So while the pilgrim's breakfast is minimal, it's very important.

There are so many lessons on the Camino. We saw Dotty and Kristen while eating. When she woke up this morning, Dotty's shoes were not in the common area cubes where she left them. She suspected someone grabbed the wrong pair but it was so early in the morning that there were still tons of shoes on the shelves so it was hard to know for sure what happened. Either way, she wasn't going far without them. I would have been panicking if I was her. Your shoes are an extension of your body out here. They mean everything to you. But she was calm and cool. She arranged to take a cab to the next large town and buy another pair. No big deal. I admired her for that and took note of her response to the stressful situation.

We walked in silence early this morning watching the fog roll over the hills. Eventually, the sun burned off the clouds and poked through, highlighting our path. I love hiking in the early morning. There are few pilgrims and the air is still fresh and cool. This morning we entered Castrojeriz, home of some beautiful castle ruins that sit impressively atop a large hill.

By 10:30am, the sun was already heating me up just in time for our biggest incline. I saw a huge hill in front of us and thought I could take it without stopping, but it was about five times longer than I expected. Every time I wrapped around the massive hill, the path stretched higher than before. I felt so victorious when I reached the top.

Much to my surprise, we were greeted by a Camino angel (a Dutchman, of course) who handed us the best cup of sweet tea in the world. These random acts of kindness make my heart swell. This guy drives around in a truck, providing pilgrims refreshment and rejuvenation just when they need it most. We took a much needed break at the top and then took pictures to capture our victory.

Once we got over the mountain, we looked down the other side and saw the Meseta. The true Meseta. Literally miles of walking in front of us. No picture could capture the vastness. For hours, we walked with the sun beating down on us. I passed time by listening to an audiobook Nikolai had on his phone, *How to Make Friends and Influence People*.

"You should listen to this book. I think you have not many friends." he jested.

I focused on the audio, and tried to ignore the three new hot spots forming on my feet. Just when I felt I couldn't go much more, some trees offered shade in the middle of the field. Big stone picnic tables gave us a place to rest and a fountain allowed me to wet my Frogg Togg and wrap it around my dust covered neck. It was a well-deserved break.

On another note, my body is a machine now. As long as I'm properly fed, hydrated, and somewhat protected from blazing heat, I can go for hours. I can't feel the additional 20 percent weight of my pack anymore and my legs are so strong, they never feel strained. I can do the big climbs without trouble. We climbed for nearly half an hour with no relief this morning. I was concerned, however, about potentially overheating, which I do quite easily, so I still stopped to take a water break a couple of times. I'm amazed at how conditioned I've become in just a couple of weeks. It's empowering.

During my hours of walking today, I had plenty of time to think. But I was suddenly struck by what I was thinking about.

I broke our silence, "Nikolai, what do you think about when you are walking?"

He explained that he thinks about lots of things. He thinks about his family, his friends, his job, school. I haven't been thinking about any of that though. I have been thinking about right here and right now. I think about where I'm placing my steps, I think about my breathing, I think about the amazing scenery, I think about how the smell in the air shifts with the winds. I think about the sound of my shoes on the varying types of pavement and dirt. Other thoughts occasionally drift in and out like the tide but for the most part, I am living in the present. It occurred to me that I have never done that in my entire life. Not for any length of time. As someone who suffers from a lifetime of deep seated anxiety, this is a luxury I am completely unfamiliar with and I am soaking it up with all my heart and soul.

So far the Meseta is not the dreaded endeavor everyone says it is, but I'm only just now starting. Apparently, this goes on for days and can really take a toll on your mind. I can see another issue though. There is no encouragement to stop walking. No shade, no cafés, no streams. Just one dusty path across miles of flat fields. We will have to be cognizant of that because walking without rest can be detrimental to the body.

While the rest of my body felt great today, my feet are another story. The continuous repetitive motion of walking has turned the ground into a meat tenderizer and my feet feel pulverized. I give up on fighting blisters. I've tried so hard to care for my feet, and I fail every day. I have so many hot spots that I'm experimenting with them in the hopes that they won't turn into full blown blisters. I treat them different to see if one responds better than another. So far, nothing has been effective. My fear is that they will blister, become infected and I'll have to stop hiking like Maria did. I'm thinking positive though.

When we arrived in our final town, it looked desolate. There were only a few dilapidated buildings and there wasn't a soul in sight. My guidebook recommended an albergue called En El Camino which was hidden between the town's buildings. As we approached, it looked horrible. The massive walls around it were crumbling and it had no curb appeal whatsoever. But we were so tired, we walked through the broken doors anyways. Wow! What a place! Inside those scary walls was a beautifully maintained landscape with an acre of soft grass, beautiful iron artwork, flower gardens in stone boxes, a swimming pool, and a café.

We hurried to the counter to see if there was any availability left. We got the last two beds! The room was a bit small and dark but our bunk mates were very friendly. Tom from England, and Diane and Robert, who were a really nice German couple. My only complaint would be that Robert walked around in a speedo. Yikes! That's pretty common for Europeans though, so who am I to say what's acceptable?

Anyway, I was so grateful when the host allowed us to shower and get drinks prior to going through the check in process. He could tell we were exhausted so he welcomed us to settle in first. Another small act of kindness that goes a really long way. I wanted to hug him for being so understanding.

I loved this place! Fortunately, we got there early enough to enjoy it. We sat in the grass huddled under a small spot of shade trying to sooth our crisp new suntans. I'm pretty sure it was the only shade (and grass) in a 20-mile radius. We just hiked through miles of dust so this was a refreshing treat!

We quickly realized the place was full of familiar faces! I saw Rose and Andrew from Quebec, who I met my very first night in Orisson! I couldn't remember their names though, so as I saw them walking way across the yard I called out, "Canada!" They both stopped and looked around. Andrew threw an arm in the air trying to ensure whoever was calling him wouldn't lose sight of him. I ran across the soft grass in my bare feet and greeted them with open arms. It was so wonderful to see them. I also saw Dolores and her friends once again. We all sat together at a long table for dinner and had a wonderful evening introducing each other and sharing stories.

As usual, I inspected my feet before bedtime. I have two forming blisters between my toes, which have been the main problem since Burgos. They feel like blisters when I apply pressure but they look more like bruises at this point. There isn't much of a bubble yet so there is nothing to drain and because of their location between my toes, I can't really protect them with molefoam as Brian taught me. I wasn't sure what I should do with them, so I took pictures and sent them to Brian asking for his suggestions. I knew I wouldn't get a response right away, though, so I said a prayer that my feet would be okay and went to bed. I have the sneaking suspicion that my body needs me to slow down, but I am making good progress, I'm having fun, and tomorrow I will carry on.

Castrojeriz

We made it to the top

# CHAPTER 21

## DAY 19: 26KM FROM BOADILLA DEL CAMINO TO CARRIÓN DE LOS CONDES

—

## PUSHING MY LIMITS

When I awoke this morning, I had a strong sense that I needed a short day so I could let my feet heal. The pressure to move forward is immense, though. But I want to walk because I want to, not because I need to. My problem is I want to. I really want to walk. I've been thoroughly enjoying myself, I've learned that I can go the distance, and I've been pushing myself for the last three days. But now I need to learn that I don't have to push just because I can. I completely understand now how people get addicted to the mileage.

"I hiked 32km yesterday. I can do it today and tomorrow too."

I don't really have a reason to push forward, though, so I planned to stop at Fromista for the day, which was only 6km down the road. But when we arrived, the town did not appear to have anything of interest. I didn't want to kill my high with a zero day (a day of no hiking) in a town that wasn't noteworthy. So instead, we stopped at the *farmacia* and *banco* as per our usual mid-sized town routine and then had second breakfast.

We pulled out the map and discussed alternatives. There were several towns we'd be passing throughout the day. We could stop anywhere along the way if I felt I couldn't continue. That sounded like a good idea. I'm trying really hard to not get too wrapped up in plans and to trust the process. I'm trying to think more like Nikolai on this trip. He's spontaneous and a free spirit. In fact, I don't think he even has a map on him. It's interesting to me that despite the simplicity of life on the Camino, my anxiety does not completely dissolve itself out here. You will carry your weaknesses with you the whole way. The Camino does not have the power to make you perfect. It does, however, have the power to highlight all of your humanity for better or for worse. I struggle with anxiety in my normal life and I will continue to struggle with it here. It is very different here, though. The things I worry about on the Camino are things like *where will I sleep* and *is my body working?* These concerns seem more natural to me. Even warranted.

I love the interaction with people on the Camino. They are all so loving and spirited. While at the *farmacia*, I bought about $30 worth of second skin and applied it all over my feet wherever I had a hot spot. While sitting outside the store bandaging myself up, three other people came by, including a couple from Florida named Michael and Linda. Another guy also came by and he asked me if the pharmacy had a remedy for blisters. That struck me as funny because we pass probably five pharmacies a day and none of them have a "remedy." Why should this one be any different?

We are all hurting, though, and we are all desperate for a cure. I learned that I'm actually in better shape than most. I'm hoping to avoid the full-blown feet problems others are forced to deal with. I am fascinated by how helpful everyone is, sharing their supplies and methods (none that work, obviously, but nevertheless, very kind).

Nikolai still has no pain or major problems, so while the rest of us were talking about blisters and wounds, he was inside buying himself a new pair of aviator sunglasses which he was immensely pleased with. "I'm so cool. I'm like a guy who flies planes."

"You mean a pilot?"

"Whatever!"

We are both experiencing the Camino in very different ways.

My feet were really hurting today so I had to stop frequently. In the next town, we stopped at a café that had an outdoor seating area. I took off my shoes and socks and rested my feet on one of the big shiny red chairs. A German man stopped by and told us in broken English that he had three blood blisters. When I showed him my two forming blisters, he scoffed at them like they were nothing. He said I needed aloe and pulled out an aloe vera plant! It seemed so random that this man was carrying around a plant in his pack!

Since he didn't speak English well, he and Nikolai went to work on my feet. I had no idea what they were doing or saying. All I could do was watch in amazement as two people who owe me nothing tried so hard to make me feel better. When they finished, Nikolai explained that they put chunks of aloe between my toes and I was to keep them there for a half hour before removing them, letting it dry and then applying moleskin. The man told Nikolai not to be jealous but that I would think about him all day because my feet would feel so much better. He was so sweet. I thanked him in German and he went along his way.

I am still so overwhelmed by the kindness I continuously experience on the trail. I turned to Nikolai and asked why he was being so helpful. He just shrugged.

"I really need to know. Why do stay with me when I'm always hurt and I'm so slow? Why do you take care of me? You could be so much further on your Camino if it wasn't for me. Just tell me why."

"I don't know" he explained. "We are friends. You are strong, you have a lot of energy, and you always talk to everyone which helps me learn English. You are fun."

I knew it wasn't easy for him to say these things, but I was glad he did. I struggle to accept such kindness. It's not something I'm used to. But I have decided not to question a good thing. For whatever reason, people are just better on the Camino.

Soon after, while my feet were still propped up, the German couple, Robert and Diane, who we shared a room with the night before, stopped by the outdoor café. They started chatting about the condition of my feet in German and examined them carefully. This trip has been a total cure for my fear and hatred of feet. I used to think feet were so disgusting (healthy feet, even!) and I didn't like mine to be exposed. Now they're out for display regularly and I inspect other people's broken feet as if it's totally normal. It is normal here. It's all we talk about. It's blister season on the Camino.

By our third stop, I was acutely familiarized with another Camino challenge: sunburn. In 3km I managed to get a blazing red sunburn on the back of my legs. I walked through the Meseta under the same sun all day yesterday and had no problems. Suddenly two hours in the morning sun today meant more pain, more blisters. I applied lotion provided by a kind pilgrim sitting near me and reluctantly zipped the pant legs back onto my shorts. It was going to be a sweltering 90 degrees. On the upside, we each ordered a whole pizza and had ice cream under the shaded dining area during that stop. Michael and Linda were there, too, so we got to talk with them a bit more.

Late in the afternoon we stopped in the shade of some trees at a site with great historical significance but the blisters on my feet were so angry, the pain was all I could think about. Nikolai was doing handstands and taking creative pictures with his phone, carefree as a child. But I wasn't remotely interested in joining in the fun. It was a very tough hike today. I didn't enjoy the scenery, I didn't read about the history, I didn't talk to anyone. It was just me, my pain, and my God. But I realized that this wouldn't mean anything if it were easy.

If I had no pain, no struggle, I would just be walking. I wouldn't be as compelled to talk to God or search for meaning as much as I was. I wouldn't be forced to experience all of my strengths and all of my weaknesses.

Today was very powerful for me. I was faced with myself. I dug deep within for an answer and one thing came back loud and clear: "I can do this." I mustered up all my strength, sucked it up, and powered through the last 5km with energy to spare. I am strong. I am powerful. I am courageous. Everything I need is inside me. Seeing our destination finally on the horizon warranted a fist bump between me and my hiking partner. I did it.

It was a good thing I had energy to spare. By the time we reached town at 5:00pm, three of the four albergues were booked. My feet were screaming in pain and I was limping so pathetically. Somewhere between the third and fourth albergue we were rejected from, we walked by a church. The massive double doors were wide open and the air conditioning from within came rolling out and hit me square in the face.

We both stopped dead in our tracks. There was no way we were continuing on without resting in the coolness of the church. We took a few steps down into the beautiful architecture and sat quietly on the stone staircase as several nuns began singing. It was one of the most beautiful sounds I've ever heard. I closed my eyes and took in all my senses. The church smelled as wonderful as it felt and sounded. I thanked God for helping me this far in my journey and for giving me a moment to rest. At that moment, I was struck by how much comfort these Spanish churches bring me.

We managed to find a couple of beds at Albergue Espíritu Santo which is run by nuns. I believe this is the place where the nuns play beautiful music for their guests and even take requests! But we got there so late and I was in so much pain that I didn't even think about it at the time. The kind nun who took us in didn't speak English but she was so very patient and kind with us. The check in process took quite a while, but then the nun showed us to our room. The dormitory was a bit scary at first glance but, despite its simplicity, it was actually quite nice. It was also only partially full and two of the other pilgrims were Robert and Diane.

I put my bag down on the chair next to my bed, unrolled my sleeping bag and sat down on the bed. All of the internal strength and power I embodied while hiking today evaporated the moment I unwrapped my feet and inspected the damage. One look and I knew my hike would suffer. On both feet, between my big toes were massive swelling blisters that wrapped around to the balls of my feet. The mere sight of them was painful. Diane, Robert, and Nikolai looked at my feet and talked about possible options. It was evident I needed a doctor before both feet became infected.

As they continued to discuss options, I quickly gathered up my things and hurried to the shower hoping no one would notice I was on the brink of tears. I cried quietly in the shower as I tried to figure out my next move. I'd have to find a doctor that speaks English the next day and either way, there was no way my Camino would continue in my condition.

There is however, no privacy on the Camino. Apparently, Nikolai was in the shower next to mine and he must have overheard me. He looked so sympathetic as we ran into each other and asked if I was okay.

"Oh, yeah. I'm fine." Yep, I'm great. I'm just a ball of positive energy. No problems here. Last thing I wanted to do was draw attention to myself or the fact that I had become completely useless on the Camino.

But everyone already knew what I hadn't said yet. Diane was standing by my bed with another man when I returned from the shower and said she found an emergency doctor who was available to pilgrims this time of day. The other man would take me to him. Again, I choked back tears. Not tears of sorrow though; I was just overwhelmed by how helpful everyone was and fortunate I was that there happened to be a doctor available to me in my time of need. I waddled behind the guy (who was waddling himself— it was clear why he knew where the doctor was) and entered a building not far from my albergue.

The man who fixed me up didn't speak any English and he was pretty rough with me. I could tell he worked on pilgrim's feet regularly. He cleaned up both feet and started explaining in Spanish how I needed to care for them. In perfect timing, Nikolai walked in with a woman who was fluent in both Spanish and English. She translated for me. No walking for three days. Bandage this, bandage that. Yada yada yada. I had a hard time concentrating after the no hiking for three days comment.

The tears flowed in front of everyone and there was nothing I could do about it. I felt so defeated. Nikolai wrapped his arm around my shoulder trying to comfort me as we exited the building.

"I'm so angry," I choked out, still fighting back the tears.

We both knew what had to be done. I would take a cab into León, the next large town, and he would continue walking without me. I really hope I see him again. It is hard to put into words just how quickly you bond with people on the Camino and how someone you've known for such a short period of time can mean so much to you.

I felt the need to tell him how special his friendship was to me but I was afraid he would misinterpret my words. I also knew he wasn't the type to talk about feelings. So instead, I thanked him for being such a good friend. The thought of not walking with him anymore is painful and I wondered if he felt the same way or if he just saw this as an opportunity to finally move on at his own pace. I didn't ask, though.

When we returned to the albergue, all of my friends were sitting in the courtyard outside eating dinner. Nikolai had bought things from the *supermercado* and had a nice spread waiting for us, which I was so grateful for because I hadn't even thought of food yet.

As we all talked and laughed through dinner, my spirit lifted just a bit. Okay, what's the worst thing? I spend the next few sweltering days in a nice hotel room in a hip town and make more friends? That doesn't sound so bad. In an effort to stay positive (or to at least keep up the appearance of being positive) I helped Robert do the dishes and I cut up the watermelon for everyone.

I had a silly interaction with a complete stranger, too. Many other pilgrims who stayed in our albergue were passing through the courtyard where we were eating. One nice woman stopped by and began speaking to us in a thick Spanish accent. I thought we were talking about the doctor who had just helped me but apparently we changed the subject and I missed it! I thought she said the doctor did not speak English well at all.

"Yes!" I agreed emphatically. She looked at me with slight confusion and walked away. I looked over at Nikolai and Diane.

"You're not very friendly," Nikolai jested.

"No, not at all," Diane agreed.

I didn't know what they meant. Apparently the poor woman was apologizing to me and told me that she did not speak English very well. And there I was agreeing that her English sucked. I felt so bad! I jumped up and ran through the albergue with my bandaged feet looking for her so I could apologize. Meanwhile, my friends laughed at me as I desperately tried to right my wrong.

When I ran into her, I gave her a big hug. "*Lo siento! Lo siento!*" I tried to explain that I misunderstood but I think she only half followed what I was saying. She just laughed and said she sort of understood. Fortunately for me, she was a very nice woman. Nikolai took pictures of me begging for forgiveness.

Oh, I should mention three other people. First, there was a guy named Thorsten who was already resting in the bed next to mine. He said he thinks he has heat stroke. He was exhausted and couldn't stop throwing up. The poor guy. Also, while we were all sitting together at dinner, I met two other Germans named Tina and Marco. Tina is a beautiful hairstylist from Munich and has a great spirit about her. Marco is a Camino angel but I didn't know that at the time. More on that later.

Before bedtime, Diane offered me some powerful sleeping tablets to help ease my concerns. I was sad about my new Camino path, but I declined and decided to settle in for the night naturally. *Tomorrow will be better*, I told myself. *I can do this.*

# CHAPTER 22

## DAY 20: ZERO DAY IN CARRIÓN DE LOS CONDES
—
## ROCK BOTTOM - NO WONDER THEY CALL IT CARRION

Dear God, please tell me this is rock bottom. Please tell me it will get better. I don't think I can do this anymore and I don't want to. This is misery. I signed up for it, though, so I suppose I deserve whatever I get.

I went to bed last night prepared for the fact that I would have to take several days off the Camino and would be severed from all the friends I have made thus far. That was painful enough.

But around 1:00am, I was rudely awoken by another problem. For whatever reason, my body decided to purge itself from any direction it could of anything I had put in it. I raced through the dormitory in the dark and fumbled for the bathroom (which is nowhere near my bed), barely making it in time. What the heck was this? Was it something I ate? Did I get too much sun like the guy next to me? Was it my nerves?

Whatever it was, it was fierce and I was up all night running back and forth in the dark hoping not to wake anyone or trip on anything. The Camino is not a place to be sick. Not only were the bathrooms far, but there is always a shortage of soap - or toilet paper. Fortunately, my brilliant husband convinced me to bring a roll. It never occurred to me that I would be in this kind of need!

It was strange how the sickness crept up on me. I was lying in bed half asleep when my stomach started feeling upset. At first I thought it was just hunger pains. As I drifted in and out of sleep, I dreamed that Diane came by my bed with a golden retriever and a bread roll that she offered me. Of course in my dream, I didn't question this weirdness at all. I reached out in my sleep to pet the dog and take the bread. The moment I took a bite in my dream, I jolted awake. Nope. It wasn't hunger. I was going to puke. I sprinted for the bathroom multiple times for the next few hours.

Around 6:00am my friends all packed up and carried on as I would have done myself if I was healthy. But there I was, clenching my stomach and praying for the pain to stop. I didn't tell Nikolai I was sick. I felt like a complete failure. Instead, I pretended to be asleep and watched out of one eye as he pulled on his pack and walked out the front door into the dark morning. *Adios amigo.* In the meantime, Thor, who was sleeping in the bed next to me, didn't stir. He was sick as a dog, too.

About an hour later, one of the nuns came into the room and asked in Spanish something about why we were still there. I gave her some body language indicating I was sick, and she told us we were welcome to stay as long as we needed. At least that's what I assumed she said based on her gentle body language. I was very grateful because some albergues will kick you out first thing in the morning regardless of your condition so they can prepare for the next wave of incoming pilgrims. I rested for several hours.

In the meantime, Marco, the nice guy I met at dinner last night and who is friends with Thor, stayed behind. He didn't continue his hike and he was perfectly healthy! Instead, without my knowing, he went to the *supermercado* and picked up some food and drinks for us. He woke us occasionally and encouraged us both to drink.

The more I watched our symptoms, the more I realized my illness could be due to too much sun as it was with Thor. I have had heat exhaustion twice before and Stephen was telling me my tolerance to heat deteriorates each time that happens, so he cautioned me to be careful. And what did I do? I gave myself a killer burn on my legs. Really smart.

The good news was, I knew it would pass and I just needed to rest. The bad news was, my only concern was where the nearest toilet was. Not where I'd stay, what I'd eat, or what my next move would be. And that's why Marco was my Camino angel. After a few hours of rest, he woke me and asked if I was strong enough to walk. I said yes. He asked me to gather up my things. I thought perhaps we were finally being asked to leave. I haphazardly stuffed my sleeping bag into my pack without bothering to roll it up.

Marco picked up my pack and asked me to follow him. I insisted I could carry my own things but he ignored me and told me to just follow. You have to understand the state I was in at that moment. I had no idea where I was or what I was going to do. I was sick and injured. All of the people I knew had hiked on without me. I had no choice but to trust this near stranger. I followed him through the streets like a displaced puppy.

As it turns out, Marco took it upon himself to walk through town, find a nice hostel and reserve two rooms for Thorsten and me. This would essentially provide us some privacy while we were sick, which I desperately needed. Then he even carried my stuff to the hostel for me. When we arrived, he checked me in, walked with me to my room and gave me some fruit to hold me over for a bit, along with a town map where he wrote down all the usual places a pilgrim would need to find (supermarket, bank, pharmacy, bus station, etc.).

I gave him a hug and the most genuine thank you I could muster up. I couldn't believe how fortunate I was in a time of such misery.

At my absolute worst moment, I experienced what was probably one of the greatest acts of kindness I've ever seen. Marco continued on his hike once we were settled in. It's strange to think that my lowest point on the Camino was also one of my highlights. I'll never see him again but I will never forget him.

Outside my hotel room was a flea market with tons of vendors and happy shoppers. Music blared all day long but I actually found it soothing to be reminded I wasn't alone and the world didn't suck quite as much as it felt. Despite the noise, I slipped into a deep, drool-inducing slumber.

Around 2:00pm, Thorsten knocked on my door and asked if I wanted to run some errands with him. I was surprised he thought to come to me. With the exception of hobbling through the streets to the hostel together, we had almost no interaction at all. I jumped on the offer immediately. I didn't even know what town or hotel I was in and somehow I had to find out how to get a bus the next morning to León. I had stopped throwing up at that point so I knew it was safe to leave the bathroom for a bit.

We walked through town looking for the bar Marco had told us about. Apparently bus tickets are purchased at a bar in this town. As Thor was purchasing his tickets and talking about his complicated plans, I got nervous about how I would find my way around León even if I managed to get on the right bus. Then I remembered something Brian told me. Money solves problems. I decided I would pay the extra money to take a cab to my exact location (not that I had any idea where that was yet). I tried to communicate with the woman about how to get a cab in *la mañana* but I just couldn't understand her. I left the bar feeling nervous and frustrated.

That's my life here in Spain though. I struggle with everything. I don't like not understanding. I have enough of my own weaknesses to deal with. For example, as I followed Thorsten to the *supermercado* next, once again I had no idea where we were, where we came from, or where we were going. I was following a stranger on blind faith for the second time today.

Part of me gets very angry. Why can't I intuitively find my way around new places like other people can? Why is everything so much harder for me than it seems to be for everyone else? Why? But another part of me thinks, so what? I'm still out here experiencing the world. Maybe other people are better at things than me because they only stick to their comfort zone. I'm always outside my comfort zone. I don't know why. Maybe that's something I'll contemplate over the next few days while I sit around healing.

Once I returned to the hostel and had a tiny bit to eat, I ventured out into town again, only this time at my own pace. I found everything I needed and my irrational fear of being lost subsided. The town itself was actually very cute. I wish I could walk around more and explore but my feet needed the rest. When I got back to the hostel, I found an English-speaking woman working there who called and arranged a cab for me in the morning. I took the moment to remind myself that things do have a way of working themselves out. Everything was going to be just fine. My last order of business for the day would be to find a hotel in León. It would take several phone calls to find something available. León was booked solid.

I'm in my hostel room now. I thought I'd be bored but I think my body was in desperate need of some rest. It's nice to relax. My windows are wide open. They have no screens in Spain because they don't really have the bugs here that we do in the U.S. This time of rest has given me time to reflect on all that's happened in the last day. Yes, last night was the absolute worst for me, but my God, I have never experienced the kindness, generosity, and love as I have over the last 24 hours. The Camino brings out the very best in people. They love and care for one another without prompting. People are their best selves here and I love all of them.

At this moment, I hear a big storm rolling in and church bells off in the distance. It must be time for Mass. I wish I could go and thank God for getting me through this rough patch but I don't feel like getting out of bed. I can understand why people go to church here every day. I grew up going to church every Sunday and yet I was not prepared for the healing powers of the churches on the Camino.

I'm also hearing barred owls just like the ones that live in my yard. They remind me of Brian! His trail name is Owl and he has a healthy obsession with the animal. Hearing them today is so comforting. Not a bad ending to such a tumultuous day.

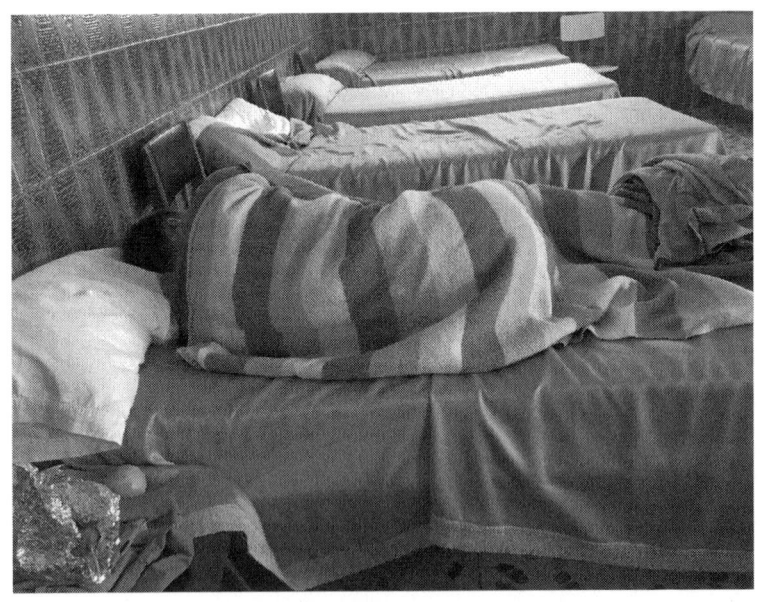

Too sick to move

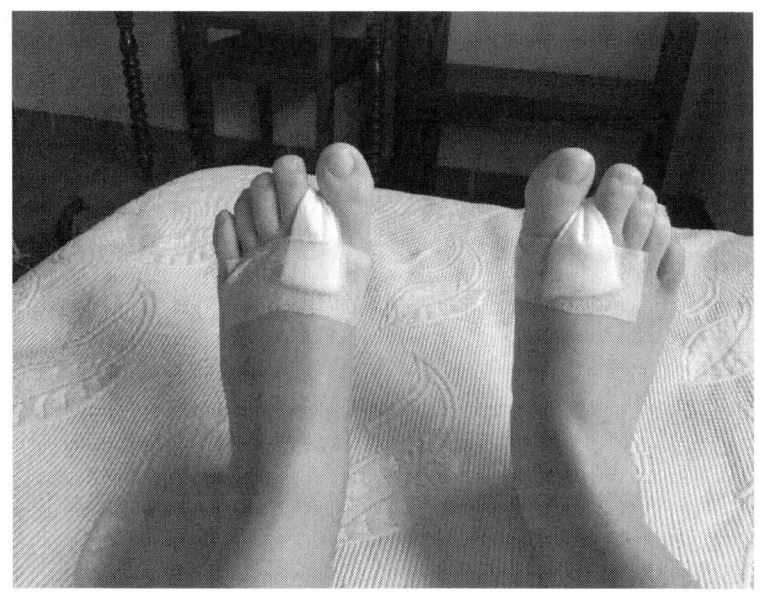

No walking for three days

# CHAPTER 23

## DAY 21: ZERO DAY FROM CARRIÓN DE LOS CONDES TO LEÓN

—

### FEELING BETTER

I woke up feeling very refreshed this morning. Then I looked at my phone and I realized that today is exactly one week from the day that my husband is going to join me on the Camino! The thought brings so much relief and excitement to me all at once.

I love my husband, I love my house, I love my dog, I love my friends, and I love my life. So usually after three or four days of being away, I start to feel really homesick. I have worked really hard not to think about my life at home for this reason. But this morning I couldn't avoid it. I really miss Brian and I cannot wait to see him. I am hoping to be nice and refreshed because I know he's going to be chipper and ready to go just like all new pilgrims are. I don't want to be tired and broken when he sees me.

Since my cab wasn't scheduled to arrive until 10:30am, I took my time getting ready in the morning. I turned the tv on and, to my surprise, found an English-speaking channel. It was just a cartoon about three old fishermen but I didn't care. It was nice to hear something in English for the first time in weeks so I sat and watched the entire episode. The men kept accidentally hooking each other, dragging them under the boat, reeling them in soaking wet and saying, "Eh, throw 'im back." For some reason I found it absolutely hilarious and laughed out loud as I sat there in my room alone. I think I really miss the U.S.

Just before 10:30am, the woman working at the hostel came to my door and informed me that my cab arrived. I gathered my things and headed out. It was a peaceful rainy ride into León. I sat up front with Antonio, the sweet cab driver. He put my pack in the trunk of the car which made me very uneasy for some reason. I'm never more than a few feet from my pack and everything I live by is in that bag. I was so uncomfortable without it.

I was also extremely cognizant of the hills. Every time the car puffed up an ascent, I thanked God I wasn't walking it. In my pre-Camino life, I wouldn't have even noticed the hills. Finally, I noticed just how fast we were moving! Even though it was raining and Antonio's speed was probably slower than average, I felt as though I was moving abnormally fast. It occurred to me that I have not been in a car in nearly three weeks and I haven't moved faster than three miles per hour in quite some time!

Antonio and I spoke only a little since I don't speak Spanish and he didn't speak English, but we had fun trying. He was a sweet older man with a soft gentle smile. With the help of the translator on my phone, I managed to explain that I was injured and my friend moved on without me. He assured me that I would make new friends and I sincerely hoped he was right. I'd to have to find yet another trail family.

When I arrived in León, I stepped out of the cab at the famous Parador hotel, and who did I see sleeping sitting up on a bench? My faithful walking companion, Nikolai!

"*Mi amigo! Mi amigo!*" I tugged on Antonio's sleeve and pointed him out in utter disbelief. Antonio laughed out loud and rejoiced with me. I was so happy to see my friend again. Nikolai hiked nearly

70km in 24 hours and took a bus the last few kilometers, arriving in León before me.

We greeted in the courtyard in front of the Parador. I told him I didn't think I would ever see him again, and he said, "Of course! I'm like a dog. Feed me and I'll follow you anywhere."

Of course he said it in horrible broken English and it didn't actually sound anything like that but I knew exactly what he meant. We are Camino partners and we stick together.

I was overwhelmed with emotions I didn't quite understand. I have always considered myself a loner and like most things in my life, I was fully prepared to hike the Camino by myself. It was scary to think I'd be traversing a country by myself, but I thought it was the only way possible, so that's just how I envisioned my journey. For whatever reason, I know now that I am not meant to experience this important part of my life alone. Everyone should experience the magic of the Camino. The world would be a different place.

It only took a few seconds to see Nikolai was hurting. Limping and exhausted, I could tell he had a rough time. As it was, he walked through the entire night in the rain without stopping. I'm not sure why he felt the need to push himself so hard but I realized then I'm as helpful to him as he is to me.

Antonio carried my stuff into the Parador for me where I booked a double room. Today would be a day of rest, but first we had to find our room in the massive castle. Despite his condition, Nikolai insisted on carrying my bag. We limped up and down the stairs and through the long hallways before finding our room.

Day two of healing was pretty boring. I watched videos on my phone, listened to music and chatted with Brian all day. We talked excitedly about how we plan to meet up when he arrives next week. Because I walk slower than anticipated, Brian will actually get to walk further with me than the last 100km. I am still several days from reaching Sarria.

For a while, I watched a young comedian on my phone with my earplugs in. I didn't want to wake Nikolai, who slept the entire day without stirring. As I attempted to hold back my booming laughter, tears streamed down my cheeks and I gasped for air in silence. It did disturb him, though, because he woke up and said he wanted to laugh, too. I replayed the three-minute scene and howled as I watched it for a second time. God, I miss home!

Unfortunately, I think the humor was lost in translation. Nikolai said it was funny, but he was too tired to laugh. Oh, well. I was glad he was awake, though, so we could go out to dinner. I was starting to go stir crazy. My mind and body were ready to go, but my feet do the majority of the work so they got the largest vote. One more day of doing nothing to go.

We looked for somewhere close for dinner. Both of us were injured and didn't feel like walking much. I didn't realize how much Nikolai was hurting until he asked me to slow down for him. I've never walked too quickly for him, and he certainly has never asked anything of me. He must have really messed up his feet during that long hike.

Dinner was fascinating. The restaurant was decorated like a massive living room with big comfy couches which made it quite unique. I ordered a veggie sandwich which wasn't at all what I was expecting. It was loaded with cooked asparagus, carrots and broccoli and the bread had an egg cooked into it. It took me a while to figure out how to hold the thing but it was very tasty once I got the hang of it.

I have to say I was sorely disappointed with my room at the Parador. For the money I paid, I should at least have a nice couch to sit on. I didn't realize it when I booked the room but this is the famous Parador where they filmed *The Way*. I mentioned this earlier, but to give you some background, *The Way* is an American movie about the Camino starring Emilio Estevez and Martin Sheen. It is what has made the Camino so popular among Americans in recent days. Apparently, it made the Parador very popular, too, because there is a lot of Camino hype about it. I wasn't impressed though. It made me miss our awesome hotel in Burgos. I'll have to see if I can find somewhere cheaper and nicer to stay tomorrow but, as of last night, most hotels were booked. León is huge for tourism.

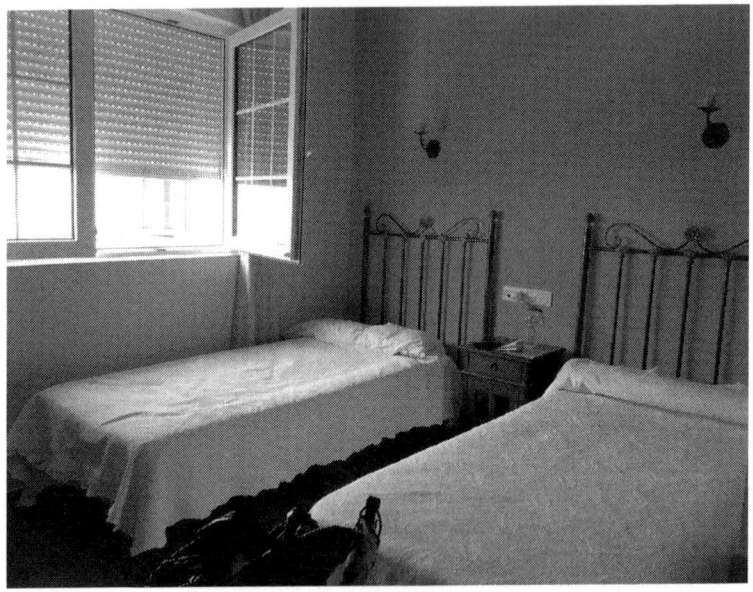

My hostel in Carrión de los Condes

Cathedral Santa Maria León

# CHAPTER 24

## DAY 22: ANOTHER ZERO IN LEÓN

—

## THE SPIRIT OF SPAIN

I'm trying to figure out what exactly makes something a five-star hotel. I have nothing else to do with my time, so why not? Is it that the two little chairs available in the room are so rickety you're afraid they will break if you sit on them? Is it that the glue holding together the wood floors crack every time you step on them? Is it the fact that when you sit on the bed the headboard falls forward? Is it that when you put something in the outlet you accidentally pull the entire thing out of the wall? Is it the fact that the door doesn't lock appropriately? Is it the fact that the bathroom door pops open while you're on the toilet and you have to yell "don't come over here!" Or maybe it's because they decorate the walls with the same fabric in the window treatments. Yes, that must be it. Why are people willing to pay a lot more for really old stuff? I don't get it.

The building itself is spectacular, yes. I highly recommend you come to see it if you hike the Camino. But my room leaves much to be desired. I was completely ripped off. Oh, and they charged me €67 to wash my underwear! I'm so out of here. We found a nicer hotel that costs a bit less.

A leisurely stroll to breakfast and a half hour walk to the new hotel; that was the extent of my morning. I'm getting bored but, at the same time, I'm losing my drive to walk. I noticed when I walked up four flights of stairs I could feel a tiny bit of strain in my thighs. I'm losing strength fast. And I'm terrified I'm going to keep hurting my feet. I hate hurting myself. I have come to love my body like it's my child. I worry about making sure it's happy and healthy. I worry about its well-being. I feel terrible when I do something to inflict pain and I mourn when there's nothing I can do to make it feel better. I'm so scared I'm going to keep hurting myself. Tomorrow I will start slow but it's 21k to the next major stop. Brian said the first day hiking after a zero day is the worst, so I'm hoping it doesn't completely crush my morale.

Actually, the stroll this morning wasn't all that leisurely. Something eventful always happens. We stopped at multiple pharmacies looking for lamb's wool I could put between my toes to keep them spaced and dry. Brian recommended it to me after asking for suggestions from several of his hiker friends back home about how to treat blisters between the toes.

We met the sweetest couple who spoke English fluently. They heard me struggling to communicate with the pharmacist and eagerly asked if they could help. I explained to them what I was looking for and they tried to translate. The pharmacist said she'd never heard of it. They pushed their 11-month old baby in a stroller all over town for us trying to find a pharmacy that knew what I was talking about. To make a long story short, Spain's never heard of lamb's wool. If you want lamb's wool, bring it with you. So I didn't find what I needed, but it was fun to chat with locals and see once again how friendly and helpful people are. The man used to be a professional basketball player until he hurt his knees. That didn't surprise me because he was about 6'7". We got to chat a bit as he showed us around the heart of León. He pointed out a beautiful building by the famous architect, Antoni Gaudí, called *Casa de los Botines.* He explained the León is actually a pretty small town but I don't know;

It looked pretty big to me compared to the other towns I've seen walking across rural Spain.

Shortly after we parted with the nice local couple, we got lost. Had I been alone, I probably would have been pretty worried, but for some reason things aren't as stressful when you're with other people. We just stopped for drinks at a local cafe that had Wi-Fi and pulled up our hotel on Google Maps. While Nikolai tried to figure out where we were, I people watched as we were sitting in the corner of a massive outdoor market, and enjoyed my pineapple juice which was a cold, frothy treat served in a big fancy glass with a massive straw.

After checking into our second hotel, which was super small and only slightly nicer yet a fair bit cheaper, we headed out for lunch. Right next to the cathedral we found an outdoor café that was open during siesta. It was peaceful and quiet because very few people were out walking around in the heat of the afternoon. I sat back and enjoyed the view as I had my tapas and listened to the music (Milky Chance, "Stolen Dance" - a current favorite!). Life is good. It was another instant when I wished Brian was here to take it all in with me. I took many pictures, but just couldn't capture the moment.

Inside the cathedral was astounding. I was surprised at how taken I was by it. I listened to the audio tour and learned all about the beginning of the gothic era and the change in building architecture and I held my breath as it talked about the 14-year renovation the building needed after nearly collapsing on its congregation. Mind blowing. The cathedral in Burgos was far more spectacular from the outside and had more chapels on the inside, but the stained glass in the León cathedral is enough to make you cry. Every bit of this architecture and lighting was perfectly deliberate.

Following the tour we strolled all over León. We ran into Michael, a guy from Florida we had met multiple times. His poor wife Linda was stuck in the albergue throwing up. The poor thing caught something. It crossed my mind that perhaps I caught some kind of stomach bug before Carrión de Los Condes and that's what had me throwing up the other day. After all, that's super common on other hiking trails. It's very possible we're all passing something around. That certainly made more sense than heat exhaustion.

When we ventured out for dinner, I realized the difference between Spanish cities and American cities. People are just happy to be out and about in Spain. They act as though they haven't a care in the world and they are just genuinely thrilled to be alive. Everyone is dressed up, there is singing, there is dancing, there are weddings, there are random celebrations of young people just enjoying the evening. So lively. So spirited. It's just wonderful. I watched newlyweds and their wedding guests pour out of the Cathedral de Santa Maria into a sea of celebration. Clapping, shouting, crying, confetti, rice. I had to watch. The joy was infectious.

Gaudí's *Casa de los Botines*

# CHAPTER 25

## DAY 23: 8KM FROM LEÓN TO
## LA VIRGEN DEL CAMINO

—

## DON'T WORRY 'BOUT A THING

I slept in this morning, knowing today would be a short walk. I wanted to ease myself back into hiker mode. Upon passing the Cathedral de Santa Maria de León (the one with the amazing stained glass), the bells rang and I realized 10:00am Mass was about to start. How cool would it be to go to church here? I asked Nikolai if he was interested in attending Mass with me and he agreed. We followed the crowds of dressed up people into the cathedral with all our gear on our backs.

When we entered, the cathedral looked completely different from yesterday afternoon. The stained glass threw brilliant colors all over the room from the morning sun, and unlike yesterday when the cathedral was staged for tourism, it was now staged for worship. All the areas were open and free for use.

That said, the place was mobbed with people. There was a big class of children getting their First Holy Communion and their families flooded the cathedral. The main area is surrounded by large iron gates. I managed to make my way to the gates and get a few pictures of the altar, but it felt more like a rock concert than a church as I was pushed into the iron work. So after only a few minutes, I stepped back from the crowds and listened from behind.

The choir voices soared as many priests and clergymen filed onto the altar. I really wanted to receive communion, but the place was so packed I couldn't figure out how I'd ever get to the altar. But when the time came, the priests scattered throughout the cathedral and people flocked to them. It looked very primitive for some reason. I pictured people gathering around Jesus as he blessed everyone. Once things settled down a bit, I walked up to receive communion myself.

When I returned to the small space where Nikolai and I had been standing, I saw an older woman on her knees praying. This woman, who probably did not have the most capable knees at her age, was kneeling on the hard concrete floor, with her elbows resting on a large column. There was nowhere for her to sit and there was no hope she could see the altar from where she stood. But there she knelt in this holy place with all her devotion. The whole experience gave me goosebumps.

When Mass was over, we followed the long procession of priests through the massive cathedral doors. Outside were men all dressed up carrying flags and playing instruments. I assume this was a big to-do for the children receiving their First Holy Communion. I can't image every Mass being such a big deal. I also noticed the whole thing was being televised so somehow we witnessed a very special ceremony. I didn't understand the words but the meaning was clearly written on the faces of everyone around me. They all took it very seriously. We lingered in the moment for a while before starting our hike.

The walk out of León was not fantastic. We hiked in the heat through dirty neighborhoods and industrial lands. The walk is never great upon entering or exiting a city. There was nothing noteworthy about it, with the exception of some huts we passed on a hill. They looked like massive hobbit houses buried in the hills, but clearly no one lived in them. I'm thinking they were used to store and cool food, but I'm not sure. Either way, the short but sweltering walk was far from amusing. We stopped at the first opportunity for shade and drinks.

In the meantime, we ran into a nice German guy whose name I never seem to catch. He pointed us to the nearest albergue, which wasn't far at all. I was very disappointed my day would be so short and everyone was continuing on, but I've made the mistake of pushing myself before and I lost two days for it (though I wouldn't say those days were truly lost. I loved León almost as much as Burgos, but I would have loved it more if I could have enjoyed it without being injured). So we stopped early.

For six euros, the albergue was pretty nice. The check-in process took forever as there was a line of people looking for a bed. I was surprised how many people were stopping so early in the day. That said, it was pretty hot out, so it made sense. Ugh. Plus, everyone was really sweaty and gross. I noticed that some of the men were wearing cotton and they were the sweatiest of all. I couldn't imagine hiking like that. I gladly let them check in before me.

Anyway, back to the albergue. It had a nice library with a seating area and a kitchen. We decided for dinner tonight we would just walk to the *supermercado* and pick some stuff out that we can eat back at the albergue using the kitchen supplies. We dropped our gear and headed back out. It was way too early to call it a day. We headed into town to pick up some *vino* and snacks for the night and there was plenty of fun and silliness as we decided on what to have for dinner. What's more responsible than having potato chips and watermelon for dinner? Then we had lunch at an outdoor cafe. The local couple sitting next to us noticed my bandaged feet and made sympathetic faces. The waiter said something to them in Spanish about us being *pereginos*. For a moment, I was proud of my wounded feet. It was proof that I am a pilgrim and I'm still hiking.

While eating our salads, Nikolai and I discussed our goals. It's something we reassess with each other every few days to make sure we're both happy with our personal journey. I have two goals at this point: 1) to meet Brian at the earliest point possible and cash in on some much needed hugs and 2) to walk into Santiago with Brian and Nikolai. Nikolai would also like to meet Brian (though not for the hugs I'm sure) and to hike with us into Santiago, too. But his latest goal is also to hike another 75k, only this time starting at night. After learning he holds the current Camino record for the longest (and perhaps craziest) hike in one day, he is compelled to do it again, only better.

We pulled out our maps and planned how far we have to walk to meet Brian on Friday and realized that barring any more injuries, we'd be right on schedule to meet him at the train station in Ponferrada. At some point after that, Nikolai will probably walk ahead of Brian and me and then meet us in a major town somewhere so we can all finish together.

When we returned to the albergue, rather than setting up my bed, showering, and doing laundry like I usually do, there was only one thing I wanted to do: sit in the shade. I popped in y headphones, listened to some Bob Marley and took a siesta … *Don't worry 'bout a thing, cuz every little things gonna be alright.* Nikolai found some glasses in the albergue kitchen and a knife to cut up the watermelon. We found a big tree just outside of the albergue, unrolled Nikolai's sleeping pad and rested in the shade with a bottle of *vino.*

As we were enjoying the early evening, another German guy we've run into multiple times stopped by. The guys talked for hours. I just listened to my music, got drunk slowly and smiled. There was nothing to contribute to the conversation but that was totally ok. I was just grateful to be a part of the international experience. Then some Austrian ladies joined us for chips and watermelon and it was the perfect evening. They talked all night.

Side note: The Austrians affectionately nicknamed Nikolai *Simon* because every time they see him, he is helping someone, much like Simon helped Jesus carry the cross. I thought that was really sweet, except, they don't pronounce it the way I am accustomed to hearing it. Instead they say "semen" and I can't help but laugh every single time they say it. Now every time they see us coming, they call out "Semen!" with such love and affection! I feel like a jerk because I can't stop laughing, but I was too embarrassed to tell them why. I did eventually explain it to Nikolai. Now he blushes whenever he sees them coming.

While I'm on the subject of language barriers, here's the latest one: I recently realized that while sometimes Nikolai says things with a strong accent, sometimes he says things completely wrong. I realized this yesterday when I learned he's been looking for a pair of pans all week instead of a pair of pants. So now if he says something that sounds off, I ask him to spell it. Today he said he wanted to work on his tan (we have ridiculous tan lines from hiking in the blazing sun all day). But he said it all wrong. I asked him to spell it. T-A-I-N-T. He needs to work on his taint. Of course I laughed until I cried and everyone at the cafe was looking at me. It wasn't until later I could explain why it was so funny to me. I'm amazed sometimes that we're even able to communicate.

After a few hours of hanging out in the grass, I decided to find other friends whom I could talk to. I informed the group that was I going to hunt for some English speaking friends. They all laughed and wished me a good night. I wandered around the common areas of the albergue until I bumped into a nice young woman from Lithuania named Vita. She told me all about camping in northern Norway and how the sun dances all over the sky day and night but never actually sets. It was so exciting to meet someone who has camped in Norway because that's one adventure I may not get to in this lifetime.

This cathedral is known for its stained glass

Spending the evening with friends is the best part of the day

# CHAPTER 26

## DAY 24: 23KM FROM LA VIRGEN DEL CAMINO TO VILLAVANTE

—

### I GET IT NOW

I slept in again this morning, but only until about 6:30am. People were packed up and gone by 5:30am. This really does a number on my nerves. I worry a lot about my feet and the fact that I move even slower now than I did originally. It's literally a race to the beds and I lose every day. I never realized just how much slower I walk than everyone. And it's not that I'm walking slowly. I actually move quickly, but my legs are so short that I take four steps while everyone else takes two!

Anyway, back to the beds. Yes, we find beds, but I hate being the last one in town walking from albergue to albergue looking for a place to put my things. Today is another short day so I wasn't too worried about sleeping in, but tomorrow is a 30km day and I'm very worried about it. I really hope my feet hold out and I can find a bed when I finally get into town.

I've been thinking a lot about the foot situation. I spoke to so many people yesterday who are walking on busted feet. What blows my mind is that no one has a solution. I walk with physicians, paramedics, and EMTs, and no one can help. I was frustrated with all the bad advice out here. I have come to learn by trial and error that threading your blisters is a bad idea, vaseline is a bad idea, and aloe vera plants (while wildly creative) are a bad idea. Many people swear by them, but I stand firmly in the bad idea camp. These remedies may make sense in our daily lives where you can rest your body, but on the Camino, where you walk day in and day out, these solutions can actually create more problems as you continue onward. I realize now that the only answer is to not walk. You aren't supposed to walk on open wounds. It's as simple as that. But that's just not an option out here, which is why none of these remedies actually work for us. The best thing you can do is surround your blisters with molefoam during the day in an effort to protect them from continued trauma and drain them and air them out at night when you aren't walking.

Now would be a good time to mention Stonehearth Open Learning Opportunities (SOLO) and the National Outdoor Leadership School (NOLS.) These two companies teach wilderness first aid, including the proper method for treating blisters, and I recommend learning from them. Brian learned everything he knows about blister care from SOLO and I should have just followed the advice he gave me from the get go.

The walk in general today was wonderful and thought provoking. The sun was hot but there was a nice breeze. By 8:00am, though, we were already sweating and in need of water. All along the Camino, especially in small villages, you can usually find fountains that gush with ice cold water. It's everything you can do to keep from throwing yourself under them to soak up all their refreshment when you find them. Interestingly, I'm learning to sniff them out. I'm not sure what it is about the surrounding areas of fountains but I'm learning to recognize where I can find one. It's a useful skill I've developed along the way.

During our second breakfast stop, I ran into the man who walked with me to the doctor several days earlier. I spoke with him and his trail family and we learned that many of us got sick and were throwing up in Carrión de Los Condes. Whatever it was, it hit a bunch of us. The conversation confirmed my thoughts that perhaps we were all passing something around. I was so relieved to be past that point in my journey.

Two random observations: first, in small towns where there is no baker, a bread truck will drive in like the ice cream man and lay on his horn. Residents run out to purchase their bread, eggs, or whatever goods he may be carrying. The first few times I saw this was very confusing because no one came out. I just saw a truck roll up next to us and lay on his horn. After this happened in two or three different towns, I realized what was going on. Second, apparently there are a lot of cuckoo birds in this region of Spain. Over the last three days, I've been amused by several on my hike. *Cuckoo cuckoo*! Just like the clocks.

Once we arrived in the town where we planned to stop for the day, I was feeling pretty good. If we continued another 10km, we could shorten the 30km day we would have tomorrow. As we drank our *cervezas*, I called to the one albergue 10km away and reserved two of the eleven beds available. This would allow us to walk at my snail's pace and not worry about having a bed. We also ran into some folks from Boston, which is always a good time. Lots of cheers as if we all know each other or just won the Superbowl. They were stopping for the day. The afternoon was too hot for them to continue and the next stretch is nothing but road walking for miles. While the accommodations were tempting in town, we still decided to push on.

About three-quarters of the way there, we came across a massive tree (dressed with the white fuzzy things) that gave us the shade we needed and the perfect spot for me to take off my shoes and rest my feet. As we sat there quietly in the warm breeze, I reflected on how we are approaching the region where that American woman was abducted in April. I reverted to my old ways, contemplating the various ways one could be abducted. Miles of nothing but a road where few cars travel.

With every passing vehicle, I thanked God I wasn't alone.

I thought about many things today, but as I was walking that last 10km in the afternoon heat, something hit me like lightning! I get why people do this now! I get it! So few people in the modern industrialized world have the opportunity to find out who they really are and what they are truly capable of within their lifetime. But when you push your mind, body and spirit to do something extraordinary, like hike for hundreds of miles across unfamiliar territory, you reach a level of self-awareness that is not possible in an average life.

As I continued to walk today, I was met with myself again. "Oh, I remember you," we greeted like old friends. I continued to push myself. Meanwhile there was nothing for miles. Just the road stretched before me, the crops surrounding me, and a mirage the size of Texas taunting me. I get it. This is why I'm here. This is what I was hoping for.

When you slow things down and remove all the extraneous things, your perspective changes. Your life changes. Simple things become spectacular. Things you take for granted normally are appreciated, adored, loved. Every day I count my blessings. My blessings are different now. They are many. The shade of a tree, the brilliant color in flowers, the welcoming smell of a church, the energetic fist bump from a friend, the cleansing effects of rain, the head nod from a supportive local, the attention of a stray cat or dog, a piece of watermelon provided by a Camino angel, five uninterrupted minutes of privacy, a healing cry, a five-minute shower, the sight of wheat crops waving at me in the breeze, the breeze itself. These are all missed when you move too fast. I'm so grateful I have the opportunity to slow life down and see how beautiful the world is. I can't even describe it. Everyone should be able to experience the world like this. What an absolutely amazing hike today.

After settling into the albergue, which was most interesting because of the talking parrot- *HOLA*!- we sat out in the front with the other pilgrims catching up and watching the goings on of this very small town. The town is so small in fact, there isn't even a grocery store. Across the street was apparently where the locals frequent. Several Spaniards sat in the shade and talked all evening long. And why not? What else is there to do here?

After dinner we spent most of the evening talking outside with Sarah the Russian and a very eccentric German guy whose name I never caught. Niko and I then took a late night walk around the town to confirm that there really was nothing to see. Confirmed. We did notice one strange thing though. While the buildings were not all that impressive, all of the doors were really nice. It was as though they put all their investments into the front door and had nothing left for the rest of the house. Or perhaps they already knew what I discovered today. There is immense beauty in simplicity.

I'm looking forward to reaching Astorga tomorrow where we will tour the famous chocolate museum!

Painted on the road

# CHAPTER 27

## DAY 25: 20KM FROM VILLAVANTE TO ASTORGA
—
## A HOMELESS ANGEL AND A BULLY

I woke up feeling amazing today. Yesterday's hike was bursting with positive thoughts and realizations about myself as well as the world around me. I had a great night's sleep and today is my eighth wedding anniversary! And while I'm not spending it with my wonderful husband, I'll see him in just a few short days. I can image how romantic it will be to celebrate together in Spain!

Adventures for today: shortly after our first stop, we came across a credentials booklet that a pilgrim must have dropped on the ground. It was full of stamps. The poor guy. His name was Miguel Angel and he was from Spain. After looking at his credentials more carefully, we deduced that he must have been a biker because he was in León this morning. No one could walk that far in a day.

So we stopped the first biker we came across, a nice Italian man. With horrible broken Spanish and the worst game of charades you've ever seen, we explained to the man that a biker dropped his credentials and he was probably well on his way to Astorga. As walkers, we could never catch up with him. The nice man agreed to take the credentials into town with him and communicate it to everyone at the albergue. I'm confident Miguel will get his credentials back. The Camino provides. And so do the pilgrims.

At our second stop, we ran into Roy, a pastor we've bumped into several times in the last week. We all assessed each other and decided we all "look great!" When someone tells you you look great on the Camino, it has a different meaning than usual. I absolutely love it when people tell me I look great because it means I'm strong, healthy, and more likely to have a *Buen Camino*. It's the best compliment you can receive, and I was so happy to hear it after my recent setback. It was validation that I'm moving past it.

When I told Roy he looked great, he pulled up his pant leg and exposed his knee, which was all wrapped up in tape. He explained to us that he fell in the Parador shower. Holy crap, Roy! We heard that story through the Camino gossip line, which is filled with stories of how fellow pilgrims are doing. We didn't know it was Roy, though! We joked that falling in a five-star shower was yet another way to die on the Camino.

We walked part of the way with a nice couple from Dublin. This is their third section hike of the Camino, and they intend to walk the rest of the way to Santiago this time. I told them that today was my eight-year wedding anniversary and I am so excited because soon my husband would join me on the Camino. They were very excited for me, and said they enjoyed walking together.

Today we crossed the Orbigo bridge, which is the largest Roman bridge on the Camino. There are many bridges on the Way but this one is the most impressive by far. The sheer size of it is enough to impress anyone. A nice man took a picture of Nikolai and me in front of it, but the bridge is so long he couldn't fit it all into view. It occurred to me as we were passing over that beautiful bridge that millions of people have done the exact same thing, and I now have something in common with each and every one of them. We also passed an old field that was used centuries ago for jousting. We scored some cool pictures there and read up on the history.

Later, as the day was heating up and we were walking through a field of dirt, we came across a half-dressed man who had a table set up full of fruits, veggies, and other wonderfully delicious snacks for pilgrims. His little food cart had hand painted on it, "*la llave de la esencia es la presencia*," which means something like the key to essence is presence. A couple of weeks ago I would have found the message cheesy, but today it makes perfect sense to me.

I noticed the man had a hammock and he was in the process of building a structure behind it. After talking with him for a while, we learned that he's actually homeless. He lives out in the field with nothing more than his hammock and the friendship of a homeless dog. "The dog is free. He exchanges friendship for food," he said. The man has been there for six years and spends his life handing out treats to pilgrims and building them a place to sit. He was quite a character and I'm so happy I got to meet him. I sat on the structure he built for us and chatted with some other pilgrims including a Californian named Christian. Nikolai was unusually reserved.

I think we are finally exiting the Meseta. We are starting to encounter rolling hills and slightly better scenery. For a week or so, I've been immensely bored with the views. I thought I was becoming jaded, but then I remembered reading that the Meseta drags on for days and really messes with your mind. I'm glad I made it through that section. The Meseta greets you just when you reach that point in your head when you ask yourself, "Why am I doing this?" I'm very fortunate, I think, because I found my answer out there in the Meseta. I know why I'm here. I know what I'm gaining from this amazing journey.

As we approached Astorga, dark clouds loomed over the town and we heard loud thunder claps. The prospect of walking into town during a thunderstorm was exciting. I put my headphones on and continued walking - it didn't rain on us though.

When we arrived in Astorga, Nikolai decided instead of sharing a hotel like we usually do in larger towns, he would stay in an albergue. I didn't mind that he wanted to stay in an albergue, but I was annoyed that he didn't feel the need to tell me that he was changing our routine the previous night when he knew I was booking a double room. As his hiking partner, I felt like I deserved to know if he planned to change something. Instead, he waited until we reached the hotel, said, "I'm going to stay in an albergue," and kept walking without breaking stride. He was probably just trying to avoid confrontation but it didn't really work. It was at that point that we had our first major disagreement as hiking partners.

As we talked about it throughout the evening, I realized what happened. It is very common on the Camino for friends to share a room to cut down on the cost. But Nikolai is in graduate school and has limited travel funds so normally I pay for the double and he buys me dinner in exchange. I think not paying his full share was beginning to weigh on his conscience. This was exacerbated by a run-in we had with a not-so-friendly man the night before. For some reason, the guy had it out for Nikolai and he teased him relentlessly about several things. At one point he called him a freeloader, which was ironic because the man himself was a proud self-proclaimed freeloader. Although he didn't say it, I could tell the guy really bothered Nikolai last night. I didn't give it a second thought, personally. What do I care what someone thinks of my Camino? But when I realized how bothered Nikolai was by it, I tried to convince him that the guy was just being cruel and there was no merit to what he said. But Nikolai must have taken it to heart and carried it with him the entire day today which would explain why he was unusually quiet the whole time. I wish he would have told me what was bothering him all day.

I could respect him wanting to pay his own way, so I accepted our new routine, but I was angry that someone hurt his feelings so badly and there was nothing I could say to make it better. The whole ordeal really threw me off and I wasn't sure how to handle it at first. Dealing with the bully the night before was one of the only negative experiences I've had on the Camino. But after fumbling through a long conversation and some arguing at dinner, we decided we weren't going to let it bring us down. Despite the language barrier and cultural differences which clearly got in the way, we worked through it and were stronger friends when all was said and done.

But backing up a bit: after dropping me off at the hotel, Nikolai returned later in the evening so we could explore Astorga. I had a chance to speak with Brian on the phone briefly while I was settling into my room. First, we wished each other a happy anniversary! Strangely, we never seem to be together on this special day. One of us is almost always traveling either for work or for pleasure. But that's ok. He'll be here in just a few short days.

I explained to him our run in with the bully and how much the entire experience bothered me. Brian encouraged me to think of all the positive people I've met along the way and to try to forget about this one horrible person. He also discouraged me from trying to force Nikolai to see my perspective and run the risk of damaging our friendship. Despite my stubbornness, I knew he was right.

Moving on to better things, Brian did an online search to find some great restaurants in Astorga for me. He recommended a place for us to try and I was looking forward to checking it out. Brian has the amazing ability to find the best places in town to eat regardless of the country he's in!

Astorga is pretty cool. First, we had to do some shopping. Nikolai wants to swim in the ocean when he reaches the coast, so he had to purchase a pair of swim trunks. Then we went to a chocolate museum, which was pretty anticlimactic with the exception of the actual chocolate tasting. Note to self: do not go to museums if you can't read the language! All joking aside, though, it was pretty interesting. It featured an excellent video on how chocolate is made with English subtitles, which I found fascinating and entertaining. They also displayed all the old-school machines and tools that were used to make chocolate, which was fun. We toured the building with another random hiker we met in town who got lost on her way to the museum. At the end of the tour, we took pictures of each other trying the various chocolate samples. The tasting was the best part of the tour, of course!

After the museum, we parted with the other hiker and looked for the place Brian recommended for dinner. When we found it, much to my dismay, it was closed. So we ended up at the restaurant next door, which turned out to be a very nice- and very expensive- restaurant. It was fantastic! Holy cow, the food was the best I've had in Spain so far, and the owner was very proud of his restaurant. Since we were there early compared to most Spanish diners, we had the restaurant to ourselves. The owner gave us the royal treatment. He pulled cuts of meat out from the kitchen to show us firsthand since we didn't understand the menu and he brought me into the kitchen to watch him cook.

Nikolai tried to order a small cut of meat to keep the cost of the meal down, but the owner insisted that a man needs a big meal. Their interaction was hilarious. When I ordered *vino*, I thought I was ordering a glass based on the price. Much to our surprise, the man brought us a full bottle. It was actually at this restaurant where we resolved our dispute from earlier in the evening. The owner could tell we were arguing when we arrived so he kept interrupting us and plying us with more wine. He was very charming and made it difficult for us to be in a bad mood. We sat there for hours enjoying our food and drink. Then we finished the day with a somewhat drunken stumble through the beautiful quiet streets of Astorga. So while the evening began a bit rocky, it ended quite well.

Orbigo, the longest Roman bridge on the Camino

Astorga chocolate museum

# CHAPTER 28

## DAY 26: 20KM FROM ASTORGA
## TO RABANAL DEL CAMINO
—
### WORDS DO MATTER

Last night, as per my usual big city routine, I checked myself into a beautiful hotel. Only this time, for the first time in 25 days, I had the room completely to myself. I passed out drunk and naked as the day I was born and it was fabulous. That is, until my alarm clock went off at 6:00am. I spent most of the night trying to sober up and listening to the wicked bad thunderstorm, knowing I'd be walking in it the next day. I seem to be in the habit of drinking too much on the nights I stay in a hotel. Maybe I'll never learn but hey, I'm on vacation right? It can't all be about the walking!

Sarah texted Nikolai last night and asked if we could all hike together out of Astorga. This is the region women are cautioned against hiking alone. Since we all stayed in different places last night, it took us some time in the morning to rally together.

I took a picture of the Astorga cathedral and moved out of town quickly as the weather was quite terrible. Apparently just next door to that absolutely gorgeous gothic cathedral is the Episcopal Palace built by Goudi. I would have loved to see it, but I completely missed it as we marched on by with our heads down. I suspect this town has much more to offer than what I was able to see. It poured and the thunder and lightning were right overhead. Despite the frequency of the thunder, I still flinched every time. I was genuinely scared walking in a storm like this but I didn't bother to consult with my hiking partner. I knew he would either be unfazed by the storm or unwilling to discuss it if it did bother him. So I said a prayer that we would make it to the next town safely and uneventfully and moved onward.

I'm not quite sure the purpose of rain clothes. Yes, they keep you dry from rain water, but you still end up soaked in your own sweat. Not to mention, my bright blue rain clothes are so big on me, I can pull the pants all the way up to my bra with room to spare, and the legs drag so far behind me, I had to use safety pins to hold them up. It was humbling to say the least. When the three of us stopped to take shelter in a nice little bar along the way, Nikolai tore his pack apart looking for items to hold up my pant legs with. The safety pins I attempted to use failed because there was so much loose fabric and part way through the walk, the bottoms of my pants soaked through.

Niko gave me the elastic bands that kept his sleeping pad tightly rolled against his backpack. He folded my pant legs up and strapped them down at the ankle. I looked like a clown and felt like an idiot, but it was necessary, so I shrugged the humiliation off and continued walking. In the meantime, while I was walking around dressed like a clown Smurf, Nikolai was asked for his autograph for the third time on the Camino. Everyone thinks he's Jake Gyllenhaal. He was thrilled and talked about it for the next 20 minutes. As I said, we are both experiencing the Camino in very different ways.

It's nice to have Sarah along with us. She brings a special spark to the team. She walks hard and fast and is generally 100 or so meters ahead of us. This is probably a good thing, because she smokes like a chimney and sings Russian songs at the top of her lungs. She's a great deal of fun. Nikolai and I joked that it was like a game trying to figure out what the heck she was singing. She also possesses this jaw-dropping natural beauty that everyone seems to notice instantly. I wouldn't want to mess with her, though. During second breakfast, a minor misunderstanding about the bill - complicated by the language barrier - turned into a strained altercation between Sarah and the two women working behind the counter. In the end, Sarah just paid more, but she held her ground and refused to be bullied. I would have given in much earlier just to avoid the confrontation.

I ran into Vita from Lithuania again and was happy to see she found someone to hike out of town with. It appears that most women received the warning loud and clear about the recent abduction and are taking the proper precautions. (Postscript: it pains me to say that after months of searching and investigating, local authorities found the remains of the American woman who was abducted the month before I began my hike. She was murdered by a deranged local in the Astorga area who lured her off of the official Camino path. This was quite a blow to the Camino community. Local authorities have since increased their numbers and presence to help hikers feel safe once again. Please remember that while this act of violence is horrible and one should always err on the side of caution, the Way is still one of the safest places in the world and this incident has in no way diminished the magic spirit of the Camino. Rest in peace, Denise.)

One entertaining thing we dealt with today were the flooded streets. While walking alongside the road, we gambled with oncoming traffic. Would the driver slow down and pass us peacefully, or would he be more "spirited" and blow through the puddles, drenching us? It was fun watching pilgrims scatter when the latter occurred.

About 10km into the walk, it became apparent that Sarah was drastically unprepared for the cool, windy, rainy weather. Under her super thin rain-resistant shirt, she had nothing more than a tank top.

I gave her my coat and hat and Nikolai gave her a couple of shirts to layer with. She must have been feeling much more comfortable because she slowed her pace to a more reasonable speed. I silently thanked Brian for helping me pack. Not only did he know exactly what I should bring to be comfortable, but I was able to provide for others in their time of need.

Early in the hike, we came across another café. We had just stopped only about 3km before and I was feeling good, but I knew there would be no more stops for another 10km. I was nervous that if I didn't give my feet a rest now, I would be really hurting by the next stop. Sarah did not want to stop since we hadn't walked very far. I got the sense Nikolai wanted to keep moving too, but I knew if I wanted to stop he would. So reluctantly I carried on. It turned out to be a great lesson. I realized I have been babying myself because of my recent blister disaster, but apparently I don't need to anymore. I was fine!

Despite the rain, being soaked to the bone, and the mud (oh God, the mud), the walk was super easy. I wish you could have seen the worst of the mud. It soaked through my shoes and I squished and squashed all the way into town. It's the worst feeling ever when you sink into a three-inch pile of mud and know you'll be carrying it in your shoe for the next ten miles. Anyway, 20km suddenly feels like a stroll.

Oh, and all my blister problems? Gone. I switched back to wool socks as I was wearing the first two weeks (when I had no blisters yet) and for the last three days, my feet have been great. Even today as they were swimming in mud, they were ok. I think my synthetic socks were too tight and squeezed my toes together, which created the blisters. I'm so grateful that I've had three pain-free days. Granted, my original chronic foot pain still exists, but that's an easy fix. I just stop walking every few kilometers. Blisters are a different story. There is nothing you can do about walking on open wounds. I'm hoping that's all behind me now, but you never know.

Sarah forged ahead of us for a good portion of the walk. I was concerned Nikolai may be getting bored walking at my snail's pace so I let him know that I would be okay if he wanted to walk ahead of me to catch up with Sarah. He huffed at me, "Theresa, how long have we been walking together?" He had a point. I should know by now that our routine is to walk together but the reassurance was heartwarming.

We came across a large stone pool. When we've seen similar pools in the past, Nikolai would approach the pool first and pretend to splash me with water. I would squeak and flinch only to find the pool was empty. This time the pool was full of water. But it was the dirtiest water I've ever seen. It was thick with green.

"You wouldn't!" I shouted.

Just at that moment, he threw a handful of filthy water at my face. It was cold and got in my mouth. The thought of drinking and wearing the sludge shocked me.

"Son of bitch," I said under my breath. All I could think as I wiped off my face was that I'm probably going to catch giardia or some other awful waterborne illness. But I had bigger problems to deal with at the moment. Nikolai was stunned by my harsh language. It was the first time since I've been on the Camino that I swore like that.

"You don't even know my mother," he said as he began walking on without me.

At first I laughed a bit. "Nikolai, I didn't mean anything against your mother. I was just startled by the water and it was a reflex. It's just a saying."

I told him I was sorry but he said, "No, I don't believe this. This is not from your heart." I realized he wasn't joking. He was genuinely bothered by what I said. I struggled to keep pace with him as he charged forward.

"I'm sorry. In my country sometimes we say that, but it doesn't mean anything," I explained.

"You must be more careful with your words!"

I stopped walking. He was right. Maybe it was just a reflex and maybe I didn't mean it literally, but there is no room for abrasive language like that on the Camino. In one sharp phrase, I'd broken our friendly peaceful bond. I wanted to apologize again and ask if we were okay but instead we walked in silence for the next few hours. Sometimes silence is the only way to clear the air. It was a small but important lesson for me. Words do matter. Especially here while we are on this spiritual journey. Eventually, Nikolai must have accepted my apology, because we resumed our usual pleasant conversation and finished the walk side by side.

We caught up with Sarah in Rabanal Del Camino. We planned to do at least five more kilometers today, but this town has so much history and there were so many familiar faces at the bar. Many pilgrims in the past have stopped here in this town after the ascent (which I have to say was barely noticeable at this point). They sought refuge here from wolves and bandits that plagued the León Mountains. The Knights Templar ran a fort here to protect the pilgrims. How cool is that? I told Nikolai I'd like to stop for the day and as usual, he was okay with that. Sarah only has a few more days to finish her trip, but she still decided to stop for the day.

The albergue came highly recommended, and while it may be really nice when it's warm out, I did not enjoy hand washing my clothes outside in cold water and I found the stone walls of my room to be cold and damp. I showered quickly, put on my last clean pair of underwear and climbed back into my dirty clothes. It's too cold to wash both of my outfits and be stuck wearing only my dress. Not only that, but if I washed both outfits and they don't dry in this damp air, I'll have nothing warm to wear in tomorrow's rain. So I went with the lesser of two evils and decided to go dirty over wet.

I put my coat on and climbed into my top bunk for a nap. I think the cold wet weather had the same impact on everyone. The seven other people I shared a room with were already in their sleeping bags napping. Nikolai and I agreed that if one of us got up to do something fun, we would let the other know. The Camino won't last forever and I don't want to miss any of it.

At 7:00pm, we got up to go to church. Sarah began chatting with Nikolai in the courtyard and I got the sense she took a liking to him. I didn't want to be the old married lady who interfered with young love so I snuck away and leisurely strolled over to church talking with some other pilgrims on the way. I've met so many amazing people on this journey of mine, and I took note of the fact that while I recognize a lot of people, I seem to be walking with a new set of pilgrims too. I think most of the people I know have moved on at a faster pace.

The church was very small and dilapidated but carried a unique charm. Nikolai entered just before service started and we listened to the monks chant through most of it. It was pretty cool but not exactly what I was expecting. Halfway through the service, a man got up and began speaking English. He said we've been walking in rain, wind, cold weather, and mud. He asked, "Why do you torture yourselves? This is an important question every pilgrim must ask. Why do you do this? A pilgrim is someone who is searching for something. You should not be running from something. You must know why you do this." It was thought provoking. I know exactly what I am getting out of this amazing journey. I understand the benefits I am experiencing but I still do not have a clear reason for why I am doing this. I don't think my answer is any more complicated than it was three weeks ago. I'm walking the Camino because I should.

His talk made me wish I could understand the rest of the service, which was not in English, because he probably had many thoughtful things to say. When the service was over, all the lights shut off and we had to find our way out of the building. It was an interesting experience. I'm not quite sure what the point was. Everyone shuffled their feet and bumped into one another as we slowly made our way towards the glowing evening light outside. On the way out, I bumped into a woman who was so happy to see me. She gave me the biggest warmest hug and I felt so bad because I can't remember for the life of me who she is or how I know her.

Someone told me yesterday that Santiago is only about 10 days away. My heart sank a little when I heard that. I'm not ready for this to be over. I planned to take a bus to the coast after reaching Santiago, but if I continue to feel good, I may extend my trip on foot and just walk there. I think it's only another three day's walk. From there, it's one day to Muxia.

Cathedral of Astorga

# CHAPTER 29

## DAY 27: 16KM FROM RABANAL DEL CAMINO TO … SOMEWHERE NOT FAR ENOUGH

—

## CRUZ DE FERRO ON A SOUR STOMACH

Oh my God, I am such a jerk. I don't know how it happened, but somehow my alarm clock was set on my cell phone and went off this morning. It wasn't the gentle vibrate kind of alarm either. It sounded like a loud obnoxious roar at 7am. What made the situation worse was that my cell phone was on the other side of the room. Outlets were limited and I was lucky to have gotten one at all. I recognized the alarm as my own and bolted out of my top bunk, banging my knees on the way down. I scooped up my phone and turned it off as quickly as I could. It was just my luck that everyone in the albergue slept in and were all still in bed. Several people stirred but no one got up or said anything to me. I'm sure someone was silently cursing me though. What a rough way to be woken up.

Once fully awake, I felt really uneasy. At first I thought it was because of how I jolted out of bed so suddenly. We sat with another woman for breakfast in the albergue and while she was cheerful and delightful, I had little interest in talking. She and Nikolai were talking about the treats on the table, provided by the albergue. There was a large bottle of Vegemite. I'm familiar with Vegemite because my husband hiked the Appalachian Trail with a few Australians and he came home with a bottle of it. Nikolai slathered the stuff all over his toast. I cautioned him to be sparing with it. It's extremely salty. He shook his head, disregarding my warning and took a big bite. Despite feeling a bit down, I couldn't help but giggle as I watched his face contort. "Oh, my God," he said under his breath.

"Oh, no. Is it salty?" I pretended to be concerned. He put down the toast. The other woman laughed at our interaction. It was a typical silly start to the day.

The day's hike was extremely difficult for me and it should not have been. Yesterday, despite the weather, I hiked 20km and barely noticed it. It was a cat jump, as the Germans say. Today we planned to do 26km. The sun was shining, the air was cool, the inclines feel gentle now, the views were gorgeous and my feet were cooperating. Yet I struggled every step of the way.

At first I thought I was just tired and needed more coffee. When we stopped for second breakfast, I ordered a *café con leche* and a chocolate-filled croissant. These are common breakfast items on the Camino and usually I'm quite excited about them, but this morning, I just couldn't get them down. Nikolai kept saying "Eat! ENERGY!" with a big smile on his face as if he could inspire me to change my mood by acting excited himself. I could appreciate his efforts and I tried to be positive but something just wasn't right with me today. It wasn't just my attitude. I finally gave up on eating and let Nikolai finish my second breakfast.

As we started walking again, my stomach started doing somersaults. For the rest of the day, I weaved in and out of the bushes prepared to throw up at any time. I was sick…again.

Today was the day of the iron cross, too. *Cruz de Ferro*. It's a landmark stop on the Camino and one I've been looking forward to. It's a tall wooden stake with a small iron cross on top that sits at nearly the highest point on the Camino (5,000 feet above sea level).

What makes this cross significant is that people carry rocks from home or from the start of their pilgrimage with the intention of leaving it at the cross. The rock is meant to carry a prayer or a sin. Leaving the rock at the cross represents leaving behind the weight of your prayers/sins. The mound of rocks was enormous. Millions of pilgrims have carried their rocks from all over the world to this one location.

I carried my rock over 300 miles for this special moment and it was being spoiled by a sour stomach. Not only that, but I lost my rock. I tore the outer pockets of my pack apart looking for it and it was nowhere to be found. I was so upset with myself. So I backtracked on the trail (something you never do unnecessarily) to find a rock. Apparently I'm not the only one who lost my rock because there wasn't a single loose pebble for hundreds of meters. I finally found the smallest pebble, brought it back to the cross, and tossed it into the massive mound of rocks for good measure. I was expecting so much more from this moment but because I happened to be having a bad day, it was completely anticlimactic. Oh, and I found the freakin' rock at the next stop in a pocket I didn't think to check. I was so pissed. A friend of mine from work asked me to bring him a rock from Spain. He better appreciate my sin rock which I will have carried for 500 miles!

The next place we stopped is another landmark of the Camino. Tomas, the Knight Templar of Manjarin, runs this rest point. He was an eccentric and friendly man who I would have thoroughly enjoyed had I not felt so badly. We only stayed briefly. We bought a couple of oranges, which I struggled to hold down, rested at the shaded wooden picnic table that overlooked the mountains, and played with the dog chained to the small wooden hut. I knew I wasn't well because normally this unique stop would have sparked my enthusiasm. I missed being the person I usually am on the Camino.

I tried to take in the views of the mountains on the way back down the mountain. I haven't had scenes like this in over a week. The mountains were covered in yellow and purple wildflowers that popped where the sun made its way through the clouds. Also, the very rocky path back down the mountain was covered with marble. I've never seen so much marble outside of a church. I should have taken a picture.

We made multiple stops along the way. As I said, this should have been the perfect hiking day. But there I was feeling sick the way I was just before León. Only before León, I was sad and feeling sorry for myself. Today I was just pissed. What contaminant has the right to interfere with the last few precious days of my *Buen Camino*? Is it any surprise though? Thousands of people from all over the world, none of them using soap or toilet paper. I shudder at the thought.

My mood was sour and I tried not to infect anyone else with it, but poor Nikolai had to deal with me all day. I felt like the worst hiking partner on the planet and he played on those emotions for his own sick enjoyment.

"Next time, I take two-year-old with me. It be easier." Or, "Your character is difficult for me today!" But I suppose I deserved his taunting. I also lost my well-loved headphones. I was beside myself when I realized I may have left them at the last albergue. How would I get through a day like today without my music? Nikolai gave me his headphones to borrow and within two minutes, they fell out of my pocket and onto the trail. Fortunately he was trailing behind me the whole day as if I was a toddler who needed constant supervision. "Theresa!! A child is easier!" I know, I know. I suck. I was in rare form for sure.

We arrived in a town and stopped for lunch. I hadn't eaten pretty much all day because I struggled to hold anything down and I was starting to feel uneasy as early as last night, so I ate very little then, too. Just as we entered town, other symptoms presented themselves. I rushed to the nearest store and asked to use the bathroom. They said no but I was only asking to be polite. I was using that bathroom! I thanked them as if I didn't understand what they said and I ran to the *baño*. I felt bad that I disregarded what they told me so I made sure I left the place sparkling and I thanked them wholeheartedly before I left the store. They didn't seem too angry. I think they realized I wasn't just trying to be a jerk.

The little village of Acebo was full of multiple nice albergues, cafés, and happy pilgrims. I thought for sure we made it. I nearly cried when I looked at the map and realized we barely made a dent in our progress. How was that possible? I trudged all day up and down mountain after mountain and I only walked 16km? I told my hiking buddy that I had to stop. It was already 3:00pm and I couldn't take the uneasy stomach down the rest of the mountain. It was quite a descent into Acebo.

We met Kelly from California and Mitch from Washington at lunch. I had a delightful conversation despite feeling like crap. When Nikolai was done eating everything he could possibly get from the café, we looked for a place to sleep. We ran into some German friends of his. They've never spoken English so I didn't really get to know them myself. They recommended to him the last albergue just before leaving the village. As we passed all the very nice albergues with pictures of beautiful private bedrooms, all I could think was, "this place better be amazing." I was in no mood for subpar accommodations.

When I got there, I knew exactly what it was. It was a donations-only albergue like the one we stayed at last night. What this means is they don't charge a fee and people pay whatever they want. It has been my assumption that these places are not as nice; at least that's what I was thinking while in the worst mood ever. I was not happy at all. These places are for college students and freeloaders and I am neither of those things! But whatever. I was too sick to protest. Besides, as long as they had a washer and drier since I was wearing dirty clothes from yesterday, I could deal with everything else.

Oh, yes. They have a washer and dryer! The sink is over there and the clothespins are over there. NO!! I was furious. I was sick and there were about four better options in town. But Nikolai was just chatting up a storm with the German hospitalero. Is everyone here German? Apparently! I sat silently as I stewed in my own fury.

The place wouldn't even allow you to bring your bags up to the sleeping quarters. You had to leave them in the entryway (yeah, that's safe) and only bring up what you need. The bathrooms are also on a different floor which is fantastic when you're sick. I think Nikolai was a little afraid of how angry I was so he avoided eye contact. We both knew we should have gone to a different albergue but we were already checked in. I grabbed my sleeping bag and stomped upstairs. Despite my agitation with the place, I actually found a really nice spot to sleep in a dark quiet corner that was close to the stairs that led to the toilet. I threw my bag down and crawled into it with my dirty clothes on. I slept for three hours.

When I awoke, I was still feeling sick, but my rotten mood had dissipated. I saw another woman I met this morning at the previous albergue. We had breakfast together. She was also sick. But because she was German, she and her friend had a conversation with the very helpful volunteer, Renate, who was running the place, and got medicine, tea, and some hard crackers. After a few minutes, I pulled together some strength and went downstairs to talk to the volunteer myself. When I got there, she was speaking in German to the friend of the other sick woman. They looked at me with a familiar face and kept talking.

I could imagine what they were saying. "Oh, she's the one I was telling you about. She's been peeing out of her butt all day, too." I'm sorry to be so graphic and disgusting, but this is my life right now and if I can live with it, you can stand to read about it. The two women went to work bringing me medicine, making me tea, and preparing some bread. I was so relieved and grateful they were willing to help me because I was too weak to do anything myself. Renate scolded me like a mother that I needed to drink more, and it can't be water, and that I couldn't come back in the building until I ate all three pieces of bread.

She carried my tea and bread to a pleasant area out back and told me to eat everything. I thanked her the best way I knew how. She understood. I felt kind of bad that I was so angry about the accommodations earlier since she was being so helpful now.

It took me over an hour to get everything down, but I was feeling a tad better by then. Nikolai texted me and asked if I wanted to join him for dinner. He was out exploring all afternoon. I really wanted to say yes, but I told him I was afraid I would just spoil his fun so I would stay in for the rest of the night. "But you are every time welcome!" he insisted.

When I returned inside with my bread eaten and my tea finished as required, Renate shuffled me into the dining room and made me sit at the large U-shaped table with the other pilgrims who were well into their evening meal. "You eat more," she said. She brought out another big cup of tea and four more pieces of bread. Everyone else was eating lentil soup and none of them spoke English, but they all understood. I looked like I'd been hit by a car and I was served breadcrumbs for dinner!

They all yelled at me in Italian, French, Korean, and German that I had to finish. It was quite funny. No one spoke the same language, but we playfully talked with body language. The charming man next to me recognized me as Italian and I had to embarrassingly explain that I'm an American Italian, which means- with the exception of my nose and my temper- I've lost my heritage almost completely. He was very sweet, though, and spoke in broken English.

I didn't finish my bread, but I saved it for tomorrow. When dinner was over, we were told we had to do our own dishes. All the men jumped up and insisted they would clean. They playfully threw all the women out of the kitchen and we visited until the dishes were done. It was a nice end to a rough day.

At 9:45pm, Renate offered to take people on a short walk to see some highlights of the small town. Nikolai had just gotten back and we were chatting in the kitchen, so we went together. We saw trees that were over a hundred years old, rows of national flags on a hill, and the beautiful sunset over Ponferrada, the town I'll walk to tomorrow. While we sat quietly watching the sunset, Niko told me he was very sorry, but he took me to the wrong albergue. The one his friends recommended was further down the road.

"But I think this is a good experience for you …" he explained defensively but with a nervous smile. I'm pretty sure he was about to say, "Because you're normally really spoiled," but I cut him off. It was a really good thing I was feeling better! Actually, I recognized that he put up with me all day, so how could I be upset with him? Plus, this place was actually pretty nice once I was feeling better. We laughed about how awful the day had been.

I hope tomorrow will be better. I'll meet Brian in Ponferrada, and get a hotel so he can get some sleep after his long trip. I was hoping to only have 6km to hike so I would have time to get a hotel, shower, and give my clothes a proper washing but as it is now, I have another 16km to go.

I just found my headphones! They were in my jacket pocket.

… well, I almost made it through the day without throwing up.

Cruz de Ferro

Entering Acebo

# CHAPTER 30

## DAY 28: 16KM FROM EL ACEBO TO PONFERRADA

—

## SAY HELLO, SAY GOODBYE

I slept like a log last night. With the exception of waking up once to throw up, I slept better than I have in weeks. According to poor Nikolai, who didn't get much sleep, the woman in the bed next to me snored louder than anyone we've shared a room with, but I didn't hear a thing. In the morning I awoke to opera music coming from downstairs. It sounded so beautiful. I think I may update my alarm clock when I get home. It was so peaceful to wake up to those sounds. Then I was smashed in the face with a pillow about ten times. I'll give you one guess who that was. I'd become accustomed to pillow bashings and apparently I was not exempt from them just because I had been sick the night before. I ripped the pillow from his hands, nearly pulling him out of his top bunk, then I curled up with it and snoozed for 10 more minutes.

I had more chamomile tea and hard bread for breakfast, and we headed out. Prior to leaving, I decided it was a good time to inspect my pack and determine if there were items I could discard. I realized that much of my first aid gear was no longer needed. Since I have been blister free for several days, I could donate some of the pads and antiseptic. I also got rid of the jar of Vicks Vapor Rub I had purchased. I stopped using it only after a few days of trying it. I had no problem finding someone who was interested in taking it off my hands though. As I explained before, you'll find that there are two camps of people - those who swear by vaseline on the feet and those who swear if you don't get blisters by slathering cream on your feet, you're lucky. I'm now in the latter camp. I believe that the best way to care for your feet is to take off your shoes and socks regularly, allowing them to bask in the sun and air. So I was happy to donate my Vicks.

It was a very brisk morning. Even with my coat on, I was chilly. Nikolai must have been freezing because since he was out of clean clothes, he was resigned to wearing his swim trunks. The walk to our first stop was unusually fast. I was feeling great. I was so excited to see Brian and thrilled that I was feeling better. I even started feeling hungry for the first time in two days which was a really good sign.

The walk itself was tough, though. It was a continuation of yesterday. Downhill on rocks and slate. Every step was carefully calculated. I have no idea how I did it yesterday while sick. I'm so glad I decided to stop when I did. Apparently, we climbed more yesterday and today than we did in the Pyrenees, which I find shocking. I struggled so much more in the Pyrenees, but I guess it's because I'm in better shape now. Even being sick yesterday, it wasn't as hard as my first two days on the Camino.

Nikolai's knees were really bothering him on the way down the mountain. He wouldn't admit it but I've been walking with him for three weeks. I could tell just from the sound of his footsteps that something wasn't right. It was only after we finished hiking for the day that he admitted he was really hurting. I've learned over the weeks that for whatever reason, he never expresses when he needs something. This is a new experience for me. My husband is a strong verbal communicator and I never have to guess what he needs or wants, so hiking with someone who rarely speaks up created a new challenge for me. I had to learn to sense when my partner needs something and find creative ways to help without appearing to actually be helping.

So, although I was feeling fine to continue walking, I told him I needed to rest my feet, knowing that he would stop and rest with me. I hoped the stop would give his knees a bit of a break. I used this same tactic when we were hiking with Ginger and Drennan, too. I knew Nikolai was hungry, but he would never burden the whole group by asking them to stop for him. So I told everyone I needed to eat and of course they all agreed to stop with me. It's a simple thing, but it's also one of the few things I could do to be helpful.

We stopped for breakfast two or three towns into our walk since we were making such good progress. As we were sitting at the bar waiting to order, we ran into a German man named Uli who we have seen multiple times on the trail. I was admiring his Camino bracelet. When he saw me looking at it, he took it off and handed it to me, "for the lady." I couldn't believe it. He just handed it over. A Camino gift! We sat with him for breakfast along with some other Germans alongside a beautifully maintained lot of grass and a stream. I took in deep slow breaths, enjoying the smell of freshly cut grass.

We walked the rest of the way into Ponferrada with Lio, a German woman who lives in Switzerland. Lio and Nikolai walked a bit ahead of me chatting away in German while I listened to my music and lagged behind. At one point, Nikolai started walking back towards me and then veered off the path towards a tree. I called out to him jokingly, "you can't pee there. We can see you." He jumped up into the tree and disappeared between the branches. A few seconds later he jumped down from the tree and brought me a handful of cherries. How sweet! Another Camino gift! He knows how much I've enjoyed cherries along the way. I hadn't even noticed that I was passing a beautiful cherry tree. We enjoyed our fresh cherries and then he sped up again to walk with Lio the rest of the way into town.

The three of us had lunch together once we reached Ponferrada. Lio wanted us to join her to see the Knights Templar castle that was in view across the street from where we had lunch, but I knew this was something Brian would really want to see, so I told her I wanted to wait for him. She understood and moved on without us. I hope I see her again. I really liked her.

Nikolai and I then walked the entire stinking town looking for my hotel which we learned much later was literally 200 meters from the restaurant where we just ate. I'm not sure what happened. Nikolai is usually a great navigator but he seemed really off his game today. When it was clear that he wasn't in any state to find the hotel and he had us wondering like Moses in the desert, I stopped, pulled out the map and figured out how to get to the hotel. "What's with you today?" I teased him. I didn't actually mind though. We got a great tour of the town.

My room was pretty basic and unimpressive but I didn't mind. "Are you sure you're going to be ok here, Theresa? This hotel isn't five stars." Nikolai teased me as he peered into the room before leaving. Very funny. The double doors opened into the Ponferrada Plaza, so I kicked my feet up on the banister and basked in the sun as I watched people pass by. It's Friday and kids were just getting out of school. This place would be jumping with people soon. I FaceTimed with my mom for a bit while Nikolai headed for his albergue. We met up again just before 3:00pm so we could walk to the train station to get Brian.

The 20-minute walk to the train station felt awkward. Nikolai was quiet and distant as he is when something is bothering him. I kept asking him if everything was ok and told him he was acting "different." That's a word he understands. But he insisted he was fine. As I sat patiently on a bench awaiting Brian's arrival, Nikolai paced back and forth on the train platform. Finally, he stopped and sat beside me.

"Why am I being different?" he asked. I didn't know what to say. I just knew he wasn't being himself. Before I could even respond, the train came screeching into the station. Nikolai got up and walked towards the train looking for Brian.

Dozens of people streamed out of every train exit when it stopped. I eagerly looked for Brian. It was so wonderful to see him after four weeks. I spotted him in the crowds and rushed in for some long overdue hugs. It's amazing how much you miss affection from someone who loves you when you've gone without it for so long. This has been such a long journey and all the emotions of it flooded me the moment Brian scooped me into his arms.

I introduced the guys but it was as though they already knew each other. I had FaceTimed Brian multiple times, so they had spoken to and seen each other before. Brian told us all about his travel adventures as the three of us walked back to the hotel. We agreed to meet later for dinner.

The next few hours were spent getting Brian settled in. He was exhausted and dehydrated from his long trip. He showered, took a nap, repacked his backpack, etc. Around 7:00pm, Nikolai showed up at our hotel with Tina, who was staying in his albergue. I haven't seen her in days but it feels like weeks! We would all have dinner together. Since our hotel was right on the plaza, we didn't have to walk far to find a place for drinks outside and then a second place for dinner.

While Tina and Brian were getting acquainted at dinner, Nikolai told me he was thinking he would keep hiking tomorrow (while I plan to take a zero day so Brian can catch up on sleep). "Is this ok with you?" he asked.

The question made me sad. Of course I didn't want him to go. We always talked about walking into Santiago together. I didn't fully understand his sudden need to leave and I could tell by the way he asked that we will not be walking together again. I assume he grew tired of walking with me. I always did fear that I was quite a burden on him - always injured or sick, always walking slowly and yesterday was the worst. Now that my husband is here, I think he can take comfort in leaving me behind knowing I won't be walking alone. I can't tell anyone how to walk the Camino though. I couldn't ask him to stay with me anymore.

"Sure," I said. And that was the end of the discussion.

It was great getting to know Tina better. We ran into each other a couple of times on the Camino, but we only hung out once in Carrión de Los Condes, the night I had to go to the doctor to get bandaged up and when I got sick. After spending more time with her now, I feel like I have a friend I'd like to visit in Munich. It's amazing how quickly you bond with people.

Brian commented later that evening that he could tell Tina was in a very reflective state on her Camino because the dialog with her tonight was very philosophical. I was hoping to keep the discussion light and fun but you never know what you'll get on the Camino. Instead, we debated everything from love to war. She spoke of the deep realizations she's been having while walking. She explained that she's been single for a while now and while she has been happy with that in the past, seeing all the couples on the Camino, has made her realize that she would like a companion in her life.

She seemed sad about being single now. Nikolai protested that finding love on the Camino was a bad idea. He told her she should focus on herself and not be distracted by love. I argued that she wasn't saying she wanted to find love on the Camino and assured her that there's nothing wrong with wanting a partner in life. She deserves to be with someone wonderful and I hope she finds her match one day soon.

We debated this for a while before the conversation shifted to more worldly issues. Nikolai explained that he's learning that regardless of where people are from around the world, we're all essentially the same. He wondered why there are wars when we all have the same wants and needs. Brian interjected that wars would end if all new world leaders were required to experience a long-distance hike. It would destroy the notion that people from different backgrounds or with different belief structures are somehow less valuable.

Tina also talked a lot about her Camino family that consisted of Thorsten and Marco, the two amazing men who helped me while I was sick in Carrión de Los Condes. She was telling me how they walked together for two weeks and they stay in touch always now. She spoke so highly of them and I asked her to say hello to them for me. She sent a picture of me to them right then and there and they responded. I was glad I had the chance to reach out to them one more time.

As she talked about how much her Camino family meant to her, I felt this deep emptiness and sadness creeping into my chest. Today was my last day hiking with Nikolai. We knew each other for a month and we were inseparable for three weeks. We walked over 200 miles together but suddenly, he would be gone. We never said a word about it, though.

Tina commented multiple times throughout the night that it must be so hard for us knowing that we'd say goodbye tonight. She explained that she walked with her friends for only a portion of the time we spent together and she is heartbroken they are gone now. The truth stung, but Nikolai seemed unfazed as he sat quietly, interested only in his meal.

With nothing more than a quick hug and a flippant "I'll see you in a few days," after dinner, we parted unceremoniously. I tried to be okay with that. I've had to say goodbye to a lot of people on the Camino. I could do it again. I made it all the way back to the hotel when my tough facade melted into a puddle of tears. My heart felt heavy and it ached terribly. I clenched my chest, curled into a ball, and cried. My ever-so-loving husband tenderly picked me up and held me.

"This is going to hurt for a long time," he said. He understands the loss someone experiences when they say goodbye to their trail family. He said goodbye to his own trail family nearly a year ago, and I know he still misses them immensely. As much as Nikolai's been a part of my life this last month, he will soon be nothing more than a distant and cherished memory. And that hurts like hell.

Despite being jet lagged and exhausted, Brian hand washed all my clothes so I wouldn't have to wait until morning to go to a laundromat. I found that I am not good at ringing out my clothes thoroughly enough to be dry the next day so I use machines whenever I have the option. But Brian always takes such good care of me.

While I am disappointed I had to say goodbye to my previous hiking partner, I am also overwhelmed with the excitement that Brian is finally here. I've anticipated this for weeks, and now that I've seen my share of Spain I'm excited to sit back and watch him explore the things he is most interested in.

Ponferrada plaza from my room

Knight's Templar castle

# CHAPTER 31

## DAY 29: ZERO DAY IN PONFERRADA

—

## HIKER'S LIMBO

Last night we slept with our balcony doors open to the plaza. I didn't realize that probably wasn't the best idea for Brian. I've become accustomed to sleeping through the all-night partying and then the street cleaning crew that comes through after, but poor Brian isn't used to the noise yet. He was up all night despite being so tired from his long trip. Tomorrow night we will close the doors. It made me realize that he's in a very new place and I've actually learned a lot along the way. I'm going to have to take good care of him.

Ponferrada is an okay town. I can see why the guidebooks recommend just walking through. With the exception of the Knights Templar castle, there is very little to see and do here. A couple of things made this town different from others. There's more graffiti here than other towns (which I actually find artistic most of the time), and I've seen more cars here than anywhere. The dogs also run off leash here, but don't seem to pose a problem. This is definitely more of a city than most places on the Camino.

We checked out the castle first, of course. It was cool, but kind of anticlimactic when we saw the real remains of the actual castle which was a small pile of rubble. It made me wonder what we just spent an hour touring. It was all in Spanish, so what would I know? Actually

I find the history of the Knights Templar extremely fascinating and I read about it before coming here, which I'm really happy I did. Otherwise I think the experience wouldn't have been as cool as it was.

Brian and I took our time walking through the castle, sitting on the stone benches, looking at the views of Ponferrada from up high and sharing stories about what we learned about the Knights Templar, the Spanish Inquisition, St. James, and the gnostic gospels. I know that I will see and experience more on this trip now that Brian is with me. He loves history and he doesn't like to miss a thing. He will point out every building, every shrub, every interesting thing he knows about along the way.

We also spent some time hanging out in the plaza as the crowds thickened a bit. It occurred to us eventually that we were amidst some kind of demonstration. We never found out what it was for, but it appeared to be pretty peaceful. We took our cue from the police. As long as they looked relaxed, we didn't mind staying. This place cracks me up, though. Even the demonstrators have limited energy and ambition. As soon as siesta began, they tore down and went out for drinks. The protest was over as soon as it began.

I've been in limbo today. Not hiking on a perfect hiking day and seeing other pilgrims pass by leaves me feeling lost. I also have this sense that the Camino experience I had before is over and I'm waiting for a new one to begin. I'm so happy Brian is here, and I'm really looking forward to walking with him, but in the meantime this one day off makes me feel like I'm wasting away.

That's normal for zero days though. I felt like this in León. The feeling will pass. The other reason for my uneasiness is because I'm no longer with any of my original hiking people. I feel like I've lost my old friends and I'll have to forge new relationships all over again, and I get the sense that'll be harder now. We are nearing the last 100km of the trail, which is considered the official Camino. To get "credit" for hiking the Camino, you technically only have to walk the last hundred kilometers from Sarria to Santiago. So there will be far more people on the trail from here on out. But people who hike 500 miles have very different intentions than people who hike 60. I can't explain it, but the crowds are very different and I find that I can relate much more to the long-distance hikers. Also, the atmosphere is changing from loving and caring closeness to tourism and commercialism. It makes me very uneasy, indeed.

That said, while we were sitting in the plaza, I saw Jenny, who was hiking with Nancy, another woman I met several times! They must have lost their path because we weren't actually on the Camino. I was so happy to see familiar faces. I introduced them to Brian and asked about all the others. Apparently, some of the crew I hiked with, including Ginger and Drennan, was not far behind. Staying a day in Ponferrada may just be the zero day needed to see all those familiar faces again as they all catch up. The possibility lifted my spirit!

I'm really enjoying watching Brian take in Spain for the first time. He's having similar experiences I had a month ago. Everything is amazing and confusing at the same time. It's nice to experience the country all over again through someone else's eyes. He keeps asking, "Is this how it always is?" He wants to be fully immersed as soon as possible!

Siesta time! For the first time I actually followed Spanish time. We strolled around and then took a nap in the middle of the day! It was perfect, too, because that's when it started raining.

Once we awoke nice and refreshed, it was perfect timing again for drinks and tapas to hold us over until dinner, which wouldn't be until 9:00pm. The evening was wonderful. Not only did I run into several people who I walked through the Pyrenees with (Misha and Pam!), but there was live music and fantastic food and drinks. I'm finally getting to share this amazing experience with the man I love. It's priceless.

We went to a very nice restaurant Brian found, Taberna San Andres. The owner was very sweet and seemed to speak every language his customers did. He explained to us that he grows all of his vegetables in his backyard and then gave us a free shot of Galician liquor. We had a fantastic time.

View of Ponferrada from the castle

# CHAPTER 32

## DAY 30: 25KM FROM PONFERRADA
## TO VILLAFRANCA DEL BIERZO
—
### BRIAN'S FIRST DAY ON THE CAMINO

What a great day for hiking, through and through. It's amazing how easy this has become for me after all the body and mind struggles I had to work through to get to this point. Today was cool and it occasionally sprinkled, which was refreshing during the heat of the day. I was so thrilled because this is Brian's first day walking and I want it to be perfect. The Camino has been such a spiritual journey for me and I want it to be just as wonderful for him. We had a lot of fun learning how to walk together. I have been walking for a month, so my pace is pretty much set. I'm accustomed to walking side by side with my partner in near silence.

Brian, on the other hand, is bursting with excitement and walks much faster than me. He walks ahead and comes back to me, walks ahead and comes back to me, all the while pointing at everything and talking about everything on his mind. He reminds me of an off-leash puppy. He is so cute. He is also super strong. I've always been impressed with how easily he carries his pack and marches forward. I hope I'll be able to keep up with him. He has boundless energy.

One thing I should mention, though, is having him enter the hike more than halfway through does present some challenges. My energy levels have slowly dropped over these weeks as I've had time to reflect and center myself. Brian on the other hand is thrilled about his new adventure. Several times throughout our first day together, I felt like his language and demeanor were abrasive and sometimes even aggressive. Of course, he wasn't saying or doing anything wrong, but for some reason, his energy seemed to be too much for me. I would ask him to calm down or not talk so swiftly. We had to adjust to being together again.

He noticed some things about me. He said he could tell I was a seasoned hiker now by how fast I recovered from inclines. I'd be out of breath by the time I reached the top, but unlike other hikers who are just starting, I don't stop for a moment at the top. I keep walking and have my heart rate back to normal in no time. That's not something I noticed about myself. He also said he is impressed with my ability to remove my coat, put it in my bag, and put my pack back on without breaking stride. I'm sure these skills are useless elsewhere but they make me feel like a badass out here. But most importantly, I feel like I have finally joined the ranks of my husband and our friends who are long-distance hikers. I'm one of them, and I love that Brian and I have this in common now.

It was a great stretch of walk for Brian's first day because it was an easy hike with cafes every 3km! It is crazy how densely packed the stops were in the beginning. I think they're becoming more frequent because more hikers are joining the trail at this point. We are quickly approaching Sarria, where the official 100km of the Camino begins. We walked right past many of the cafés since my feet were cooperating and Brian doesn't need to eat constantly. That's another important factor to take into consideration when hiking with someone. I went from hiking with someone who has a dangerously fast metabolism and has to eat every 40 minutes to someone with the slowest metabolism ever and only needs to eat twice a day. We're just not stopping as frequently as I did earlier in my hike.

We were walking through one town when an elderly man flagged us down tirelessly. We walked over thinking he needed help, but he just wanted to let us know that we were passing a church and should stop in. I couldn't tell it was a church from the outside so I was glad he let us know. We stopped in, took a couple of pictures, and said a prayer before continuing on. I noticed that for Brian, this was just a cool place to tour, but for me, these churches have great significance and I feel the need to pay my respects in as many as I can. Everyone's Camino is very different though and I wonder what the churches will mean for Brian. I gave the man a couple of euros and he stamped our Camino passports.

Around lunch time, we hit another town. There were a few nice-looking restaurants we wanted to stop in, but we were not getting a friendly vibe at all. The locals wanted nothing to do with pilgrims. They acted as though we were invisible and even though we were carrying heavy packs, we had to step off the sidewalk to let others pass by. So we kept walking until we found a restaurant with a pilgrim's menu. I assured Brian that most locals are very accepting of pilgrims.

I don't know if I've mentioned the pilgrim's menus, but while they are easy to order from and pretty filling for the low price, after several weeks of the same menu, they aren't super appetizing. They try to Americanize the menu by adding grease, fat, and sugar, and you generally get the same selection of meals regardless of where you go. The menus have been destroying my stomach these days (I live on Imodium now), but we didn't feel we had a better choice in this town. I ordered the spaghetti because I never learn. I love spaghetti even when it's bad and if it's an option, it's mine regardless of how sick it makes me later. Today's dish actually wasn't bad, but it's hit or miss with these places.

Brian ordered a massive dish of *pulpo* (octopus), which is not only very popular in this part of the country but also a special dish between the two of us. I ordered octopus on our first date. I was afraid he would think I was weird, but I had never been to a restaurant that served octopus before so I took a chance and ordered octopus. Brian asked me, "Do you usually order the weirdest thing on the menu?" Somewhat defensively I said yes. Fortunately for me, he thought that was pretty cool. So now we always order octopus when it's an option.

The view today was one of the most beautiful I've seen on the Camino so far. The weather contributed to how spectacular it was, too, because the sun was shining but the sky was bursting with dark rolling clouds all day. We walked up and down rolling hills and passed beautiful vineyards. We are passing through the Bierzo region, which consists of villages tucked between mountains. The placement of the mountains themselves create microclimates that are ideal for vineyards. Brian and I stopped frequently to take pictures.

We reached Villafranca del Bierzo in record time and were feeling great. The town was adorable! It was a mix of old falling-apart buildings and super-updated buildings that still maintain their old charm. Many of the houses were built right into the sides of the mountains which gave the town a cool feel. If I lived somewhere along the Camino, I would choose Villafranca.

Heading into town, we came across an albergue with a symbol with an A and a T. It was identical to the official Appalachian Trail symbol. Brian got so excited. "We have to stay here!" he exclaimed. So we entered the beautiful Leo albergue and asked for two beds. As a bonus, the *hospitalero* was gorgeous. Brian was quite smitten. He asked her about twenty questions upon arrival, of which only five were actually relevant to anything. But this is Spain. What can I say? The people are beautiful. I still had to tease him a bit when he was done. He couldn't wipe the smile off his face long enough to deny anything.

Today, I learned the benefit of traveling on the Camino with your husband when it comes to albergues. We were able to combine our money power and drastically improve our room arrangements. Not that the arrangements have been horrible at all; I have come to enjoy the community feel you get when you share a room with lots of strangers. And the beds are usually fairly comfortable.

But tonight, we got a tiny room all to ourselves, with a super modern feel to it. Granted, we still had bunk beds, but who cares? We each had our own shelf, locking cabinet, wall outlet, and overhead light. Super cute, too. The albergue had a nice warm, welcoming fire which was nice since it was raining by the time we made it in and we were starting to chill a bit. The showers and bathrooms were also super modern and clean! I took a nice long shower. The only complaint I would have is that the showers had no privacy. The glass walls were only slightly frosted, but I was fortunate enough to have the whole bathroom to myself the entire time. Plus, I took such a hot shower that the steam provided plenty of cover for the modesty in me.

By 5:00pm we were showered, had done our laundry, had adequate Wi-Fi time, and were ready to see the town. It was cold, windy, and pouring by then, and most pilgrims were hunkering down, but the town was too unique to miss and we were excited to explore Spain together. So we pulled out our ultra-light umbrellas and hit the streets. I told Brian how much I appreciated him telling me to pack an umbrella. It's my favorite item!

First, we visited the botanical gardens and the town plaza. These are unique in every town. Then, we just strolled around looking at the old architecture and all the artwork built within the walls. It wasn't long before we wanted dinner. I've learned to ask the locals where they eat so, before we left the albergue, I asked the beautiful Maria where she eats. She recommended two great places. We ended up at El Casino and it was wonderful! We watched the soccer game on TV and drank our wine with our meals.

Brian's first day on the Camino

Even the graffiti is friendly

# CHAPTER 33

## DAY 31: 30KM FROM VILLAFRANCA DEL BIERZO TO O'CEBREIRO

—

### ON HORSES

We were the first ones up this morning, rising at 6:00am. The noisy Asian kids who were up late last night were still sound asleep when we left. I've got my morning routine down to 15 minutes. Brian is still working out his routine, so it took him a bit to get going. You have to develop a system for pulling every little thing out of your pack and then repacking it exactly the way you had it. It takes a few days to get the hang of it. I waited patiently by the warmth of the fire in the dark hallway. I'll miss this albergue. It's beautiful.

It was cold when we left and I wished there was a way to camel up on the cool air that I would be craving once the sun came out later. There were two routes to choose from this morning. One added a couple miles to the trip and had a very steep incline, but hikers are rewarded with beautiful views of Villafranca below. The other route was a more subtle road walk that followed a rushing river. We opted for the rushing river. At first I thought we had made a mistake, until I saw the beautiful valley we were passing through and one of the best trout fishing streams I've ever seen. The sound of the rushing water and sight of the foam made me miss my fly fishing rod. We talked about how cool it would be to have our rods with us. Brian had brought one for the last section of the AT and thoroughly enjoyed catching his dinner in the hundred- mile wilderness.

It's interesting how most people are super friendly, but others are not remotely interested in talking. The culture here on the Camino is very friendly and open. It's customary to strike up a conversation with strangers when you run into them. *Where did you start? Where are you finishing? How are your feet? Where are you from? Where are you staying tonight?* These are the common questions. Almost always, you find something in common there and a natural discussion emerges.

But occasionally you get through all those questions (or sometimes only halfway through), and realize that the other person has no interest in talking. I ran into a woman who was from Alexandria, Virginia. When I told her I used to live there, she wasn't remotely phased. Yesterday, on the other hand, I ran into a woman from the same city. When I told her I used to live there, it provoked a ten-minute conversation with lots of smiles and hand motions. You never know what to expect from people. I love finding out though.

I'm so proud. Some Spanish guys just walked by and said hello. I had very little interaction with them, but they said they were surprised I was American because the little bit of Spanish I did know sounded so authentic. They thought I was Spanish. Yay!

Dear God, even the garbage men here look like models. I wish I got a picture. It was hilarious. A man rode by on the back of his garbage truck in his fleece turtleneck, waved at me and said, "*Hola*" somewhat flirtatiously.

Brian just looked at me and said, "Don't even say it." Wasn't gonna.

I hadn't noticed, but Brian was the one to point out that this area must be known for its hunting and fishing. There were fishing signs all along the streams and all the bars had taxidermied animals.

Somewhere along the way, we ran into an awesome trail family. I was listening to my music through my headphones when I heard a very noisy group coming up from behind me. At first I thought perhaps I should remove them and be more social, but I decided against it. As it turns out, it was my headphones that sparked up a conversation that would form new friendships.

One of the three people asked me what I was listening to, and I said I have every kind of music. "Oh! Do you have Bob Marley?"

Why, yes, I do! They asked if I would play it loud for them. So I played "Three Little Birds" and we all sang along as we hiked together. It was so much fun and so spontaneous. We learned that Vito and Marco are from Italy and they met CiCi who is German. Vito was the sweetest, most talkative guy. He said he started his Camino three days ago in Astorga and hoped to walk to Santiago by Sunday. He would then take a bus to Finisterre where he would see the ocean for the first time in his life. How exciting for him!

He talked all about how emotional the Camino is and how it's only been three days for him. He said he couldn't imagine the experiences I've had over the last month. I can't believe them myself! We walked together and talked for several miles, but then had to separate because Brian and I hadn't taken a break in several hours. Brian's feet aren't broken in yet and he was starting to have some issues. We hoped we'd run into each other again. Either way, we exchanged names and numbers so we could find each other on WhatsApp. I had never heard of the app before, but it's very popular in Europe and I use it all the time now to keep in touch with my new friends.

Brian's been struggling today. He says it's because he brought the wrong shoes for so much road walking, and that may be a contributing factor, but I think he's just experiencing the same issues we all deal with in the beginning. Your body needs days or even weeks to break itself in. He's having foot pain and chafing just as I did when I first started. Interestingly, all those issues seem to work themselves out over time. I haven't had any problems in several days. My feet have been cooperating and I never feel tired, so I need fewer breaks. I just go. I almost forgot how many issues I've had along the way because everything seems to be working as it should be now. My body fell in line, finally. I'm going to have to be patient with Brian as he breaks himself in.

I think he is also having trouble managing his expectations. I don't think he was expecting to be walking on a road for the majority of the day, and that was a real demoralizer for him. He's accustomed to walking in the woods on a loosely defined path. I felt bad because there's not much I can do about that. Yesterday was amazing, but some days are not as spectacular as others. I wish I could give him whatever it is I have that makes me so content with how things are. I've walked through all kinds of environments and while some are better than others, as long as it's not pouring down rain or blazing hot, I'm happy. We've been blessed with amazing weather lately.

But as I've learned before, the Camino provides. Just as Brian was feeling at his lowest, there was a big spray painted sign that said, "Do you need horses?" Why, yes, we do need horses! Finally, something I could do for my husband!

I called the number immediately and spoke to the nice man on the other end. Fortunately for me, he spoke English. About three towns away, this guy has several horses that he's been working with for years. He takes people up and over the next mountain and into town. This world is so simple. He told me he would be back in his town in about three hours, so to wait for him. I didn't give him a name or anything. We just started walking and had faith that we would find our way.

Sure enough, after about an hour and a half of walking (and the time we spent having a great outdoor lunch) we arrived in Las Herrerias and stopped in the store to ask for directions. I ordered a drink and a banana as the guy explained how to find the horse farm. It was right up the street. I called the horse owner again and let him know we were there. He asked us to enjoy our snacks and to wait for him to return in an hour. No problem. We basked in the sun and talked to the nice store owner down the road.

That's when I realized I left my puffy coat behind somewhere. As the day warmed up, I must have removed my coat at one of our stops. I know exactly which stop it was, too, because it was the one and only time I did not look back to make sure I didn't leave anything behind, something I always do. I remember telling myself that I should look back, but I was chatting with Brian and didn't think twice about it. I was so sad to have lost my puffy. I don't usually get attached to inanimate objects, but that coat got me up and over the Pyrenees Mountains. It was symbolic for me and I had lost it.

By the time the horses arrived, three other pilgrims stopped by and wanted rides. The owner told us he needed to let his horses rest for forty minutes, and to feed them. So he was kind enough to call ahead to the hostels where we all previously made reservations and let them know we would be arriving later by horse. He was so helpful. You could tell he's done this a thousand times because he eased all of our concerns. He also called a cab and had all our bags driven ahead of us since it would be difficult to carry them on our backs while riding horses. In the meantime, we all hung out at yet another bar on the back outside patio eating ice cream and getting to know each other.

When the time came to finally saddle up, three additional pilgrims arrived. One woman said she was from Cornwall. "Oh, my family is from Cornwall," Brian explained to our new friend. The woman began talking about the history of Cornwall and explained that many people from there were expert miners. Brian told her that makes sense because his grandfather and great grandfather were both coal miners in the United States. He wondered if it was a family occupation that had been passed on through the generations.

My horse was great, but she taught me today that I have control over nothing! She would stop and eat when she wanted, gallop when she wanted, fart when she wanted. I was just a passenger. I was very nervous in the beginning when Brian and I were sitting on our horses waiting for the others to saddle up. I was so anxious that the first time my horse made a movement, I blurted out, "It's MOVING!"

Everyone laughed at me. "Yes, it's an animal." I felt pretty silly. It's not like I've never been on a horse before! Brian also had a great deal of fun teasing me about how I looked. They provided us with shower caps and helmets which we were required to wear. They were too big on me of course so I looked absolutely ridiculous.

"I don't know whether to shoot you out of a cannon or ask for more mashed potatoes!" he shared helpfully. Brian also let me borrow his vest since it would get cold heading up and over the mountains. The vest, of course, was enormous on me. So I was quite a sight. I'm getting used to looking like a fool on the Camino, though.

Riding horseback through Spain on roads built before Jesus's time is a once-in-a-lifetime experience. What an adventure! Walking up steep, wet, rocky terrain is scary in itself, but doing it on a horse is so much scarier, especially when you can feel them slip on the rocks or trip. I spent the first two kilometers holding on for dear life, but eventually loosened up a bit. My horse would get it in her to trot. The first time she did it my feet flew out of the stirrups and I was terrified I would fall off.

After a while it wasn't quite as scary, but it was still nerve-racking when she would run up hills on the steep Spanish cliffs. Oh, and what a view! I tried to take pictures when I could, but it was difficult to pull my phone out while clinging to the horse. I'm hoping some of the others got good pictures they're willing to share.

The highlight of the trip was when we encountered a bunch of bulls coming down off the mountain from the opposite direction. The bulls were spooked by the horses and began charging towards us! Fortunately, the horses were very steady and they passed the bulls without incident. I was terrified, but Brian handled it so well. He learned to ride when he was a kid so he led the group while I was way in the back.

O'Cebreiro was another awesome town, but for totally different reasons than the last. This one was a small village of massive stone buildings with thatched roofs at the top of the mountain. It had a strong Celtic influence that called to Brian. By the time we went to dinner, we knew almost everyone in the bar. We've been meeting so many people along the Way that dinner was like a big family reunion between friends from the beginning and new faces from just recently.

After dinner, we experienced hiker midnight, which is when everyone goes to bed really early. By 8:30pm the little village was dead. It was a hard hike to the top of the mountain … unless you were on horseback. That said, I never realized how much of a workout horseback riding is. Oh, and my butt is so bruised! Clearly, I was doing something wrong.

Brian and I bought a few lightweight souvenirs in the gift shop, including a Camino sweatshirt for me since I lost my North Face puffy behind.

One final note: As I was lying in bed tonight, I found myself fiddling with my blue bracelet that I purchased weeks ago. It has all the names of the major stops on the Camino. Today the bracelet means more to me than it did when I purchased it. Each of these names has a significant memory associated with it now. I'm going to keep this bracelet for a very long time.

The Camino provides

# CHAPTER 34

## DAY 32: 20KM FROM O'CEBREIRO TO TRIACASTELA

—

## A TAD OF ENTITLEMENT

I feel like we are being chased by taxis. They're everywhere. The closer we get to Santiago, the lazier the pilgrims get. I know it's not my place to judge and everyone must hike their own Camino. I can even see the mild hypocrisy in my ways; after all, I took a cab to León when I was injured. But when you have your bags forwarded and you cab your way from town to town, you're essentially abandoning your spirit on the Camino. You cannot possibly embrace the Way of the Camino from a vehicle.

I'm noticing other differences too. Now, if we want a bed, we have to call ahead and reserve, whereas before you strolled into town with nothing more than a little faith that you'd find a bed. I'm so glad I have had a month to practice Spanish because this morning I had to call ahead and reserve a room for us. I explained that we are married and needed them to hold a private room for us for eight hours (which will give us plenty of time to hike there). I did pretty well! Of course now that I'm finally getting comfortable with Spanish, we are in the Galician region where people speak a completely different language.

I don't believe I've mentioned this before, but the hotels along the Camino are unlike hotels in most places. The Camino is such an accommodating place and hotel owners really know their market. They know that the majority of guests are probably sharing a room with a friend they met along the hike, so it is standard for the rooms to come with two twin beds. I was told that if I want a normal sized bed, I have to tell the person upon check in that I am married. It feels weird to offer up personal information to a stranger but I thought I would give it a try. We still ended up with a double.

The landscape was pretty cool today. As we were leaving town, we passed through a holloway. Here, the path has been beaten down by the millions of pilgrims who have walked the Way for centuries, so much that the path itself has sunken into the earth by about fifteen feet. It felt as though we were walking through a tunnel.

We walked with a variety of different people today. First, we walked a bit with a couple from Michigan who were section hiking the Camino. They had their bags forwarded. I noticed that even without packs, they needed more breaks than we did going up hills. They were fun to talk with for a while but I'm finding it harder and harder to find people who are walking the whole Camino and with all their own gear.

Brain and I separated for a while after meeting a great couple from New Zealand. The men blazed ahead while Anne and I brought up the rear. Partway through our long walk with them, we ran into an old local woman who made this wonderful sugar bread. Yum. A great midday snack. It was funny, because at first we thought she was a trail angel and we thanked her for the treat. But she yelled at us and told us we owed her money. Oops! We paid her and thanked her for the wonderful snack.

At one of our stops, I became painfully aware that I am now in the minority. All of these people came on tour buses and were clean and bright. Some semi-hiker "touragrino" wearing a Camelbak on his back and an iPod on his arm told me to make sure I keep my feet dry and to have a *Buen Camino*! I wanted to plant him six feet under. What does he know about hiking? He just started and his luggage is in a suitcase in some town three miles away.

I really miss my Camino friends. I miss my Camino family. Where are all the hikers in this sea of spoiled tourists? I'm trying really hard to be positive and to not feel so entitled. I'm failing miserably. I just keep praying for grace and patience as my Camino changes. I have to remind myself that the actions of others do not change my intentions or minimize my own accomplishments.

I just read a section of my John Brierley guidebook that was written specifically for me. It talks about the changes we will see in people on the Camino. It reads, "beware of signs of irritation at the intrusion on 'my Camino' - remember that many of the new arrivals may be nervous starting out and the last thing they need is aloofness built on a false sense of superiority. A loving pilgrim welcomes all they meet along the path with an open mind and open heart without judgement" ... shit. I've been out of line.

The hike today was a beauty and yet again we had a perfect day with regard to weather. There was some road walking, but mostly we hiked up and over mountains of pastures. We passed lots of happily grazing cows and horses.

Highlights: During second breakfast, Brian and I sat with a French guy who walked all the way from Le Puy-en-Vela, France. What this means is he walked nearly twice the distance I have (about 1,000 miles total). I realized that while I'm frustrated with the pilgrims who are entering the Camino from Sarria, he was probably frustrated with all the pilgrims who entered back in St. Jean-Pied-de-Port, France, where I began. It put things in perspective for me a bit.

Second breakfast was also fun because there was a beautiful border collie who hung out next to our table, hoping we would throw him some scraps. We joked about how some Camino books warn about the "vicious wild dogs" but all we've seen are friendly pups who are looking for love and affection. Brian is a huge animal lover so we spent some extra time there so he could play with the pup.

This dog was not wild though. He clearly belonged to someone. In fact, we got to see him work! As we were exiting town along the road, we saw two older women commanding the dog. The dog sprinted across the street and up a steep hill that sat alongside the road. The field was filled with fat, happy cows. We watched curiously as the women yelled commands at the dog and the dog herded the cows from one side of the field to the other. It was quite amazing to watch. What a brilliant pup!

Once again, the town we stayed in was awesome. I can take pictures but I really can't explain the unique charm that each of these villages bring. This one was cool because there were multiple restaurants with outdoor seating lining the one street the village had to offer. We said hello to all of our friends as we passed through to get to our hostel.

The hostel itself was great. Since I had called ahead and asked for a room, it's essentially a charming little hotel room.

After our shower and sending our clothes to be washed, we headed out to explore the town. That's another thing that's different now that Brian has joined me. I'm not hand-washing my clothes anymore or sitting around by the washer and dryer. Most of the places where we've stayed since he got here have a laundry service. For a small fee, someone will launder your clothes and when you return, they are folded neatly on your bed. I would normally be against using the service, but it's giving me more time to hang out with my husband and explore the towns. My Camino is definitely changing.

The first place we went to was church. I prayed and meditated until all my ugly thoughts and feelings had passed. Then we went straight to the bar for drinks and appetizers. While there, we decided to have dinner since we knew every single person on the street. It was an awesome evening. All the others were drinking heavily, something I personally stopped doing a while ago because it makes hiking the next day hell. Anyways, they all thought Brian and I were rock stars because Brian hiked the Appalachian Trail last year, and I was the only one who has hiked the entire Camino. We were invited to sit at multiple tables so we made our way down the street talking with everyone. Spending time with everyone loosened my attitude about the newest hikers. They're a good crowd just doing the Camino the best way they can.

O'Cebreiro

# CHAPTER 35

## DAY 33: 18KM FROM TRIACASTELA TO SARRIA
—
## THE BEGINNING OF THE END OF MY PILGRIMAGE

I was telling Brian this morning that I can't believe how much more coffee I drink here on the Camino.

"Do you think that's regular coffee you're drinking? How cute!" he said. He pointed out to me that I've actually been downing double shots of espresso. I had no idea. I thought *café con leche* was coffee with milk! I think that quantity of caffeine in real life would kill me. But here it's essential.

We ate breakfast at the hostel. We'd have a long climb ahead of us with no place to stop for food for a good 10km.

On our hike up the first ascent of the day, we passed a tiny little church for a town of ten, and carrot fields that grew along a rushing stream. There were multiple alternative routes on the Way today. We chose the route going up this time because we were feeling good. What a beautiful day - sunny and very cool. Perfect.

Brian chose to wear his kilt today, which generated a lot of interest. Everyone assumed he was from Scotland. After a while he stopped correcting them. One man kept telling him how beautiful he looked in his skirt. I would have thought he was mocking him if the man wasn't so sincere. Brian is a very confident man. He would rather feel comfortable than fit in, so he is not fazed by the stares or comments.

We only had a few stops today, but they were all interesting in some way. The first stop had nothing more than a picnic table and a vending machine in the middle of the woods. An extension cord ran for acres across a field to get to it. Everyone had to get pictures with it of course. It looked so unlikely sitting in the middle of a wooded lot. Then, shortly down the path on the way back down the mountain, we found a nice tiny bar where we had spicy empanadas. The café was so tiny, I don't think they actually make the food there. They must have it brought in from somewhere else. It was delicious!

All day long, the only thing we could smell was cow manure. It was everywhere - in the roads and in the fields. Some villages we passed through had happy cows trotting freely down the street and picking at the trees as they went by. They were free as birds, and they pooped everywhere.

My body is so programmed to go now. I have a continuous need to move forward at all times (granted, that could be the espresso). With the exception of our ice cream break, where I reclined in the shade during the hottest part of the day, I've had the urge to *go* all day . Even when we sat and ate, all I could think was *when do we move again*? And it's not that I love walking. I just have to. I can't even imagine what it was like for Brian to return from the Appalachian Trail after nearly seven months of walking. I have no idea how I'll adjust to work again, sitting for hours at a time. This has become my life now. I don't know any other way.

I've decided that even though we may not need to, we should stop as frequently as possible just to extend the Camino. Today, I got a snack at every stop. The new hiking group we run into frequently joked that they probably wouldn't recognize me if I wasn't eating all the time.

I keep forgetting that Brian hasn't had the same physical conditioning that I've had. He's always stronger and faster but for once, that's not the case. We came across a staircase of about 100 steps. I took it slow and steady like I always do. When I got to the top I turned around and poor Brian was resting halfway up. I didn't even realize the level of effort required until I saw him. I have to say it felt good to realize how strong I have become. I wish I could always be this strong.

By the time we reached our hotel in Sarria, it was super hot outside and the sun had sucked all the energy out of us. It was a two-star hotel that normally would make me cringe, but for the Camino it was extravagant. It had a bed, a toilet (with a seat and toilet paper), shade from the sun, and running water. I sat in the dingy chair and slept for an hour before doing anything else. The sun took everything out of me today. Brian, on the other hand, was eager to take a nice long shower.

Sarria was a bit of a bust for us. I was excited to get here because it marks the beginning of the end of the Camino. This is where most people begin, and it's only about a week's hike to Santiago from here. But there wasn't much to see. We had a negative experience with a restaurant owner. We couldn't seem to communicate with him and he stood in the streets yelling at us as if that would help. Then when the food arrived, it was far from perfect. I'd say it was the second worst meal I've had on the entire Camino. The first was in León (spaghetti of course) and I nearly threw up.

Then we walked to the castle, which was built in the 1400s. It's a landmark that inspired us to stop in Sarria rather than to continue on. Unfortunately, the castle was difficult to see from anywhere we were allowed to stand. There just wasn't much left of this beautiful old relic. We did, however, get to visit the monastery, which had some redeeming qualities. Brian took joy in pulling on the long rope to ring the bell and request access. Once inside, we walked around the cloister several times admiring the artwork in the walls and on the ground.

Then we found a delightful Italian restaurant where we enjoyed sangria and air conditioning. It felt like home for a moment. The two of us enjoyed our drinks and joked around without a care in the world. We spent the evening strolling around town and checking out the churches. Then we returned to the same Italian restaurant for dinner because it looked so good, especially in the sea of commercial pilgrim restaurants. We had told the owner we would be back for dinner the first time we were there and he was kind enough to reserve a table for us! We sat outside in the cool evening breeze and enjoyed a real Italian dinner. It was perfect.

The owner was such a nice man yet, he had a sad story. He explained that the town would not allow him to expand his outdoor seating area beyond a few feet from the building. The reason cited for this restriction was that larger emergency vehicles needed room to pass through the streets. That would make sense except, when we looked at every other restaurant in town, their seating areas clearly jetted out farther than this man's. When Brian pointed this out to the owner, the man said the real problem is that the town has been attempting to damage his business since he is the only non-Spanish owner. Such a pity.

As we were leaving the restaurant, we ran into a family of four we've seen a couple of times. They were walking through the streets looking for somewhere to eat. We told them the Italian place was fantastic and highly recommended it. We ran into them later in the evening and they were also quite pleased with the restaurant. They pledged to eat wherever we told them.

I'm glad we stopped in Sarria. Walking further in today's heat would have been a problem for both of us. Plus, I'm in no hurry to end my Camino. I only have about five more days to Santiago.

Speaking of Santiago, I got a text from Nikolai tonight. He made it to Santiago today! He hiked 107km in 22 hours! That's over 66 miles! I was very happy to hear from him. While we occasionally text to see how the other is doing, I spend portions of my days missing him. I told him I was sad he left, but I understood that he had to. He assured me that he enjoyed walking with me but needed some time to himself to think. I hope he found the mental clarity he was looking for during his long walks. Congratulations, *amigo*!

Vending machine in the middle of the woods

Monastery in Sarria

# CHAPTER 36

## DAY 34: 24KM FROM SARRIA TO PORTOMARIN

—

## NOT THE CAMINO I KNOW

Wow, the number of pilgrims on the Camino just exploded. They're everywhere. It is fun to see them all in various stages of readiness. Some people are here in full gear, ready to go, and others are hiking in jeans and cotton. Some are sporting their new hiking poles properly and some are over-exerting themselves by using them at the wrong length. Most are wearing cute little packs that you can tell they purchased because they were pretty and they make their butt look good.

Prices have skyrocketed and trust is gone. You now have to pay for your food and drink as soon as you order, rather than leisurely paying once you are done at the café. I ran into a woman from Canada who has also hiked from St Jean. I knew she was a long-distance hiker because the first thing she did was kick off her shoes and change out her socks. We talked for a bit about how difficult it is to adjust to the new way of the Camino. For both of us, what we miss most is the camaraderie between pilgrims, which just doesn't seem to exist anymore. Just like anywhere else in the world, on the Way the more densely populated an area is the more people are likely to behave like strangers. Later, I met a nice French guy who was also very saddened by the new Camino. We had a lot in common.

As we were exiting Sarria, we had to walk past an elementary school. It was a bit of a mess as we tried to walk around the waves of cars coming in to drop off their children. It occurred to me that it must be so frustrating to parents who have to wade through pilgrims on the streets every single day as they try to see their children off safely to school. I tried to stay out of their way and be as unobtrusive as possible.

Then we were chased by a stampede of school children for about three miles. They must have been on a Camino tour today. We tried to let them pass us, but they kept stopping to take breaks. Spanish children are as obnoxious as American children, in case you were wondering. That's at least true when they are in large groups. I have to say the Spanish children who are accompanied by parents are far better behaved than American children, though.

Highlight of the day: an old man trimming his rose bushes offered me flowers and a walnut and asked me in Spanish to please make a donation in his honor once I get to Santiago. I'll be sure to say a prayer for him and make a donation when I arrive in a few days. But I thought, how amazing is this man that 200,000 strangers walk past his yard every year and he is still kindhearted. It also made me wonder how many other women he's picked flowers for!

Today was a scorcher. Fortunately, the trees provided some shade for us most of the way. The scenery is looking more like New Hampshire here. Lots of pine-covered mountains. We stopped for drinks at a beautiful outdoor café with peaceful new age music playing. The band of children was just leaving so we knew it would be a nice stop. I kicked off my shoes, rested my head on the table and passed out for quite a while. When I awoke, I found Brian chatting it up with various people. This is one of the best parts of my trail experience, so I was happy to see him engaging, too.

An Irishman we kept running into along the way introduced us to a couple who used to live in Boston. They're here on a tour. We spoke to them for a few minutes before they headed on their way. They turned around and their poles were gone. Someone stole their poles. When I first began the Camino I was paranoid about my poles and umbrella being stolen, because I heard it was so common. But I soon learned that you could leave your gear anywhere and there was nothing to fear. Here we are now, only one stop after Sarria, where the Camino is most crowded, and someone's poles are gone. This is not the same magical Camino I know.

That said, at the same stop, an Australian guy walked by us with a feral cat on his backpack! He said the cat jumped on his pack and hitched a ride for a mile or so. When he reached the café, the cat jumped down like he'd reached his destination. You could tell the Australian was a bit sad to lose his new friend. He tried to coax the cat back onto his pack but the cat was no longer interested. It was a classic Camino moment that I was glad I got to be a part of.

Something grabbed my attention this afternoon. A cab rolled up and picked up only two of the four-person group we had been following. Something seemed different to me about the arrangement because they were clearly seasoned hikers. I recalled seeing two of them way back in Estella, and they were the family who we recommend the Italian restaurant to. I wondered if someone in their group was injured, but I was intrigued that they didn't all get in the cab together. Later we met with the two who were left behind. Susan and her daughter (from the States) began their hike in St. Jean. Their husband and other daughter joined them for the last portion of the Camino. But they found they walked at very different paces and were of different mindsets. They decided to continue the Camino separately. They still met in the towns every night but they found it very difficult to walk together.

This prompted a conversation between Brian and me about him

joining me for the end of my journey. For whatever reason, in the last few days, my adventure has turned from a spiritual journey into something that resembles a standard vacation. I don't know how much of that has to do with the fact that a) I've fallen into a bit of routine on the Camino, b) my husband has joined me, or c) because the Camino vibe is changing so dramatically. Whatever the reason may be, we agreed that Brian joining me more than halfway through the trip was difficult for both of us. We considered that perhaps it would be better if we hiked separate, but in the end there was just no way either one of us is willing to leave the other's side for any amount of time. That said, we both understood why the family chose to hike the Camino separate. It is the only way they can all enjoy their adventure.

Still, Brian and I have tons of fun together. He was cracking me up this afternoon. We were approaching the last big hill before the bridge over Portomarin and people were struggling with their knees. Brian explained to me the significance of downward hills and said the trick is to run down the hill and lean back so you don't fall. He then demonstrated the "proper" way to approach a hill by throwing himself down it at full speed. I couldn't stop laughing because some poor unassuming couple at the bottom of the hill turned around and watched in horror as a large man in a kilt, oversized hat, and bright orange shoes came barrelling towards them. They looked terrified.

His downhill demonstration worked wonderfully. However, he wasn't so fortunate later on. As we were crossing the busy bridge over the reservoir in Portomarin, not far from our destination, he got his leg caught on a sharp metal corner of the guard rail. He tore a pretty big chunk out of his leg. It obviously hurt a lot and he was bleeding everywhere, but he treated the wound as best he could right there and carried on like a soldier. I'm not sure I would have handled it so well.

Towards the end of our trip today, we took a nice long break complete with drinks, a nap in the shade, and ice cream. When we got started again, we were feeling good and refreshed. I was looking forward to getting into town and exploring the area with Brian. I actually enjoy that more than the hours of hiking!

So, I mentioned once before that the Camino is said to have three sections, one that exercises your body, one for your mind, and one for your soul. I think I struggled the most with the bodily exercise but that all worked itself out. I blew through the mind exercise walking across the Meseta with no trouble at all. But what I'm failing to understand now is how I'm supposed to work on my soul. I'm finding myself very distracted by all the changes on the Camino and I don't understand how this commercial environment is conducive to spiritual growth. I went from having a very personal journey to suddenly being bombarded with t shirts, postcards, and magnets. I guess I have a few more days to figure it out.

Speaking of t shirts, postcards, and magnets, as we were walking by a little hut filled with Camino paraphernalia, the man running the shop came outside and tried to coax us in. He promised all kinds of Camino goodies. He said we may be able to find these same items once we reach Santiago, but that they would be at least two euros more there. Brian told the man that for the extra weight he'd have to carry it for the next few days, he would gladly pay the additional two euros at the end of his journey. I think he was a little annoyed by the salesman.

I don't really have much to report on for the evening. We checked into our room, which was decent, and went out for dinner and drinks. Nothing eventful happened but we thoroughly enjoyed ourselves. My morale may be low throughout the day but I'm really trying to soak up every last minute of my time on the Camino. It's so close to being over and I'm just not ready to give it up yet. During dinner we sat outside and looked upon a church that had been relocated brick by brick in the

'60s. In fact, this entire town was relocated in the '60s, which was the biggest architectural salvage operation in all of Spain. Brian read all about it beforehand and was teaching me what he had learned. He showed me the numbers written on each brick, which was the guide they used to move the entire building.

A kind local gentleman

# CHAPTER 37

## DAY 35: 25KM FROM PORTOMARIN TO PALAS DE REI

—

### RUNAWAY COW

It was another intensely hot day. We spent a lot of time hoping for shade and swatting flies away. I also spent a lot of time thinking about my trip; thinking about what it's meant to me, how it has changed me, how I'm still the same, how this new Camino is affecting me. I've been dealing with a roller coaster of emotions these last few days. I'm sad that my trip is almost over, but at the same time, my destination is so close I can smell it ... so a lot of this feels pointless. I just want to blast through my last three to four days of hiking and get it over with. Santiago is drawing me in.

I'm so excited to reach Santiago de Compostela, but I'm also feeling a bit empty because I'll be finishing without any of the people I began with. We are scattered all over Spain at this point. This trip has been so profound and I don't want to forget or lose any of it.

I also don't want to go back to the routine of life back home. I don't understand how people can be so open, caring, and loving here, but so distant and reserved in the rest of the world. I've always struggled with the lack of connections people make in their daily lives. For example, I've lived in the same town and have worked in the same place for about eight years. I see the same people day in and day out. Yet I know nothing about them and they know nothing about me. This has always bothered me, and what's most bothersome is that others don't seem to mind at all.

I think people get so caught up in their lives, so caught up in themselves, that they completely miss the value of getting to know the people they see every day. Their priorities are different. They don't even know what they're missing by not finding how much they have in common with those around them. And then of course everyone spends their time feeling misunderstood and unappreciated. This has always been difficult for me to understand. I want to shake people and tell them they're wasting precious time! We don't live forever!

But who am I to tell someone what to do with their time? That's part of what I love about hospice. There, you are dealing with people who know their time is limited. Many people who are fortunate enough to have time to reflect back on their life realize the importance of connecting with those around them. They're stripped of all the bullshit and there's nothing but raw humanity. There's no worry that someone may not like you for who you are. There's no concern that you may look bad if you begin talking to a near stranger. There's no time to worry about those things.

It's similar here on the Camino. Our time here is limited, and we may not ever see our friends again, so we don't waste time with small talk. We jump right into what matters most. Ugh ... I'm just rambling now. That doesn't even come close to articulating what I'm actually thinking. Too much sun today, I guess.

The scenery is definitely changing. We are still passing through farm towns full of cows and manure, but we are now also passing through lush greenery along the mountainside. We walked through fern gardens that fondly reminded me of home. I'm starting to miss my home and my dog, Jersey.

Let's see, what else? We've been running into a Canadian named Don these last few days. He has a great story. He met and befriended a woman hiking the entire Camino once several years ago. Although she was from South Africa and lived thousands of miles away, they remained good friends for years. Recently she decided to take her son on the Camino for his 21st birthday. She and Don agreed to meet and do it again! So here they are, hanging out in Spain again. What a great story.

Don was struggling today though. He said his shoulders were bothering him a lot. It was clear from looking at his pack that it was riding entirely too low and the weight of his pack was pulling his shoulders down. He was slouched way forward and was holding the back of his pack up with his hiking pole. Unfortunately, he was not interested in advice. As soon as he told us his shoulders hurt, he insisted it was not his pack. We slowed our pace a bit to keep him in view just in case he was suffering from something more serious. Eventually we moved on, though, confident that he just wasn't wearing his pack right and knowing there was nothing we could do about it.

There is also a tour group we've been running into lately. They're a great group of folks and a lot of fun, too. They all know us as "the serious hikers," which I think is pretty cool. Talking with them, though, really highlights the different Camino experiences we are having. I love hearing about their hiking challenges. For example, yesterday, they arrived at their hotel around 2:00pm wanting nothing more than to go swimming, but they couldn't because their suitcases that were taxied forward were locked and their sister who had the key was still hiking into town. They had to wait two hours in the heat before they could get in the pool! I couldn't relate and I knew they wouldn't be able to relate to my blister challenges. It was a reminder that we all hike our very own Caminos. Every pilgrim's experience is very personal and very different.

Highlight of the day: as we were leaving one of our stops, we saw a baby cow walking down the road. She clearly didn't belong there, but there was no owner in sight. Several of us tried to surround the little cow to keep her from running while others looked for the owner. I walked around the building and saw a woman walking swiftly with a stick. I yelled "cow" to her but of course she didn't understand me. She started yelling something in Spanish. I forgot the word for cow so all I could think to do was moo at her and point in the direction of the cow! "Moooo!"

"*Gracias!*" She thanked me and started running. The poor baby cow was so scared and mooed at every person she came across, but the cars had her terrified and she would run in any direction she could regardless of how unsafe it was. One car stopped and put its flashers on but then a huge truck came barreling down the road and swerved around the car towards the cow! What the heck was he doing? I thought he was trying to hit the cow but it became apparent that the driver was somehow affiliated with the farm and he was just trying to block the cow. The driver jumped out of the truck and several people jumped on the baby cow. She made it back home safely.

Once we arrived in town, Brian really wanted to see an old church, *Iglesia Bomanica Vilar de Dones*, that was several kilometers out of town. So we actually did it. We took a cab. But it wasn't on the Camino! It was an alternate route! When we got there, we learned that the church was one of the oldest things near the Camino. It's a tomb for several Templar Knights and dates back to the 12th century. Pretty cool!

When we got back to town, we learned that our accommodations did not have laundry. Since we were out of clean clothes, that meant we would be spending our evening looking for some machines. We asked for directions to the laundromat, but failed horribly at finding it. We were hot and tired and in the end, I convinced Brian that we should walk into another albergue as if we were guests and just use their machines. It worked like a charm. The albergue was very nice, too. We hung out in the common area and greeted other pilgrims while our clothes were in the machines. I kind of miss staying in albergues, since lately we have been staying in hostels with private rooms.

Dinner was fantastic fun! Brian found a great non-pilgrim restaurant that served *pulpo* (octopus) to celebrate our anniversary. The service was great. The guy didn't speak English but my Spanish has really improved and ordering was a pleasant exchange. I translated for Brian and helped him order. We started with free tortillas, which were so tasty. Brian absolutely loves tortillas, by the way. Then we got to watch them prepare the octopus right in front of us. It was the best we've had so far in Galicia! Brian is so good at finding great restaurants!

We will be going to bed early tonight. Tomorrow will be a longer day.

Runaway cow

Water fountains are plentiful

# CHAPTER 38

## DAY 36: 30KM FROM PALAS DE REI TO ARZÚA

—

## GALICIA IS SPANISH FOR SEAFOOD

We intended to get up early this morning, but I didn't set my alarm so we slept until 7:00am. It was nice to wake up naturally, but that means we lost over an hour of early-morning hiking, which we would need on a day like today. It's been very hot during the day and this would be Brian's first 30km day. The morning was a great hike though. Our path was blessed with lots of shade and cool breeze. Along the Way we saw horse farms, cow pastures, and eucalyptus trees that filled the air with their scent. We also crossed another old Roman bridge.

Walking has become super easy for me. I no longer have any problems with my body, so that gives me plenty of time to focus on other things. I spend a lot of time deep in my head. When I'm not swimming in my own thoughts, though, I like to play games. For example, one game I play is to figure out where pilgrims started walking from.

If they have fresh sunburns and hiking boots, they just started in Sarria. There are a lot of pilgrims who started in Sarria. They are also all on a mission. They put their heads down and walk as fast as possible. It makes me wonder what they are getting out of the trip. They're not seeing much and they certainly aren't meeting all the great people on the trail. Many of us were like that when we started the trail, too. You feel like you're embarking on this insurmountable journey, so you thrust yourself forward thinking that's what you need to do in order to succeed. But eventually you learn to look up and enjoy your trip. It was around the eighth day when I learned that lesson for myself. The pilgrimage from Sarria will be much shorter, though, so I hope these new hikers learn to stop to smell the poppies sooner than I did.

About halfway to our destination, we stopped in Melide for lunch. The town is known for its octopus. As we were trying to decide where to eat, a man making octopus right on the street called us over to try his. It was great marketing because I was convinced I wanted to eat there. Brian teased me for being so easily swayed, but he humored me. We ordered more octopus and a huge plate of salted peppers. Yum. I also ordered a Coke. I'm not a big soda drinker at home but Coke tastes so much better here in Spain.

After lunch, we strolled through town feeling good. We were enjoying ourselves so much that we lost sight of those beautiful yellow arrows. We made the mistake of following a pilgrim we recognized for a bit. Eventually she turned around and said in broken English, "I hope you're not following me because I'm going to the *farmacia*." Oops. We were so far off course we had to admit to her that we were blindly following her. We all had a good laugh and then Brian and I headed in the right direction again.

For several weeks, I have been running into Lisa and Kathleen. The other day, Kathleen's husband Joe met her in Sarria to finish the hike with her just as Brian is doing with me. At that point, Lisa decided to give them room and continued on her own. We saw her several times today with her new Camino family. I overheard her talking to them at one of the stops. Apparently she had her bags forwarded to a different town from where they all planned to stop.

She asked them if they would be willing to wait for her to catch up in the morning so she could hike to Santiago with them, but they said no. I felt so bad for her. I know what it's like to feel left behind because I'm such a slow hiker, but I completely understand why the others said no. They have to hike their own hike.

Hours later, I ran into Lisa again and she told me she decided to pick up her bags and taxi to the next town where her friends are staying. She decided it was more important to stay with her friends than to walk every mile of the Camino. I told her I totally understand that, and I'm happy she will get to hike into Santiago with her friends. It also made me really grateful that I'm with my husband because I know I'll be hiking in with my best friend regardless of what day I get there!

The afternoon was extremely hot. We spent our time chasing shade like those giant Iraqi camel spiders, but there were large stretches across fields where we scorched in the open sun. I felt bad for the new hikers who are developing killer sunburns. I got through my sunburn phase weeks ago, so I'm charred to a crisp now and don't have much to worry about with regard to burning.

Brian's been doing a good job with the sunscreen and while he is very light skinned, he has avoided burning so far. He wears a long-sleeved shirt, which helps a lot. Actually, I noticed today that I have raccoon eyes from wearing my sunglasses all the time. I considered walking without my glasses for a bit to even out the tan, but then it occurred to me that I don't care. My vanity died about 450 miles ago.

During one of our stops, Brian checked the weather on Wi-Fi. It was 38 degrees Celsius. I know that I prefer walking in 20 degrees, 25 degrees is warm, and anything over 30 degrees is miserable. When Brian told me it was 38 degrees, I almost passed out. No wonder our progress was so slow. That's over 100 degrees Fahrenheit. We had to stop so many times just to get through the 30km.

One of the churches we passed along the Way was from the 11th century. I can't even process how old that is. The paintings and iron work were amazing.

Totally random note: it's getting much harder to go to the bathroom on the trail due to the number of people. It used to be so easy! Now I have to hunt for a private spot. However, it's evident that many people have found those private spots before me. The areas are littered with toilet paper. This is one of those differences between people who hike 500 miles and people who hike the final 60. Those who hike 500 miles don't use toilet paper because that's just extra baggage they have to carry and because it's unsightly to leave it behind. But I'm seeing a lot of toilet paper scattered along these last few miles. We were walking along what looked like a cliff and Brian suggested there might be a beautiful view, so we both walked off the trail eager to see our vantage point over the edge, only to find the little area had been considered a *baño* for many previous hikers. Brian was disappointed and appalled at the soiled earth.

With only about 5km left, we were in need of a break. The sun was kicking our butts and we had just hiked up a long, steep incline. The shade from the café down the road was calling to us. We stopped for ice cream and so Brian could treat his blisters. He had learned how to treat blisters on the AT, so it was no big deal to bandage himself up. I was impressed with how quickly and precisely he could tend to his wounds. It made me wish he had been with me when I was having trouble with my feet.

While we were trying to cool off and catch our breath, a nicely outfitted English couple sat down next to us with a bottle of wine talking about how absolutely lovely the day was. They had just gotten out of a taxi and were squeaky clean. I said *hola* to them, but they just looked me up and down, said hello and went back to their conversation. I could have strangled them if the sun hadn't sucked the life out of me. Instead I sat there sweating and panting, feeling all funky. I was so wasted.

At another stop where we found some nice shade, there was a small farm dog. At first, I thought he was shy so I completely ignored him and gave him space. But when I sat in the grass to relax, the pup walked up to me and laid right against me. He was the sweetest little thing that demanded to be petted and loved for a good 15 minutes. I love the animals I encounter out here.

During our final stop of the day (it was 5:30 in the evening and we still weren't to town yet!) I struck up a conversation with a South African woman named Jay. She had a bad blister on her heel. I gave her my molefoam and told her how to treat it. In the meantime, another hiking buddy of hers, Rory, came into the bar. He's a pretty cool guy we have run into multiple times. We then followed them outside where the rest of their five-person family was hanging out. Everyone was great!

After talking for quite a while, we decided it would be great if we all stayed in the same town tomorrow night and possibly walked into Santiago together the following day. Prior to this conversation, Brian and I were considering walking straight through to Santiago tomorrow by pulling our first 40km day. I've never hiked 24 miles in a day before, and I thought my last day on the Camino would be a nice poetic challenge for me.

But the temperature is supposed to be even hotter tomorrow than it was today, which is downright dangerous for hiking. So stopping halfway to meet up with friends was sounding like a better option. We said goodbye to the group and told them we would see them tomorrow night. They were stopping for the day, but we planned to continue on.

Because we took time during that stop to refresh ourselves, I was ready to go again. The sun was beating down on us but for some reason I was feeling pretty good. I was hot and tired but I was pulling through. I had my umbrella, but part of me wanted to take whatever the Camino has to throw at me. I only have two more days on this beautiful path. I felt like I should just endure and soak in every last ounce of the Camino. But then it occurred to me how silly that was. So I popped open my umbrella, turned my music up and enjoyed the rest of my walk in semi-comfort.

Arzúa had a lot of new construction. There was a long road walk into town. When we arrived, we checked into a nice hostel with a very fine restaurant attached to it. We felt very self-conscious when we walked into the restaurant. We noticed the patrons were all dressed up. Brian asked the hostess if we were dressed appropriately. She said of course we were welcome and seated us at a very nice table in the middle of the restaurant. Brian ordered a wonderful steak smothered in their soft Arzúa-Ulloa cheese. I highly recommend trying their famous cheese if you are ever in this region of Spain.

Best Camino family ever

Friendly farm dog

# CHAPTER 39

## DAY 37: 20KM FROM ARZÚA TO O PEDROUZO

—

### HEAVY HEART

Well, today will be difficult. We stayed in nice accommodations, but I had a lot on my mind and I didn't sleep a wink. That's going to make for a very difficult hike today. Having not slept at all only confirmed our tentative plans to not walk the full 40km to Santiago. Instead, we would hike an easy 20km to the next larger town, have dinner with friends and head for Santiago tomorrow.

Arzúa was jumping with people all night long. I know because I was up to hear all the partying. But when we left our hotel at 7:00am, the town was dead. Even the cafés were not open yet. I'm thinking because it's Sunday, places must open later or perhaps not at all. We checked the map and there was supposed to be a café about 5km into the hike. You don't normally want to go much farther than that on an empty stomach.

When we arrived to the general area where the café should be, many sad pilgrims were standing around not knowing what to do. The cafe was closed! We all moved on, knowing the map didn't show another stop for another 10km. It would be a hard walk without food. Everyone was in good spirits, though, which I was grateful for. I was going to need the positive energy to get me through the day. The trail was packed with pilgrims, so much that when a cafe not mentioned on the map appeared in the distance, it started a chain reaction of cheers. We heard about the cafe long before we actually reached it. When we got there, it was packed with every hungry pilgrim on the trail, which was really nice because we ran into all our new friends there.

I walked with a very heavy heart today for personal reasons. I was told last night that my grandmother was diagnosed with pancreatic cancer and is deteriorating quickly. Even if I left today, I most likely would not be home in time to say goodbye to her. This tragic news, coupled with the hottest day of my entire trip, made today one of the hardest I've ever had. I imagined my day before reaching Santiago to be very different than it has been.

I imagined I would feel like a child the day before Christmas, all excited about what's to come, but also feeling a hint of sadness knowing that all this anticipation will have built up and then disappeared in an instant. I thought that's how it would be, but I just couldn't get my head in the game today. People kept passing me and saying, "You better hurry. You'll want to be out from under the sun before it really heats up!" I felt like I was trudging every step of the way, and I just couldn't move faster.

Brian is my strength, though. He was gentle and sweet, but kept me moving forward. I could tell he wanted to move much more quickly than I was moving, but despite the insane heat he stayed with me the entire day. I tried to listen to music and talk to friends and sometimes those things helped temporarily, but overall, I just couldn't get into it. All I could think about was the news of my grandmother and all of the wretched family drama that immediately followed. I know family feuds are common at the threat of a loved one dying, but I just can't bare it right now. What does it mean when the matriarch of an Italian family dies? What will this mean for us? My family will never be the same. We will not recover from this. God, I hate today.

My mom told me last night that my grandma has been enjoying my blog, and it's the one thing that has kept her going during these scary times. So while part of me wants to collapse on the hot pavement and surrender, another part of me drags onward. My grandmother's condition only strengthened that anxious voice I continuously hear in my head *Life is short. Do it all.* I have to continue my trip. I have to finish.

My grandma and mother did not want me to find out about this while I am on pilgrimage. My grandma did not want me to worry. She did not want the news to interfere with my journey and dammit, I cannot allow that to happen. I have to shake this! My time on this amazing journey is so limited! And so I struggle struggle struggle. God, what a horrible day.

The evening was a tad better, but not by much. We ran into all of our Camino friends in town - Jay, Rory, Lizzie, Ad, and Maureen. I am so grateful for these people right now. They'll never know how much I need them right now. We drank and were merry. Brian relaxed in the hot shade with the others while Maureen and I walked from restaurant to restaurant to find the best place for dinner. We got a fantastic recommendation for the pizza place by some nice younger hikers who were eating whole pies.

When we returned to the restaurant where we left the others, we found them now inside the restaurant and drinking sangria. We eagerly joined them! We all made grand plans to see each other again, as well as plans to hike into Santiago tomorrow. We are all leaving at different times in the morning to compensate for our varying speeds, and plan to meet in the town just before Santiago so we can walk the last few kilometers together. I'm so excited I don't think I'll be able to sleep tonight. As we walked back to our room from dinner, we ran into several more groups eating outside. I feel like I've had a chance to see everyone one more time before we take our final walk. Still, in the back of my head is the nagging grief that continuously threatens my entire Camino experience. I'm fighting so hard to remain present.

Celebrating with my new Camino family

# CHAPTER 40

## DAY 38: 19KM FROM O PEDROUZO TO SANTIAGO DE COMPOSTELA!!!

—

## SUNRISE IN SPAIN

I made it!! We are in Santiago!

Brian and I woke up at 5:00am and were on the trail by 5:40am, giving us plenty of time to reach the agreed gathering point with the rest of our friends just before reaching Santiago. I didn't sleep well at all, partially due to my excitement, partially due to my grief, and partially due to the fact that it was over 100 degrees in our room (that's not an exaggeration). I actually had dreams that I was hiking naked because I was so overheated all night. Brian indicated that he also had a rough time sleeping.

We began our walk in the dark, which was a new and exciting Camino experience. As we walked out of town with our headlamps on, we ran into Rory and Lizzie! Even though they have really long legs and walk quickly, they opted to start early, too, because Lizzie has a bum knee (two of them actually). We all walked together for pretty much the entire day.

In the beginning, they blazed ahead of us, but as the morning drew on, we walked more and more together. I couldn't tell if that's because they wanted to hang out with us, or because Lizzie's knees were acting up. Either way, I was happy for the company. We stopped and had second breakfast together and continued on with each other after that.

It was at that time that we learned Rory and Lizzie have somewhat of an obsession with those machines that flatten coins. They have been collecting them all along the way and had quite a few. I don't even recall seeing those machines before, but suddenly I'm seeing them everywhere. Rory also talked to us for quite a while about Holland's legal system and culture. It was all very fascinating and it made the time pass quickly. It also helped keep my brain focused on one topic at a time, which I've really been struggling with lately.

As we took our last walk towards Santiago de Compostela, we watched the sun rise over our right shoulders. The surrounding sky glowed red, silhouetting the trees and architecture that made up the horizon. It was a beautiful sight to see, one I did not plan for. It occurred to me that sunrise in Spain indeed looks similar to sunrise at home. But how poetic that we should witness this new beginning on the day we arrive in Santiago?

The air was also full of new smells. Some were very pleasant while some were … not so much. Passing through one town we smelled hot apple pie! We were so disappointed to find there was no food in that town, though. As we walked along, we all asked each other about it. "Did you smell pie in the last town? Did you find any?" We overheard several pilgrims speaking excitedly in other languages. I just know they were talking about pie too. No one found the source, though!

Because we started so early, we took our time at all the rest breaks and hung out. We stopped for quite a while at *Monte do Gozo*, "the hill of joy," which boasts having the first views of Santiago. Apparently, at one time you could see the three spires of the cathedral from this location, however that view must be blocked by overgrown eucalyptus trees because we didn't see anything. Nonetheless, pilgrims rejoice at this point because Santiago is only about one hour's walk from here.

At one of the stops just outside of town, we stopped for drinks at a café and congratulated all the other pilgrims as they walked by. At that time we found out that the rest of our group didn't get up until 8:00am! That was a little hard to hear for some people, since we all got up early so they wouldn't have to wait for us. I didn't mind waiting for them, though. I was just happy we were all going to Santiago together and I was enjoying the day with Brian. The others picked up their pace and raced in towards us so we could all enter town together!

In the meantime, Rory, Lizzie, Brian, and I crossed into Santiago (although we didn't walk to the cathedral without the others). We took lots of fun pictures in front of the famous Santiago signs. Then Rory bought us all some 17-cent beer and we celebrated on the side of the street, saying hello to all our friends as they passed. I saw Tina again! When the rest of the group arrived, we celebrated in true redneck style with cheap beer and lots of selfies. I don't think they have open container laws in Spain and if they do, no one bothered us. We were just another excited group of pilgrims celebrating our near completion of our Pilgrimage.

We all walked into Santiago together and it was truly special! I was so excited I could barely contain myself. Your first encounter with the magnificent cathedral is from the side. Technically, we had not finished the trail, but we were only a few meters from kilometer zero. We all stopped and gazed up at the architecture. We're here. We're actually going to make it. Chills ran up and down my spine as I tried to comprehend the last 38 days of my life.

We ran into so many other pilgrims and congratulated each other with hugs and kisses. I couldn't believe it. I ran into people I met the first day and every day after! Everyone was there! And they all represented different phases of my Camino, all equally special to me. It was like watching a quick recap of my trip. That said, none of my closest Camino family was there. I said a prayer for Melisa, Cristina, Stephen, Nikolai, Ginger, Drennan, Maria, Renate, Christof, Roswitha, and all the others I did not see.

After some time and plenty of celebrating with one another, we gathered ourselves and headed for the plaza in front of the Cathedral which marks the end of the last kilometer to Santiago. Bagpipes echoed through the tunnel as we passed into the plaza. Pilgrims were everywhere. The air was bursting with joy and celebration. We all stopped and gazed up at this beautiful cathedral we just walked 500 miles to see and soaked in the victory.

Our friends took pictures of Brian and me standing together arm in arm in front of the cathedral. We did it. Since I began planning for this trip, I tried to envision this moment. As I stood there, looking up at the statue of St. James, I thought to myself, *so this is what it feels like. What it feels like to accomplish something extraordinary.*

As if this moment wasn't special enough, once we arrived right in the center of the plaza, Rory got down on his knee and proposed to Lizzie! None of us had any idea it was coming. Everyone stopped to watch and cry as Lizzie said yes. It was a magical moment. There were lots of pictures and joyous tears. It was kind of funny, how it happened. I was excitedly talking with a Frenchmen I met along the way and when I turned around everyone in my group was crying. "What's wrong?" I asked. But then I saw Rory getting up off his knee and I knew exactly what had just happened. It was too perfect for words.

We all lingered in the magic of the moment, soaking in our victory, listening to the bagpipes playing, and talking to the hundreds of pilgrims streaming into the area.

The others Brian and I hiked into Santiago with were clearly a tight Camino family. They had hiked for a couple of weeks together. So Brian and I got the sense we should let them all have their time together. So we said goodbye and headed to our hotel at the Parador right next to the cathedral. I wasn't super interested in staying at a Parador since I already stayed in two of them along the way, but I felt like Brian really needed to experience at least one night in a very special place. We were not disappointed. It was a very nice room indeed, and we got a pilgrim's rate, so it wasn't outrageously expensive.

Next, we headed to the pilgrim's office to obtain our compostelas. We heard you can wait for hours, but we were in and out in exactly 45 minutes. Although the line snaked its way outside of the building, we were protected from the sun by a beautiful grape leaf canopy. When it was finally my turn to enter the building, I was greeted by a young American man behind the counter. He asked me what my motivations were for hiking the Camino. I told him religious and spiritual. I surprised myself because if I had been asked that question several weeks ago, I probably would have said for the adventure of it. But my journey has become so much more than that for me. He then asked how far I walked. I told him I began in St. Jean Pied-de-Port in France. He wrote the official number of kilometers I walked, 775. He then handed me the two compostelas in a beautiful case. One is written in Latin, attesting that I completed my pilgrimage, and the other is a certificate of distance.

We also took a quick peek at the Cathedral even though we plan to take the self-guided tour tomorrow when it's supposed to rain. It was staged for tourism rather than worship, and I've learned that I prefer to see the churches during Mass. But Brian was really excited to see it and he had a good point: I had just walked 500 miles to see the cathedral. It didn't make sense to wait another day.

The cathedral was immaculate and splendid. There was a lot of construction and restoration going on, though, so the place echoed with drilling and hammering and most of the beautiful views were obstructed by scaffolding. That said, wow. The altar was one of the most beautiful I've seen and I can't wait to attend Mass tomorrow so I can see the whole thing. The crypt under the altar, where St. James' body resides, was open. Pilgrims lined up to walk down into the dark room, kneel before the tomb and say a prayer before exiting.

We also got to walk up the stairs and behind the altar way up above where the statue of St. James looks down over the entire cathedral. It was an amazing view. Pilgrims lined up again to hug or put their hands on the statue. The view from behind Santiago's statue was beautiful. I looked down below at all the other pilgrims.

Tomorrow, we will arrive for Mass extra early so we can get a seat reserved for pilgrims. A massive *botafumeiro* filled with incense hangs above the altar. On Fridays, it's swung high over the entire church, which is an experience all pilgrims want to witness. The Catholic Church knows how to capitalize on pilgrims, though, so for a 500 euro "donation", they'll swing it on any day of the week. But they won't tell you if a donation has been made for the day so you have to go to church and just hope some wealthy pilgrim or a group of pilgrims made a donation. It's quite the scam, actually. People hike over 500 miles to see it. They should swing that thing every day. Be that as it may, we will go to church tomorrow and hope they swing it even though tomorrow is not a Friday. I'll be very happy if I have the opportunity to witness it.

We had a very nice early dinner outside of the cathedral and returned to the Parador to freshen up for the evening, which would undoubtedly be a grand celebration with all the others. And man, did we celebrate! All through the town, pilgrims celebrated through the night. We had second dinner at one restaurant and hit a couple of other bars for drinks (and more food) after. Everywhere we went we ran into pilgrims we saw all along the Way.

I was explaining to Lizzie, Rory, and a couple of others what Geocaching is and told them I really wanted to find a cache in Santiago. Rory and a couple others followed me as I embarked on my first international scavenger hunt. Unfortunately, we were unable to find the cache. I was really hoping to show them how much fun caching can be but they still seemed to enjoy the idea of it, even if we didn't actually find the cache. We returned to our table of thirteen pilgrims to continue the celebration.

Tonight truly was an endless celebration across the entire city. Everyone was eating and drinking to their heart's content. It was also a sad time, though, as most pilgrims are traveling back home in the morning and everyone knows they will most likely never see each other again. I had many bittersweet goodbyes throughout the evening. For example, I got to see Lio again! She is leaving for her home in Switzerland tomorrow morning. Even though we only hiked together for the one day going into Ponferrada, we shared a very sad goodbye. We will stay in touch via email.

Today was an awesome end to an amazing adventure. And Santiago at night is a beautiful, romantic city. I am so happy to be here with Brian. I'm looking forward to exploring it more tomorrow. That is, after I've slept in as long as I want for the first time in over a month.

Monte do Goza

# CHAPTER 41

## POST HIKE DAY 1: SANTIAGO DE COMPOSTELA
—
## THE PROCESSING BEGINS

So this is it. The day I begin processing my Camino. Who would have thought it would be so reflective and thought provoking? I think I'll be processing for quite some time. But first, we totally won at breakfast this morning at the hotel. Rows of meats, cheeses, breads, fruits, desserts, and quiches. I've never seen a spread like it. We were somewhat intimidated when we first walked in because everyone was all dressed up. We thought we were the only pilgrims there, but after overhearing some conversations, we realized that most of the others walked to Santiago, too, but had their bags forwarded. Their hair was perfect, their makeup was done, their jewelry matched, their clothes were pressed, and they smelled good. We were *so* out of place. But we didn't care. Breakfast was amazing and we were blessed to have such a nice hotel to celebrate in.

After eating, I had my usual urge to walk. So we strolled all over town talking about our odds of whether or not the *botafumeiro* would swing at the 12:00pm pilgrim's Mass. It's unfortunate that it's turned into such a tourist trap. We asked several security people working in the church if it would swing the day before, but they wouldn't tell us. The reason they don't tell us is because it increases their chances of more people offering 500 euros to swing it. What a scam indeed.

Anyway, regardless of how wrong the church may be for making money off it, Brian and I were very excited at the prospect that we might see it swing. We were about two blocks from the cathedral around 10:00am when we both got a huge whiff of incense. We both looked at each other and had the same thought. We did an instant 180 and walked swiftly back to the cathedral. If there was any chance at seeing the *botafumeiro*, we wanted front row seats. There are a few rows in the very front reserved for pilgrims who bring their credentials, so we made sure to have ours with us.

We took our seats in the front row and off to the left side of the cathedral two hours early. That may seem a bit overeager, but within 30 minutes the cathedral was crawling with tourists. Security guards roamed through the crowd, reminding people to be quiet, take off their hats, and leave their camera flashes off. At one point, a security guard pulled out a microphone and in Spanish reminded everyone that this is a place of worship and to please be quiet. People respected his orders for about five minutes before their energy levels burst again. Everyone was just so excited to finally be in Santiago. It occurred to me that this must be how Santiago is every day of the week. This town is in constant celebration as new pilgrims arrive every single day.

It was odd to be present at that strange hour when tourists were bustling through to see St. James' crypt and celebrate their finale while other people were coming in to prepare for worship. It was a bit of a mess to see the groups clash. Brian and I just sat quietly in our seats and tried to wait patiently.

While waiting, I saw several pilgrims I've come to know over the last several weeks. For example, remember the four-person family that split up because they decided it would be best if they hiked the Camino at their own pace? Well, I'm happy to report that all four of them made it to Santiago. It was wonderful to see them in the cathedral. I also saw Kiki, who I walked part way into Santiago with along with Rory and Lizzie. I informed her that she needs her pilgrim credentials to sit in the first row. I saved her a seat as she ran back to her albergue to get hers. We would sit together at Mass.

So, as for the background story of the *botafumeiro*: it's said that over 100 pilgrims used to bed down every night in the cathedral after walking 500 miles, so the place would smell terrible. They swung the incense ball to overpower the pilgrim stench. You have to imagine back then, pilgrims did not have the luxury of a shower every night. The *botafumeiro* itself weighs 23 kilos (50 pounds) and takes eight men to swing it! It flies high up and over the heads of the congregation from a long rope.

No such luck seeing it, though. We went through the entire Mass and the *botafumeiro* did not swing. We were told by two pilgrims before the Mass that they knew it would swing so we were super excited. Something tells me this is a rumor that flies around town for every Mass, because as soon as we left, we also heard it would swing at tonight's 7:30pm Mass. It doesn't matter, though. Brian and I have decided we will come back to Santiago on Friday, which is the only time it swings for sure. I'm actually very frustrated about this whole situation. The church creates so much anxiety in pilgrims as they try to plan their lives around this one event, which the church refuses to talk about because they make more money when they leave people guessing.

All complaining aside though, the Mass was beautiful. It began with a nun who had the most beautiful singing voice and personality. I couldn't understand anything she was saying, but she had the entire Spanish-speaking congregation chuckling. She prepared us by teaching us the melodies we would be singing along to during the service and lead us in prayer as the priests filed onto the altar. I thoroughly enjoyed everything even if I didn't get to see the *botafumeiro* swing.

Today has been another roller coaster of emotions. I've laughed, I've cried. I think I've hit a mental road block though. I fully intended to hike to Finisterre and Muxia, the two beautiful cities on the coast of Spain, not far from Santiago. But after the big celebratory finale all day yesterday, I feel like I'm done. I just don't want to walk anymore.

On that same note, I'm really sad that it's over, and I really struggled with my decision to take a bus to the coast. Today, when we were walking through town, I came across those beloved yellow arrows and I instantly felt good. I felt like, *Oh, yes. I know what my purpose is. I know what I should be doing. I should follow that arrow.* But I didn't. It left me feeling very conflicted and incomplete.

Continuing to walk now will feel like taking a summer class after you've already graduated from school. I was told the hike to the coast is not too scenic (which I'm not entirely certain is true) and once there, there is no celebration or anything that makes you feel like you've completed your goal. That was here in Santiago. So I've decided we will take a bus to the last two towns. I am no longer a pilgrim. I'm a tourist.

I think the exhaustion has finally caught up with me as well. Sometime between visiting all the museums today, I fell asleep sitting up on a stone bench outside. I never just fall asleep like that! I even dreamed while sitting there in broad daylight and Brian had to wake me.

The inertia of this whole adventure is finally catching up with me. I'm also starting to feel the slowing of it, though, and that has me uneasy. I say this a dozen times a day, but I'm just not ready for it to all be over. We heard about the Pilgrim House, which is an American welcome center for pilgrims in Santiago. It's a wonderful little place to seek rest and shelter although they don't allow people to sleep there. The volunteers were tremendously helpful and welcoming.

They consisted of former pilgrims who have returned to Santiago for no reason other than to welcome new Pilgrims to town.

We went there to do our laundry and while waiting, Brian handed me a pamphlet on "debriefing and processing the Camino." I started to cry as I read the form. It suggested reflecting on questions like *how has the Camino changed you* and *what actions will you take when you return home to continue what you've learned from the Camino? What will you do to allow yourself to rest before re-entering your normal life? What will you miss most about the Camino? What didn't you like about your trip? Do you think you could have done it better?*

These are all questions that have been racing through my mind all day today as I pretended to be interested in museum after museum of really old relics. Could I have done this better? Did I miss something? Did other people have a better experience than I did? And if not, why do I suddenly feel so sad and empty? Am I completely ungrateful for this amazing journey? What's wrong with me? Tears were streaming down my face as I made eye contact with one of the volunteers. He gave me a warm smile as if he understood what I was going through, and continued to tend to his business.

I looked over at the counter and saw that they had about 200 copies of this form printed out and occurred to me that I'm probably having a completely normal response to my trip ending, and apparently I will need to give myself time and *an honest to goodness rest before re-entering normal life*. I was so grateful for the Pilgrim House and for the kind volunteer who, without words, managed to comfort me, even if only for a moment. I'm willing to accept that processing the Camino will be a long hard journey, perhaps harder than the Camino itself. But Brian and I still have several days left of this trip so I'm going to have to process it while continuing to make the best of this adventure.

Today, we toured the cathedral, a monastery, and a convent.

Despite being a bit burned out on this stuff, I did find some of it fascinating, and Brian loved it. We noticed interesting things, like how the church in the convent was far more colorful and only depicted positive scenes from the bible, whereas the monastery had more graphic and even violent art. We also got to see remains of the original cathedral, which dates back hundreds of years ago.

Dinner once again was fabulous! I can always count on Brian to find the best reviews and restaurants. No more pilgrim meals for me. We went to *Casa Marcelo*, a Spanish-Japanese fusion restaurant just a few blocks from the Camino's kilometer zero marker. When we arrived, we sat at the bar and the waiter started talking to us in Spanish. When he realized we didn't speak the language he rolled his eyes and walked away.

For a moment, I thought we were in for a rough night. But then the head chef came by and explained that he knows English, but he learned in Ohio so we had to speak slowly. He was delightful and very funny! He said since it was our first time at the restaurant, he would create a menu for us. We agreed that we were okay with eating raw seafood, raw meat, and very spicy foods. We were so excited. We had no idea what they would bring us.

They started us off with a bottle of red wine, which was wonderful, of course. Then they went to work making our meal right in front of us. Lots of fancy raw fish and some raw meat. Every few minutes, they would hand us another colorfully decorated dish with small amounts of fancy food. When they planned to serve us dessert, we were still hungry for more surprises. We asked for one more dish.

A few minutes later, they brought out a huge fried fish meant to be eaten with our hands! The fish was sitting upright on the dish and staring at us! It was an awesome meal and a great night! I kept having moments when I would pause and thank God for allowing me to be in such an amazing place with my favorite person. The night was so great that we opted out of all the other awesome things going on. The folks we walked into Santiago with invited us out for drinks for one last time, and that sounded like fun, but we were out until well after 11:00pm. They eat so late here. Tonight was also the night of San Juan (*Noite de San Xoan* in Galician), when the region celebrates St. John with feasts and massive bonfires all over town. People jump over fire to keep the witches away. It also coincides with summer solstice.

We wanted to join in the festivities, but we decided it would be nice to enjoy our last night in Santiago with just the two of us (Postscript: this would be my one and only regret of the Camino. You can sleep when you're dead. Never miss the opportunity to spend time with your trail family because it could be - and it was - the last time you ever see them).

Tomorrow we will take a bus to "the end of the earth" and watch the sun set there.

Giant fried fish

# CHAPTER 42

## POST HIKE DAY 2: FINISTERRE

—

## THE WORLD'S END

After another lovely breakfast, we hailed a cab to the bus station where we purchased tickets for The World's End, Finisterre. While at the station, we ran into Jutta and Helga, two very nice German ladies from my past. Jutta made me tea and toast while I was sick the second time just before Ponferrada, and Helga was sick along with me. It was nice to catch up with them again, and it was good to see that Helga's sickness did not hold them back.

I have to mention our experience getting on the buses. The concept of lines is very different here in Spain. People cut in line so frequently that while we were the fourth and fifth person in line to get on the bus, we were two of the last people to actually climb on board. It was amazing to watch dozens of people cut us off as if it was completely normal. I didn't realize how organized Americans are and how, socially, we all agree the cutting is rude and inappropriate until I experienced lines in a different culture. In Spain, it's totally acceptable to elbow someone out of your way. Brian was extremely annoyed, as he is a very orderly person and he has a strong sense of fairness. I found it frustrating too, but I wasn't willing to confront everyone who cut us off, so I accepted that we'd end up in the back of the line and I encouraged Brian to just embrace the international experience. I quoted Stephen: *It's all a part of the experience.* Brian calmed down a bit and we still managed to get decent seats on the bus. But if you ever find yourself in Spain, take note of the different social norms. It's fascinating, albeit sometimes infuriating!

I'm going to miss this city. I saw so many pilgrims. Apparently Brian and I are pretty memorable, because we had many people come up to us with open arms and wish us luck on our next adventure, but we frequently had no idea who they were. I know I've met a lot of people in the last week or so to the point that it was difficult to remember all their faces, but I have a feeling people we didn't actually meet treated us like they knew us.

One woman at the Parador kissed us goodbye and wished us well. She asked us where we were going and told us all about her plans. I'm positive that I never formally met her. I think she just heard about us and that we are both hikers because she knew that Brian hiked the AT. I will miss that kindness and genuine interest people take in each other on the Camino.

One thing I won't miss about Santiago is the beggars. I don't think I have mentioned this before. They are in most towns, actually, and they are very aggressive. They beg while you are eating your dinner outside, they stand next to cash registers and shove their empty cups in your face when you receive change, they whine at you and block your exit when you leave church.

What I find most frustrating is that some of these people actually are homeless, while others just beg for extra change, and I can't tell them apart. I don't mind giving money to the homeless, but when I see someone begging one hour and see him exiting his very nice home the next (which I did witness in Santiago), it makes me really angry that he bothered me to begin with. It all makes me very uncomfortable and there were many more panhandlers in Santiago than anywhere else.

I was very happy we took the bus rather than walking to the world's end. Every time the bus puffed up the smallest incline, I thanked God I wasn't walking it. I will never take hills for granted again! From our double decker bus, we were able to see beaches and beautiful views. I wasn't able to get pictures from my seat, but just imagine coastal Maine, only with Spanish architecture. Beautiful.

Lunch on the coast was an adventure. We found a local hole in the wall in a back alley called *Os Tres Golpes* that had a seafood assortment tray for 55 euros. The guy spoke Galician, so we were completely lost.

Speaking of languages, Galician reminds me of a softer Portuguese more than Spanish. For example, instead of saying "*buenos dias*" in Spanish, Galicians say "*bo dia*," which is closer to the Portuguese who say "*bon dia*." This was the extent of my Galician knowledge, though. I tried to use my Spanish translator but that only helped a little. One of the local guys who probably just hangs out and smokes there all day gestured for Brian to follow him into the restaurant. They pointed to all different kinds of shellfish. Brian gave a thumbs up on all of them so we had no idea what we would actually be served.

When I ordered water for my drink the owner told me "No," I would have beer. So I had a beer! He was right, though. When he came out with what would be over $200 in seafood in the U.S., I knew I would need a beer to wash it all down. We got three types of crab, langoustine lobster, barnacles, razor clams, and shrimp on one massive plate that took up the entire table. I'm not a huge seafood eater, but it was so much fun trying to make a dent in that massive plate of food.

The atmosphere here was very interesting. You could tell it was a local joint, as most of the people in the restaurant were there just to hang out, not to eat. We were just waiting for one of the locals to yell at us for doing it wrong and sit with us for an hour, showing us how to squeeze every last drop of meat from the shells. No one did, but we did get to listen to their energetic conversations in the background. I would have thought they were fighting if I didn't know how vocal the Spanish are. They have a lot in common with Italians. I felt like I was with my family. Interestingly, I did not find this to be true with the people in Basque territory. I didn't start noticing it until I was farther west.

Our hotel was closed when we arrived at 1:30pm (siesta), so what else is there to do other than eat and drink? We went to our third restaurant since entering town and had dessert and wine. While there, we talked with a nice mother/daughter team from Nashville. The sun started to poke through the clouds as we sat and watched the boats float in and out of the harbor.

We took the shortest tour ever of a small shack full of fishing paraphernalia, but it was actually one of the most interesting tours I've been on because the guy running the place was so excited to tell us all about the old ways of fishing and whaling. You couldn't help but to be excited with him. It was also fun because his English was extremely limited, so some of it was in Spanish, too. It felt like the longest game of charades ever. He pointed, gestured, and swung artifacts through the air, anything to get us to understand old fishing methods. Brian and I had a blast. The other two women who didn't speak Spanish or English were less than amused.

That evening as we strolled around town, we ran into lots of friends old and new. I got a phone call from Nikolai. He was in town! I could tell in the two minutes we were on the phone that he was hangry, so I suggested we meet for dinner. He and his new hiking partner, Cristina, met us by the harbor for more food. It was great catching up and sharing our experiences in Santiago. They had already walked to Finisterre and Muxia and even camped on the beach. I felt a tinge of jealousy as they talked about their adventures. Partly because I wish Nikolai was with me when I walked into Santiago, and partly because they continued their pilgrimage to the coast. I had to remind myself that it was okay that I chose to take a bus to the "World's End" rather than hiking those few extra kilometers.

Cristina is awesome! She's an Italian chick with lots of attitude and just beneath that "tough as nails" persona is a gentle kindness. I liked her immediately. I thought perhaps we were distantly related because her last name is so similar to my maiden name. How cool would that be, to find a distant relative in the middle of Spain? But it turns out, her family is from a different part of Italy than mine. Nonetheless, I loved the little bit of time we spent together.

Seeing Nikolai again was bittersweet. I was so happy to see him again, but something was different now. He seemed like a different person from the man I'd come to know and connected with while hiking together. Even our light discussion seemed distant and changed. It was as if the close bond we formed while hiking over 200 miles together had dissolved over just a few short days, and all that remained of him was a noticeable awkwardness towards me.

I enjoyed the four of us sitting in the evening air, sharing our stories of hiking into Santiago and I know that we will always be friends, but I was left feeling like something was missing that I can't quite define. I carried on like normal, but I'm left wondering why our last interaction was so different from all our other time together, and am saddened by what feels like a loss.

After saying goodbye to Cristina and Nikolai, Brian and I started our hike to the lighthouse at the World's End. When we arrived, multiple groups of people were burning their hiking gear on the cliff rocks. It's an old tradition people are actually trying to discourage now because it's so toxic, but it still goes on sometimes. Brian and I found a nice private rock and sat on the cliffs to watch a beautiful sunset. The clouds parted just enough to give us an amazing view. The sun set at 10:20pm. Everyone clapped. Most people left immediately but we stuck around for a while to watch the clouds change colors and to celebrate my big victory once again. This is the second of three parts to my journey. Santiago, check! Finisterre, check! Muxia, here I come!

We had our headlamps and planned to hike back down from the lighthouse in the dark, but as we were walking along the road, a car with a couple in it drove by us. They stopped and excitedly started talking to us in Spanish. I heard them say Camino. "*Si! Camino!*"

"We are also peregrinos and we saw you in Santiago yesterday!" They offered us a ride down the mountain just because they saw us twice before! I jumped on the opportunity because I was minutes from going to the bathroom on the side of the road, and it was getting cold out, too. We chatted the whole way back into town. They were impressed that I had walked all the way from France and wanted to know more about my experiences.

I was so moved by how interested these people were in us simply because we were all pilgrims. They got out of the car with us and gave us big hugs and kisses before we parted. It made me realize that all those people who spoke to us excitedly but whose faces I could not remember for the life of me really were complete strangers. Brian and I are both easily recognizable people. He's a big guy who hikes in a kilt and I'm just over four and-a-half feet tall and hike with a huge pack. You can't miss us. That totally explains the dozens of random interactions we have every day. I love all of them!

We returned to our rooms around 11:00pm and decided to stay in for the night. Nikolai and Cristina were at the "hippy beach" at a big bonfire, and we considered joining them one last time, but it was late and judging from the name of the beach, I suspected there would be a lot of drugs; I didn't really want a part of that. Besides, I felt good having the opportunity to see my hiking buddy one last time and I didn't want to have to say goodbye for a third time.

This whole journey has been surreal and I'm starting to deal better with the fact that it'll soon just be a memory. I'm so glad I decided to see Finisterre and Muxia, although they aren't technically a part of the Camino. They are providing me with a gentle transition away from what has been my life for the last several weeks.

Dinner at Os Tres Golpes

# CHAPTER 43

## POST HIKE DAY 3: MUXIA

—

### LAST STOP

Well, I wasn't sure how it would happen, but everyone is right. The Camino really does have three parts to it - one for the body, one for the mind, and one for the soul. I thought I'd struggle with the spiritual connection with all the commercialism of the final parts of my pilgrimage, but I suppose after you've worked on your mind through the Meseta, it prepares you for all the distractions. I feel I've now experienced all three phases completely.

I have learned some extremely valuable lessons in the last few days that I look forward to taking home with me. They are lessons I've had before and I try to live my life by them, but my trip as a whole has given me undeniable proof that I can be confident in my life choices, I can be confident in those lessons learned, and I can be confident that God will provide. I came to the Camino prepared yet completely vulnerable, and I was given all the love and support I needed along the Way. Undeniable proof.

So what else have I received undeniable proof of over the last several weeks? I'd say there are four things. The first three I actually have tattooed on my arm represented by three Plumerias.

1) Life is short. Do what you need to do. And do it regardless of what people think, because you are the only one who has to deal with

the consequences of your choices.

2) Always keep your husband close to your heart. Because with the exception of your mother, he's the only person who will love you no matter what.

3) Regardless of how you are doing with the previous two lessons, remember to be grateful for what God has given you.

4) Be extremely particular about who you include in your close circle of loved ones. If I've learned anything on this trip, it's that you can shape the quality of your life by deciding who will inspire you. Surround yourself only by those who have a positive influence on you, those who have characteristics you would like to emulate, those who enhance your mind and spirit in a positive way. These are the people who are deserving of your time, love, and devotion - regardless of whether you've known them for a day or a lifetime.

This is my big takeaway. You can choose who will have an impact on your life and who will fade into the background. I have met a couple of negative people on this trip and have dealt with some dreadful family drama while here in Spain, but I chose to leave them out of my story because those aren't the memories I want to keep. Those people will fade from my consciousness the quickest.

I'm so grateful that this trip has given me the opportunity to dig deep within and pull these lessons out of my own conscience.

Okay, so today we took a bus to Muxia, my last stop on the Camino! All the Spanish I've learned in the last month is barely useful anymore. People speak Galician, which as I said is more like Portuguese or Italian than Spanish. It was a bit gloomy today, but the town still sparkled. It sits just on the western coast of Spain and has no protection from the Atlantic Ocean, so the waves are fierce against the rocky shoreline. It was a bit unfortunate that we didn't have better weather, but I really can't complain because of my 38 hiking days, it only really rained for two! That's pretty darned good.

After checking into our hotel and dropping off our packs, we hiked out to the famous church that sits right on the shore. It was closed, so I said my prayers from outside the doors. Then we walked down to the rocks and visited a famous rock that all pilgrims try to get their picture taken with. There is a superstition that if you walk under it 13 times, you'll never have arthritis. I thought that sounded silly, but Brian was all about it. I was sure to take pictures of him walking back and forth. We also hung out on another famous flat rock on the shore which is said to be the site of an altar once used by the Celts.

Speaking of rocks, there is quite a bit of religious history here. Although the Catholic religion spread across the land, many of the old Celtic traditions remained. Apparently, Celtic women would hump the rounded beach rocks on this shoreline to promote fertility. The Catholic church was appalled by this behavior and sent extra priests to the region to stop the tradition. If you plan to hike the Camino, I'd encourage you to explore the history behind this region. However, I should warn you, while this particular story sounds silly and is actually a bit funny, as you can imagine with any religion, there is a very dark history. I tried not to delve too deep myself into the slayings and persecution. The stories of St. James are actually gruesome. I prefer to think of the Camino as it is today in all of its glory. It makes me realize that while we are still plagued with "holy wars" in our modern world, the Camino is a loving example of how people from all walks of life and all religions can come together and experience life in harmony. This is the spirit I hold onto.

Lunch was decent, though we had to go to two places. The first place we went should have had a "no peregrinos" sign on the door to save us some time. We sat outside for over ten minutes watching the waitress serve everyone but us. It wasn't until we watched her ignore another couple of pilgrims that we decided we probably weren't welcome. The place where we ended up was also outside, right on the water, and the service was great!

Seafood seafood seafood. I have never had more seafood in my entire life than I've had in the last three days. We also ran into a woman named Kris from Montreal again, so she joined us.

We spent the afternoon leisurely walking around town. We saw so many fish swimming in the fresh clean water. I never realized how overfished our waters are at home until I saw so much sea life here! We also found a boardwalk and followed it all the way to a beautiful sandy beach. As we were entering the beach area, I saw a yellow Camino arrow. Oh, how I love those arrows. I stopped and stared at it for a moment. "My Camino is over, isn't it?" Brian hugged me tight and then led me onto the beach. It was gorgeous and we were the only ones around. I cannot describe how blue the water is here. It reminds me of postcards from the Caribbean. We laid on the beach for hours, never seeing a single person. The sun came out, and it was the most peaceful afternoon.

Dinner was more amazing seafood and a lot of liquor. Wow, do they know how to do sangria here and then they give you a free shot after your entire meal. They do it right here! Love Muxia!

Tomorrow will most likely be my last post. I will head back to Santiago one more time just to go to the 7:30pm Mass and see the *botafumeiro* swing.

Note to self: I need to stop eating (and drinking) like I'm still walking 25km a day.

# CHAPTER 44

## POST HIKE DAY 4: SANTIAGO

—

## FINALLY THE BOTAFUMEIRO

Arriving in Santiago again was very nice. It's said that after three days of arriving in Santiago, one should move on because it's no longer your town. All the pilgrims you know have left and a whole new group comes through. I found it exciting, though, to see all the new fresh faces. This is such a big day for them. I loved watching the crowds roll in and gaze up at the cathedral that they just walked 500 miles to see.

We arrived to town super early, so after a nice breakfast at a small café, we dropped our bags off at the Parador and used their computers to plan the rest of our trip. We decided to spend the remainder of our time in Barcelona! Then we will spend two days in Madrid before heading home. We had a horrible time buying train tickets online, though, so we ended up hailing a cab to the train station and buying them in person. We then took another cab to a clothing store to buy some extra clothes, because doing laundry every other day and walking around in hiking clothes is getting old. It was another subtle reminder that I'm no longer a pilgrim.

Our cab driver told us that he has never seen Galicia so dry and we are lucky to have such beautiful weather. I concur!

We accidentally ordered white wine at lunch. After all the

amazing red wine I've had here, I don't really have a taste for white wine anymore. So we decided we were going to sit outside on this beautiful day and drink that bottle of white until it tasted red. As we sat there enjoying the day, we played a game. Who hiked the whole trail and who section hiked? We found the secret to deciphering the code. The long-distance hikers were all bundled up like me. When you spend a month sweating and constantly being overheated from overexertion, when you stop moving on a day with a nice cool breeze like today, you actually feel cold. All the long-distance hikers were wearing sweaters and sweatshirts. Very interesting.

We took a tour of the cathedral and looked at all the chapels we missed when we were here the other day. Then we took our seats extra early for Mass, ensuring a superb view of the *botafumeiro*. And what a sight it was. It was totally worth taking another two-hour bus ride back to Santiago from Muxia. The *botafumeiro* swung high and wide and people went crazy for it. We were all told photos and videos weren't allowed, but there was no hiding that everyone documented this event. We walked 500 miles to see it! There will be a record of it!

Dinner was amazing once again. We returned to *Casa Marcelo*, where the head chef recognized us and prepared for us another very special menu. For dessert, he didn't even ask what we wanted. He just ordered around the kitchen staff and told us what we would eat. Actually, he did that for the entire meal! It was all amazing and all different from what we had tried a few nights before.

After dinner, guess who we ran into on the streets? Ginger, Drennan, Dotty, and Kristen! They are all staying at the Parador, too. I was so happy to be able to introduce them to Brian. Our greetings were short though. They were all off to bed. Brian and I were still bursting with energy, so we walked around town bouncing from one live performance to the next.

Santiago is such a romantic town at night. We could also see the cathedral better at night than in the daylight for some reason. In the spotlight we could see the difference between the sections where they had completed renovations and where they hadn't. The building clearly needs work, so I don't feel as bad about the fact that it's currently covered in scaffolding.

Well, I guess this is my last post. My adventure is over, although I'll still be in Spain for another 10 or so days. Thank you so much for following along as I took my journey.

I highly recommend this adventure to anyone looking to enhance their life. Please don't hesitate to reach out to me if you need genuine encouragement. I will be a cheerleader for you as you have been for me. This has been the most amazing thing I've ever done and I will cherish it always.

Over and out.

Preparing the botafumeiro

# CHAPTER 45

## THE TRANSITION

—

## PROCESSING THE CAMINO

It's been six months since receiving my Compostela in Santiago, and I am still processing the entire experience. My Camino transformed me in ways I could not expect and cannot explain. I spent weeks trying to make sense of the plethora of emotions I was dealing with on a daily basis all the while trying to assimilate to life back home.

My first day back in the "real world" was gradual. I took an additional week off work to give myself time to recuperate, as wisely recommended by the pamphlet I read in Santiago. I figured I would get bored eventually and return to work sometime later that week, however I found that I needed every minute of that time off, and then some.

My husband returned to work immediately, so I woke up that first morning alone. I got out of bed and stood upright. I looked around the room, thinking, "I have nowhere to walk." What was I supposed to do now? I couldn't decide what to do with myself so I climbed back into bed. I did this three times. I'd climb out of bed, look around, realize there was nothing to do and lay back down. By the third time, it occurred to me that I could take a shower. Yes! There's something I can do with my time. I took a nice long hot shower enjoying the clean accommodations and the privacy. This was something I hadn't experienced in quite some time.

My routine at home was no longer second nature. I had to think about every step in the process. "Okay, I've showered. Now I have to dress myself." I walked to my closet and stood in utter shock. Why in the world do I have so many clothes? How could I possibly choose what to wear? I was appalled at the number of clothes I had and angry at the fact that I was forced to contemplate which ones to wear.

After weeks of wearing the same outfit and walking the same path, my brain had rewired itself. Not only could I not remember how to determine what clothes to wear, but this was a superfluous decision I was forced to make, which took time away from thinking about the important things that mattered in life. On the Camino, all the unnecessary decisions are removed from your life, allowing you ample time to reflect on what is important to you, what inspires you, what gives you purpose. These are the things I'd become accustomed to pondering and suddenly I had to worry about which shirt matched which pants?! It struck me as ludicrous.

I did manage to dress myself, though, and the rest of the day continued on like this. Making one ridiculous decision after another and none of them amounting to anything that actually mattered. The red shirt or the blue shirt? The cup or the glass? The plate or the bowl? The couch or the chair? The tv or the radio? The book or the newspaper? The salmon or the swordfish? And returning to work proved even more challenging. It seemed that decision-making and critical thinking had taken a vacation, and I was left feeling frustrated and anxious as I struggled to readjust to my former lifestyle.

Everything and everyone was exactly as I had left them, but somehow everything seemed different now. I was different now. I lived, loved, and learned. I grew, I was experienced. But no one knew this about me. I struggled to relate to anyone other than those who have also taken a life changing journey. I sought comfort from my

Camino friends who were also struggling to readjust to their lives back home.

I was frustrated by those around me who choose to ignore their blessings, and continue on their daily lives with little regard for how precious their lives truly are. I had to remind myself that I was the one with these new lessons. I was the one who experienced the Camino, and no one else would be able to understand what I had been through. When I tried to explain what an amazing adventure it was, people seemed wholly focused on my overall safety and whether I had felt in danger - seeming to miss the point of my journey itself. While there will always be many threats in this world, I no longer believe it is as dangerous as some people have lead me to believe in the past.

Things seemed to move needlessly fast, and I couldn't (nor did I want to) move at that pace. I no longer had the chance to stop and be grateful for my day. Everything was a blur and suddenly my life meant very little. I had to learn to slow myself down despite the world around me and take time for myself, take time for God. And let me explain that when I say I take time for God: sometimes that's just taking five seconds to count my blessings. On the Camino, this came so naturally. But at home, there is very little time for it.

The Camino consumed every moment of my day and every inch of my thoughts. For weeks, I replayed the best moments of my life in my head. They were still fresh and real, and every time I thought about them, they would bring joy to my soul. But with that joy came complete and utter disappointment when I was pulled away from those thoughts and back to reality. It seems that the withdrawal from the most significant time of my life coupled with the sudden lack of physical exertion is enough to launch oneself into a full blown clinical depression. Many hikers can attest to this, as I have since learned many of my Camino friends (as well as my husband and his AT friends) have experienced the same phenomenon in slightly different ways. Just as suddenly walking twenty miles a day is extremely difficult on your body, so is suddenly not walking twenty miles a day. Your body physically cannot manage the sudden change in physical exertion. This is in addition to the mental trauma of suddenly being thrust into a completely different lifestyle. Your mind and body struggle to process it all and function simultaneously.

If that wasn't enough, I was dealing with the loss of my trail family. I went from spending every hour of every day with these people to not seeing them at all. It felt like someone died. I'm very familiar with the grieving process and I can say that I mourned the loss of my trail family the same as I mourned the loss of my grandmother, who I am sad to say did in fact pass prior to my returning home. It all seemed too much to bear some days.

I know this all sounds dismal, and I wish I could paint a more glamorous story for you, but I cannot in good conscience talk about how marvelous the Camino is without sharing the most difficult parts. No one tells this part of the story. But here's the truth: self transformation is not pretty. It is not easy. It's excruciating, and oftentimes lonely.

So you may be asking yourself, why in the world would I want to hike the Camino if it could possibly result in so much agony? Well, first of all, many of the challenges you may come home with will dissipate fairly quickly as you reacclimatize to the life you left behind. You will rise above any mental, physical, and spiritual struggles, I promise. But know this. Once you experience something as amazing as the Camino, you do not come back the same person. Prepare yourself for that. Have a loving and supportive network to return to and know that while your friends and family love you, they will not understand this new part of you.

I have come away with so many treasures I carry with me every day of my life. If my life were a book, it would consist of two parts: life before the Camino and life after the Camino. I began my journey as a solo hiker filled with uncertainty but returned with a sense of self as well as a sense of community. In this second part of my life, my spirit is renewed and my faith in humanity is restored. That is probably the greatest gift I could have gained from my thirty-eight-day pilgrimage.

There is, in fact, great kindness in this world - and not just fleeting moments of it. A genuine deep and abiding goodness, generosity, and care-taking between complete strangers is a common thread across the entire Camino, and when I carefully examine my own life, I see that same beauty everywhere more so than I did before. I see it in my neighbors, my friends, my family, my colleagues and of course, complete strangers. Nothing has changed, only my perspective. This in itself is worth every heartbreaking moment I endured after returning from the Camino.

I've also found peace within my life and within my heart. This is something so foreign to me that I struggle to fully understand the feelings associated with it even months later. Prior to the Camino, I would have waved a dismissive hand at this notion but the Camino bestows complete peace onto its pilgrims. While I may not be able to recreate those moments every day in my life, I frequently reflect back on the peace and freedom I experienced during my pilgrimage and embrace it until my troubles subside.

I also have this intense feeling of self-satisfaction. I am 35 years old now and while I've done many things in my life I am proud of, I can say with absolute certainty that for those thirty-eight days on the Camino, I lived my life to the fullest. I don't believe that is something I will ever take for granted. I absolutely refuse to regret my life, and now…I won't.

I've received many other gifts from my pilgrimage; self-confidence, inner strength, a powerful sense of self, the overall perspective that everything really is going to be okay, a deeper love for my friends and family, the satisfaction that comes from the international experience, the reminder that while the U.S. isn't the best of everything the world has to offer, it's a darn good place to call home, as well as a much deeper appreciation for everything I have.

I've also been given the gift of lifelong friendships bonded by shared experiences. Whether I walked with someone for a day or a month, the bonds that formed in that time are difficult to compare to any other relationship. I've frequently tried to describe this phenomenon to people who have not hiked or taken a spiritual journey and I always fail to make them understand just what they're missing. To steal something my husband once told me, sometimes you form a closeness with other hikers before you've even met them. The strength of that relationship is amplified by the exclusivity of your experience. Frequently, I'm reminded of the joy I shared with my friends on the Camino and it takes my breath away. I stay in touch with each and every one of my Camino friends. My holidays are flooded with love from all over the world. I also have plans to see most of them again.

Finally, one of the most exhilarating outcomes of this adventure is the world truly does feel like my personal playground now. I have discovered an absolutely voracious appetite for continued exploration of this world I occupy. I always feel the need to be moving forward. In fact, I am already planning my next big adventure. My husband and I will be hiking the John Muir Trail in California this coming summer (the very moment we have enough vacation time saved up). What's most exciting about this adventure is that we will be joined by Stephen and his girlfriend. Stephen and I only got to walk through Spain together for three days, but we formed a kinship in that time and I think the four of us will make an excellent hiker family. I cannot wait to find out what this latest chapter of my life has to offer.

Thank you for following this most amazing journey with me. If I could pass to you a single message, it is this: your time on this planet is precious. Don't waste a moment of it. There is much to do, much to see, and much to experience. Don't be afraid. Don't let anyone else's opinions or perspectives hold you back from finding and pushing your limits beyond the visible horizon.

Life is short. Do it all!

Now, go do something amazing for yourself.

18871212R00183

Printed in Great Britain
by Amazon